Teach to Develop Talent

For teachers:

Because you touch the future.

Teach to Develop Talent

How to Motivate and Engage Tomorrow's Innovators Today

Jeanne L. Paynter, EdD

FOR INFORMATION:

Corwin

A SAGE Company

2455 Teller Road

Thousand Oaks, California 91320

(800) 233-9936

www.corwin.com

SAGE Publications Ltd.

1 Oliver's Yard

55 City Road

London EC1Y 1SP

United Kingdom

SAGE Publications India Pvt. Ltd.

B 1/I 1 Mohan Cooperative Industrial Area

Mathura Road, New Delhi 110 044

India

SAGE Publications Asia-Pacific Pte. Ltd.

18 Cross Street #10-10/11/12

China Square Central

Singapore 048423

Acquisitions Editor: Jessica Allan

Senior Content Development Editor: Lucas Schleicher

Associate Content Development Editor: Mia Rodriguez

Production Editor: Astha Jaiswal

Copy Editor: Amy Hanquist Harris

Typesetter: C&M Digitals (P) Ltd.

Proofreader: Lawrence W. Baker

Indexer: Integra

Cover Designer: Candice Harman

Graphic Designer: Lysa Becker

Marketing Manager: Stephanie Trkay

Printed in the United States of America

ISBN: 9781071812556

This book is printed on acid-free paper.

SUSTAINABLE FORESTRY INITIATIVE

Certified Chain of Custody
Promoting Sustainable Forestry
www.sfiprogram.org
SFI-01268

21 22 23 24 25 10 9 8 7 6 5 4 3 2 1

CONTENTS

Visit the companion website at
http://resources.corwin.com/DevelopTalent
for downloadable resources.

ACKNOWLEDGMENTS

The tap root for this book runs very deep in the soil of my career in education, finding its way to my first position teaching English in Baltimore County Public Schools, where I later became a gifted program coordinator. There are too many talented and dedicated colleagues there to acknowledge you each by name; I hope if you are reading this, please know that I mean *you*! However, I must acknowledge my colleague Hedy Droski, the great heart and mind behind the Primary Talent Development program. Hedy introduced me to the concept of creating targeted goals to develop "gifted behaviors" in all young children by engaging them in creative and enriching lessons, observing their responses, and documenting their growth using developmental rubrics. Resource teachers Melanie Carter and Deborah Myers have trained hundreds of teachers in this process; imagine the lives they touched! Thank you to Assistant Superintendent for Instruction Phyllis Bailey for supporting us in this work.

I founded Educating Innovators LLC with the mission to see "every child challenged, every day" because I sensed the urgency for schools to teach to develop talent. For over a decade as gifted education specialist at the Maryland State Department of Education, I fielded earnest (sometimes desperate-sounding) calls from parents, grandparents, teachers, and some school leaders who were concerned about children who definitely were not being "challenged every day." Their stories were heart-wrenching to me, and I must add that these calls from "every zip code" advocated for diverse children in urban, rural, and suburban schools. There are systemic causes for a lack of appropriate challenge, some of which I have referenced in this book. However, I believe that schools are willing to develop "tomorrow's innovators" if they have practical, effective, affordable tools.

I want to acknowledge the gifted team who collaborated with me on the talent-targeted studies that are sampled throughout this book: Joan Cable, Alexandra Clough, Barbara Kirby, Kathleen Mooney, Traci Siegler, and Kelley Smith. At that time, we didn't know that this work would give birth to a whole new approach: talent-targeted teaching and learning. Also, thank you to Sara Long and Apryl Lannigan for piloting the curriculum.

Everyone who has written a book knows what I do now: This is a hero's journey! Some of the friends "along the way" have included the following: BFF and "sis" Kimberley McMenamin and her husband Jim McMenamin (on his own writer's journey); and Kathleen Mooney, Stephanie Zenker, and Roni Jolley (the MSDE mod squad). Then there are my life mentors: my big sister Norma Reinhardt, and of course my husband Jim Farley, who shared with me years ago the wisdom that I finally heeded: Writers *write* (so get started). With his great sense of humor, Jim dubbed our two Norwegians as "service cats" for the way that they flanked each side of my laptop as I typed away at the dining room table. As for the foes, trials, and near-death ordeals: I acknowledge you as all part of the plan!

A heartfelt thank you to Corwin editor Jessica Allan, who championed my cause and believes as I do that we must cultivate a talent development mindset in and for all children. Thank you to the Corwin content development team led by editor Lucas Schleicher, who made a masterpiece of my manuscript.

Finally, I have dedicated this book to teachers, and so many of you have contributed to it by sharing your time and talents with me as students in the graduate education programs at McDaniel College, the Johns Hopkins International Teaching and Global Leadership (ITGL) program, Goucher College, and Towson University.

This book marks one journey's end, and by God's grace, I am "back home" in the place of safety, forever changed, and awaiting the next call to adventure.

Publisher's Acknowledgments

Corwin gratefully acknowledges the contributions of the following reviewers:

Ellen Asregadoo
Teacher, Grade 5
Public School 190
New York, NY

Charla Bunker
Teacher
Whittier Elementary
Great Falls, MT

Melissa Campbell
AMSTI Mathematics Specialist,
    Grades 3–5
University of Alabama, Huntsville
Huntsville, AL

Kelly A. Hedrick, EdD
Principal
Old Donation School
Virginia Beach, VA

Marcia LeCompte
Retired Teacher
Baton Rouge, LA

Christine Williamson
District Coordinator, Gifted and
    Talented Education
San Antonio ISD
San Antonio, TX

ABOUT THE AUTHOR

Jeanne L. Paynter, EdD, currently works as an educational consultant and faculty associate at the Johns Hopkins University. She is the founder and executive director of *Educating Innovators*, which partners with schools to implement unique teaching and learning approaches to engage and challenge all learners, including those who are academically advanced or gifted and talented. Previously, she served on the faculty of McDaniel College, Maryland, where she taught graduate courses in curriculum and gifted education.

Jeanne has had a wide variety of experiences in K–12 public education that have shaped her interest in talent development, leading to the design of a new approach that brings gifted pedagogy to all, talent-targeted teaching and learning. Currently, she serves as the president of the Maryland Coalition for Gifted and Talented Education (MCGATE).

As the state specialist for gifted and talented education at the Maryland State Department of Education (MSDE), Jeanne directed numerous grant projects to increase the participation and success of low-income and minority students in PreK–12 advanced programming. Previous to her work at MSDE, she was the coordinator for Gifted Education and Magnet Programs K–12 in Baltimore County Public Schools, a large urban–suburban district.

Jeanne's personal passions are motivation, creativity, and talent development in K–12 education, and she has made numerous presentations on these topics to national and international audiences. In addition, she has authored award-winning research on the topic of intrinsic, extrinsic, and moral motivation.

Jeanne earned her master's degree in gifted education and her doctorate in teacher development and leadership from the Johns Hopkins University and a bachelor of science degree in English from the Towson University. She resides in Baltimore, Maryland, with her husband and two Norwegian Forest cats.

Chapter ONE

Why Teach to Develop Talent?

Education doesn't need to be reformed—it needs to be transformed. The key is not to standardize education but to personalize it, to build achievement on discovering the individual talents of each child, to put students in an environment where they want to learn and where they can naturally discover their true passions.

—**Sir Ken Robinson**

I believe that our schools today have a talent development crisis. Do you agree?

Many leaders in creativity and innovation do. Creativity expert Sir Ken Robinson describes the state of education today as "Death Valley" in need of rainfall to awaken the dormant fields.[1] It's "one minute to midnight" on the clock that will strike the demise of our educational system.[2] Innovation expert Tony Wagner believes that our school system must be "re-imagined" to focus on the skills that matter today. "The world simply no longer cares what you know because Google knows everything. What the world cares about, and what matters for learning, work, and citizenship, is what you can *do* with what you know."[3] Business leaders continue to report that "creativity is king" in their list of most sought-after employee attributes, along with other noncontent-related skills such as perseverance, problem solving, and leadership.

Realistically, how can schools develop these talents in all students? Decades of school reform based on standards and standardized testing have left our students unmotivated and disengaged. Teachers feel the pressure to "cover the curriculum," to focus on raising test scores to proficiency level, which leaves them feeling forced to "teach to the test." Test data are examined primarily to identify deficits rather than strengths. Even with new, more rigorous content standards, the taught curriculum is narrowed to what is assessed on standardized tests.

The purpose of this book is not to articulate our education crisis, which has been articulated so well elsewhere. This book presents a solution: a paradigm shift in the way we look at teaching and learning. I call this shift *teach to develop talent* (talent-targeted teaching as opposed to test-targeted). And all schools can begin this shift now, right in the midst of their current practices, with or without changes in board policies and state regulations. This book is written for all educators (and that includes parent and community members) who sense the urgency in this crisis of wasted talent. It describes a practical approach to teaching and learning that schools can begin even in the midst of the standards movement. You won't necessarily need to throw out your required curriculum and assessments to do so. You'll see how a talent-targeted teaching approach directly supports student motivation, engagement, and developing the talent aptitudes of tomorrow's innovators today.

> This book presents a solution: a paradigm shift in the way we look at teaching and learning. I call this shift *teach to develop talent* (talent-targeted teaching as opposed to test-targeted).

Who Are Tomorrow's Innovators?

Innovators are creative problem solvers, those who produce new and useful ideas, methods, or products that are valuable and useful to those who implement them. While creativity is the process of conceiving new ideas, innovators put them into practice. Creative problem solvers can sense challenges, define problems, propose and evaluate solutions, and create a plan to implement them.

Innovation takes place in all fields of endeavor. Psychologist Abraham Maslow once said, "A first-rate soup is more creative than a second-rate painting."[4] In this sense, all of us are potential innovators, and so are our students. Don't think of innovators as just the top 1% of tech geniuses like Steve Jobs or Google founders Larry Page and Sergey Brin. In his book *Creating Innovators: The Making of Young People Who Will Change the World*, Tony Wagner writes about the growing number of young social innovators and entrepreneurs.[5]

Transformation Starts With WHY

Our students can become tomorrow's innovators—beginning in our schools—today. To illustrate how we begin, I'm going to use Simon Sinek's strategy "start with WHY." Sinek developed the concept of the Golden Circle—three concentric circles that start inside with WHY, then HOW, then WHAT as the outer circle. The Golden Circle is a paradigm for creating and maintaining inspiring, motivating organizations.[6] In your school, your WHY is the overarching purpose, cause, or reason for existing. Sinek says that most organizations focus on WHAT they do (for example, "We make widgets") and HOW they do it ("We make widgets with many features that are better than the rest"), but they don't know WHY they do it ("We believe widgets can change the world").

Have We Lost Our WHY?

Many schools today are focused on WHAT they "produce." This is either a holdover from the old industrial factory model of education or a misguided adaptation of incentive-driven business models. Sir Ken Robinson compares these schools to fast-food restaurants. Each meal is standardized to meet rigid quality control standards in order to turn out exactly like every other meal. The problem is that the products, while uniform, are not really of very high quality in a world where Michelin stars define quality.[7] Michelin restaurants, not fast food, represent the globally competitive world that our students will live and work in. They deserve, and must be given, the opportunity to strive for the stars.

It's not that we didn't start out with the right WHY. Teachers still do enter the profession to "make a difference." They believe that their work is about nurturing relationships, developing individual talents, and about inspiring their students, not incentivizing them. Given the opportunity, teachers express their moral motivation to make a difference, be a role model, to change lives.[8] And they also express their frustration with the current derailment of their mission. How did this occur? Largely because school systems have fallen prey to the mistaken belief that incentives, the carrots and the sticks, would achieve our long-term goals. According to Sinek, "There are only two ways to influence behavior; you can manipulate it or you can inspire it."[9] When our WHY is derailed, "manipulation rather than inspiration fast becomes the strategy of choice to motivate behavior."[10]

> Given the opportunity, teachers express their moral motivation to make a difference, be a role model, to change lives. And they also express their frustration with the current derailment of their mission.

Incentives are short-term tactics used to produce long-term outcomes, and they *do* produce results, if only for the short term. Manipulations can be monetary rewards (bonuses, raises, merit pay), but they are also emotional, coming in the form of fear, peer pressure, promises, or the allure of something new or different.

So, What's Wrong With Incentivizing if It Works?

Do our kids love learning, coming to school to be inspired, and wanting to inspire? If so, they'll be more productive, creative, and innovative; they'll be happier, healthier, and achieve more—in short, they can grow up to change the world. Manipulation through incentivizing, on the other hand, turns learning into—using the language of business—a series of singular "transactions" that may work in the short term but builds no "brand loyalty" to learning.[11]

The trap of incentive-driven education is that the effects are fleeting and must be repeated, each time "upping the ante." For students, each test or extrinsic hurdle is a one-time transaction, requiring us to find some new and better incentive that will motivate them next time. Their response to incentives becomes "So what have you done for me *lately*?" Educators are stressed about what they can do to maintain the gains, and the stress is passed down to the students who experience it in loss of motivation, engagement, and relationship. This obsession with short-term gains from incentives is ruining our health,[12] not to mention our relationships, creativity, and innovation.

Daniel Pink describes the oppositional effects of "carrot and sticks" incentives in his book *Drive: The Surprising Truth About What Motivates Us*:

Mechanisms designed to increase motivation can dampen it. Tactics aimed at boosting creativity can reduce it. Programs to promote good deeds can make them disappear. Meanwhile, instead of restraining negative behavior, rewards and punishments can often set it loose—and give rise to cheating, addiction, and dangerously myopic thinking.[13]

Many teachers I work with in schools and in graduate education programs tell me that they are stressed by viewing their students as data points to be incentivized instead of individuals to be engaged. Says Sinek, "More data doesn't always help, especially if a flawed assumption set the whole process in motion in the first place."[14] These teachers want to see their students as the unique individuals they are. Teachers want to return to their original passion for teaching, their WHY, to make a difference and lasting impact in children's lives. And, I would add, they really *do* want to teach to develop talent.

The Difference of Beginning With WHY

Let's look at the Golden Circles of two schools. School #1 is typical: It focuses on WHAT they do (the outside/outcome) and HOW they do it, but they have mistaken WHAT for WHY.

- <u>WHAT we do:</u> We graduate students who are college, career, and citizenship ready (as demonstrated by their standardized test scores).

- <u>HOW we do it:</u> We use rigorous curriculum standards, the latest teaching techniques, state-of the art technology, and robust data-driven accountability.

- <u>WHY we do it:</u> *Why?* I already told you: We do it to graduate students who are college, career, and citizenship ready (as demonstrated by standardized test scores).

School #1 has confused the short term (WHAT we do) with the long-term WHY (our overarching goal or purpose for existing). Their "HOW we do it" markets well to the education consumer, but it's an expensive moving target that is stressful to maintain, further distracting them from reclaiming their original intrinsic motivation, inspiration—their WHY. Having a focus on WHAT we do rather than WHY we do it limits our impact. Says Sinek, "When an organization defines itself by WHAT it does, that's all it will be able to do."[15]

Contrast this with School #2 that operates from the inside out, starting with their overarching purpose, their WHY.

- <u>WHY we exist:</u> We motivate and engage tomorrow's innovators today.

- <u>HOW we do it:</u> We teach to develop talent, creating and assessing talent-targeted instructional goals to develop students' individual aptitudes and content expertise.

- <u>WHAT we do:</u> We graduate creative problem solvers who understand and can use their unique talents in useful, beneficial, and innovative ways as productive members of society.

At first, you might say that School #2 is overly idealistic, impractical, and basically, not of this planet. School #2 definitely operates differently because it begins with a different long-term aim as its purpose: We motivate and engage tomorrow's innovators today. How? We teach to develop talent. What's the result? We produce creative problem solvers who understand how to apply learning and use their unique abilities for the good of all.

Notice that School #2's goal (WHY) and methods (HOW) aren't exclusive of School #1's. They are *inclusive* and *surpassing*. Students in School #2 will graduate "college and career ready" but so much more: They are life-ready, whatever the future holds. "The only way to prepare for the future is to make the most out of ourselves in the assumption that doing so will make us as flexible and productive as possible."[16] School #2 can use rigorous curriculum standards, effective teaching techniques, up-to-date technology, and accountability systems, but only as the means to a different end: To educate tomorrow's innovators today.

You can choose your school.

Which school would you choose? As a parent or caregiver, do you want your child to discover and develop their individual talents in order to become productive, creative, thriving adults? To find out who they can be? Then choose School #2.

Would you like to design and deliver instructional activities that motivate, engage, and guide learners to discover their unique aptitudes, instead of trying to fit them into a standardized mold that just *doesn't*?

As a teacher, would you like to focus on developing your students' strengths instead of diagnosing their deficits? Would you like to design and deliver instructional activities that motivate, engage, and guide learners to discover their unique aptitudes, instead of trying to fit them into a standardized mold that just *doesn't*? If so, then School #2 is your choice.

School #2 Can Be *Your* School

I have good news: School #2 *is* of this planet. It is *your* school! Or could be. Embrace the paradigm: We motivate and engage tomorrow's innovators. We teach to develop talent! Our graduates are tomorrow's creative problem solvers. This is your new Golden Circle. You probably wouldn't be reading this book if this message didn't resonate somewhere deep within you. Once you adopt this mission, the HOW of teaching to develop talent will become the means to your end. You can begin now, with practical steps, tools, and examples provided here.

This Book Focuses on HOW

With our purpose clear and in place, we can become very practical and focus on how—in the real world with its parameters and limitations—we can teach to develop the talents of all learners. The process we'll use is called *talent-targeted teaching and learning,* and it is based on sound psychological and pedagogical principles of motivation, engagement, and innovation. You'll learn how to create a talent development mindset in your classroom, pre-assess and set talent goals rooted in rich STEM and humanities content, and use evidence-based teaching and assessment strategies to attain long-term goals aimed at the aptitudes of innovators.

Although it's preferable that a school or system adopt the vision, I wrote this book with teachers in mind. Sir Ken Robinson reminds us: "The real challenges for education will only be met by empowering passionate and creative teachers and firing up the imaginations and motivations of the students."[17] The practical tools for talent-targeted teaching and learning are designed to empower teachers and can be adapted to your students and school context. I believe that teaching to develop talent is a creative commitment that teachers will find challenging and intrinsically motivating, just as the students will.

However, *practical* doesn't mean that the shift from test-targeted to talent-targeted is going to be easy. It isn't. I include one caveat to prepare you for possible reactions to your newfound vision:

> When we do have a sense of WHY, we expect more. For those not comfortable being held to a higher standard, I strongly advise you against learning your WHY. . . . Higher standards are harder to maintain. It requires the discipline to constantly talk about and remind everyone WHY the organization exists in the first place. . . . But for those who are willing to put in the effort, there are some great advantages.[18]

I believe that *you* are among those willing to put in the effort, and you will be reaping the advantages as you see learners motivated and engaged, experiencing the joy of learning, discovering their talent aptitudes, and developing the content expertise that prepares them to become tomorrow's innovators today.

Let's begin the journey together. In many ways, it will be a "hero's journey,"[19] one in which we are called to leave a place of safety and embark on an adventure that we sense *could change everything*. Expect that there are friends, foes, and trials along the way but that you will return with the treasure.

The process of talent-targeted teaching and learning is captured in five stages (Table 1.0) and is explored in the chapters ahead, which contain practical examples and tools that empower (and I hope inspire) you to *teach to develop talent*.

Table 1.0 Five Stages in Talent-Targeted Teaching and Learning

1. Prepare and Pre-Assess	Introduce the concept of talent development, survey student aptitudes, and begin using the language of talent development with students and families.
2. Set Goals	Create talent goals and design performances of understanding aligned with required content standards and learning objectives.
3. Develop Targets	Use the Talent Aptitude Learning Progressions to compose rubrics for ongoing assessment.
4. Design Talent-Targeted Tasks	Use the seven evidence-based curriculum "Design Essentials" and strategies modeled in the sample studies to focus your curriculum on talent development.
5. Assess and Reflect	Document student progress over time to improve teaching and learning, provide opportunities to self-assess, and set growth goals.

Chapter 2: You Can Motivate and Engage Tomorrow's Innovators

We begin with a sharp focus on our WHY: to motivate, engage, and develop the talents of our students today, the innovators of tomorrow. First, to ensure common understanding, we'll review the core principles of motivation, engagement, and talent development. Next, we'll explore HOW: *talent-targeted teaching and learning* is a new paradigm that shifts the emphasis from short-term goals for content and skill acquisition (often manipulated rather than motivated and measured on standardized tests) to long-term goals for talent development and transfer of learning. We'll see how these talent goals integrate, achieve, and exceed your current required content standards.

Chapter 3: Create a Talent Development Mindset

Stage 1 of talent-targeted teaching and learning is *Prepare and Pre-Assess*. To begin, the teacher uses a talent quiz to uncover "fixed mindset" misconceptions and introduce the concepts of talent development. Next, students use an aptitude survey to identify their strengths and set goals for growth. As teachers, students, and families begin to use the language of talent development to recognize, affirm, and nurture potential, new aptitudes are discovered and developed. Aptitude observational scales can be used periodically to document student behavior observed over time and to identify students' emerging strengths.

Chapter 4: Teach the Seven Aptitudes of Innovators

The seven aptitudes of innovators are identified from research as seminal to expert achievement and innovation across talent domains. These general or "cross-domain" aptitudes include both cognitive and noncognitive/psychosocial skills that can be explicitly taught: *curiosity, logical reasoning, creativity, insight, persistence, metacognition,* and *leadership*. Stage 2 of talent-targeted teaching and learning is *Set Goals*. This chapter is organized into seven "self-contained" sections; each one explains and gives examples of how to create motivating and engaging talent-targeted goals and performances of understanding based on required content standards.

Chapter 5: Teach to Develop STEM Aptitudes

Research shows that by the middle grades, a learner's talent development trajectory becomes more domain-specific. This is the time to identify and nurture emerging STEM talent by targeting the higher-order thinking and problem-solving abilities represented in five STEM-specific aptitudes: *engagement in STEM, investigation, problem solving, spatial reasoning,* and *mathematical reasoning*. This chapter continues Stage 2 (*Set Goals*) and presents five "self-contained" sections that model how to create STEM talent goals, performances of understanding, and assessments.

Chapter 6: Teach to Develop Humanities Aptitudes

The humanities develop habits of mind that are essential for creative problem solving and innovation, particularly in the social sphere. While the STEM and humanities aptitudes are not mutually exclusive, there are five aptitudes that are essential to understanding and creating in the humanities: *engagement in the humanities, empathy, resourcefulness, verbal reasoning,* and *communication*. This chapter presents sample humanities talent goals and performances of understanding to support the identification and development of learners' domain-specific interests and talents.

Chapter 7: Teach to Assess Talent

We know we need to teach the higher-order cognitive and psychosocial aptitudes essential for success in society and the innovation economy. The problem is that we have "too much content to cover," and even if we could focus on these skills, they are difficult to assess. This chapter develops Stages 3 and 5 of talent-targeted teaching and learning: *Develop Targets* and *Assess and Reflect*. First, I'll demonstrate how to use the Talent Aptitude Learning Progressions (cross-disciplinary, STEM, and humanities aptitudes) to compose the rubrics for ongoing assessment of talent goals. Learners use the student rubrics to self-assess and document growth over time in their Talent Development Portfolios. Teachers are reflective practitioners who systematically observe, reinforce, and document evidence of the talent aptitudes.

Chapter 8: Teach to Develop Tomorrow's Innovators Today

The paradigm shift of talent-targeted teaching and learning is epitomized in the process of creating and assessing talent goals. These new long-term aims will naturally foster the design of instruction that deepens learning. To maintain the emphasis on targets, to this point, we have only indirectly referenced Stage 4, *Design Talent-Targeted Tasks*. This chapter introduces seven "design essentials," or evidence-based practices used to design the four STEM and humanities studies sampled throughout. Some of these practices will be familiar; you may have used them before. Now, use these with fresh purpose to engage and motivate as you develop the talents of tomorrow's innovators today.

Notes

1. Robinson, K., & Aronica, L. (2009). *The element: How finding your passion changes everything* (p. 258). Penguin Books.
2. Robinson, K., & Aronica, L. (2015). *Creative schools: The grassroots revolution that's transforming education* (p. vii). Viking.
3. Wagner, T., & Dintersmith, T. (2015). *Most likely to succeed: Preparing our kids for the innovation era* (p. 223). Scribner.
4. Maslow, A. (1962). *Toward a psychology of being* (p. 128). Van Rostrand Reinhold
5. Wagner, T. (2012). *Creating innovators: The making of young people who will change the world.* Scribner.
6. Sinek, S. (2009/2019). *Start with why: How great leaders inspire everyone to take action.* Penguin Business.
7. Robinson & Aronica, 2009, p. 250.
8. Paynter, J. L. (2002). *The motivational profiles of teachers: Teachers' preferences for extrinsic, intrinsic, and moral motivation.* Doctoral dissertation. Johns Hopkins University.
9. Sinek, 2009/2019, p. 7.
10. Sinek, 2009/2019, p. 50.
11. Sinek, 2009/2019, p. 28.
12. Sinek, 2009/2019, p. 33.

13. Pink, D. (2009). *Drive: The surprising truth about what motivates us* (p. 35). Riverhead Books.
14. Sinek, 2009/2019, p. 13.
15. Sinek, 2009/2019, p. 45.
16. Robinson & Aronica, 2009, p. 20.
17. Robinson & Aronica, 2009, p. 247.
18. Sinek, 2009/2019, p. 147.
19. Campbell, J. (2014/1990). *The hero's journey: Joseph Campbell on his life and work*. New World Library.

Chapter
TWO

You Can Motivate and Engage Tomorrow's Innovators Today

Revolutions don't wait for legislation. They emerge from what people do at the ground level. . . . It's what goes on between learners and teachers in actual schools.

—Sir Ken Robinson

Although you may have recognized the systemic issues described in Chapter 1 as present in your own school or system, you may not feel adequate to undertake transforming them to be centered on engaging and motivating tomorrow's innovators. Let me encourage you: "If you are involved in education in any way—you can be part of the change."[1] Despite all the factors that you can't control, there is always one that you can: your WHY, your vision of *what should be.* When you begin to focus on long-term aims for learners, viewing them as "tomorrow's innovators," and are armed with the knowledge of what motivates and engages them, then you are thinking with a talent development mindset that transforms everything that happens between teachers and learners.

When you begin to focus on long-term aims for learners, viewing them as "tomorrow's innovators," and are armed with the knowledge of what motivates and engages them, then you are thinking with a talent development mindset that transforms everything that happens between teachers and learners.

In this chapter, we'll begin by exploring what it means to motivate and engage tomorrow's innovators. First, we examine the concepts of motivation, engagement, and talent development in order to identify key principles. We'll see how those key principles have been applied in the design of talent-targeted teaching and learning, and we'll walk through the core paradigm shift of this approach, creating and assessing talent goals. These features of talent-targeted teaching and learning are illustrated with examples from four model STEM and humanities studies, which you can adapt to use in your own classrooms.

Key Understandings

1. **Goals** focus our attention, and the nature of our goals determines whether our talents are developed or wasted.

2. **Intrinsic motivation** is supported through opportunities for autonomy, competency, and involvement.

3. **Student engagement** is fostered through opportunities for challenge, novelty, and purpose.

4. **Talent development** is a deliberate process of identifying and cultivating (over time) specific inherent abilities or aptitudes.

5. **Talent-targeted teaching and learning** shifts the focus from short-term goals for content and skill acquisition to long-term aims for talent development.

6. Educators can create, target, and assess **talent goals** to develop students' **aptitudes of innovators** in a content domain.

Teach to Motivate Tomorrow's Innovators

As educators (and parents), we often lament the lack of motivation in our students and are eager to know what we can do to "move" them into a deeper engagement in learning. Motivation is defined as "the process whereby goal-directed activity is instigated and sustained."[2] Goals focus our attention and energy and help us to visualize outcomes. Our self-esteem depends on the nature of our goals, which then shape the person we become. Without this focused attention on goals, we waste time, energy, and, ultimately, talent.[3] This is why the talent-targeted teaching and learning process begins by creating learning goals that help students visualize and focus on long-term outcomes.

Intrinsic Motivation: Autonomy, Competence, Involvement

As we learned in Chapter 1, when we rely on extrinsic rewards or incentives, we fall into manipulating rather than motivating. We may see short-term gains, but students have no long-term "loyalty" to learning. Intrinsic motivation, an internal reason for acting, comes through activities for which participation is its own reward—in other words, tasks that are enjoyable or bring pleasure. Research shows that intrinsic motivation is positively correlated to enhanced learning and long-term achievement, while extrinsic motivation can result in stress, superficial learning, and short-term outcomes.[4] To support intrinsic motivation, teachers can create a learning context that fulfills learners' psychological needs for *autonomy*, *competence*, and *involvement* or belonging.[5]

Autonomy

Autonomy literally means "self-power." When I am autonomous, I act of my own free will, independently and without outside controls. This state plays a crucial role in our students' intrinsic motivation and achievement. While all classrooms need to provide "autonomy supports," too much external control undermines autonomy and intrinsic motivation.[6]

Competence

Intrinsic rewards come through a sense of competence in my ability to do something successfully. Competence develops through accomplishing something difficult to master, overcoming challenges, and attaining a high standard. This develops *self-efficacy*, or self-confidence in future success through my personal mastery experiences, the vicarious experiences of observing others master challenges, and the social influence from the feedback of teachers and peers.[7]

Involvement

The social influence that is so important in creating competence also fosters *involvement*, the sense of belonging to a "community of learners" that shares values and beliefs and actively learns from one another.[8] The teacher builds a learner-centered environment when students are actively constructing meaning and working interdependently. The teacher models a mutually respectful environment by knowing each individual student in order to recognize the diverse talents and levels of competence in the classroom community.

Teach to Engage Tomorrow's Innovators

While motivation and engagement are sometimes used interchangeably, *engagement* can be seen as an outcome of motivation. Student engagement is defined as "the intensity and emotional quality of children's involvement in initiating and carrying out learning activities."[9] Engagement can be observed in the time and effort students spend on various activities and by asking them to estimate their levels of involvement. Educators and families are concerned about the growing disengagement seen in students today, leading them to drop out of school or graduate poorly prepared for either college or career. Student disengagement is particularly prevalent in low-income urban and rural settings.[10] How can we engage all of today's diverse learners? By designing instruction that provides *challenge*, *novelty*, and *purpose*.

Challenge and Skill: The Optimal Match

"Do you ever get involved in something so deeply that nothing else seems to matter and you lose all track of time?"[11] This state of optimal engagement, called *flow*, occurs during an activity that provides the optimal match of "high challenge/high skill." We feel our best in the state of flow when we are involved in something challenging, solving a problem, or learning something new.[12] The engagement of flow comes from having clear goals, getting immediate feedback, experiencing manageable challenge, and applying our skills in periods of concentration with few distractions.[13] Finding flow, however, requires having free time to explore new potentials in ourselves and our environment.[14]

Novelty

The opposite of flow—boredom—is the absence of engagement. Today, too many students appear and complain of being bored. They are weary of school, restless, and disinterested. This is a serious problem because we feel best "in flow" when we are being challenged and using our skills. The environment influences engagement, and the classroom can provide a context that sparks learners' interests through *novelty*, or new, different, and unusual experiences and opportunities.[15] Variety *is* the spice of life. New things engage our attention. Novelty-seeking is a component of creative behavior, and creativity is the essence of flow.

Purpose

Creativity requires unstructured time to explore, but too much free time or leisure is not a good thing.[16] Our actions need purpose, or intent. Purpose provides the reason, or the "why," for activity. But having the *right* goal and purpose is what motivates and engages us. Relevant, personally meaningful goals that invest in relationships focus our attention on external demands and engage us in a type of flow.[17] Purpose comes in doing something beyond ourselves, and it provides emotional energy and satisfaction from "doing something that matters, doing it well, and doing it in the service of a cause larger than ourselves."[18]

Teach to Develop Talent in Tomorrow's Innovators

Levels of student motivation and engagement are linked to student achievement. Students enjoy learning and do better when they are intrinsically motivated, and students who are engaged are more likely to increase their competencies—in other words, to develop their talents. *Talent* can be defined as "a complex of genetically influenced and environmentally determined aptitudes, skills, and personal characteristics that are seen by the culture and tradition as valuable to society."[19] This means that when talents are seen and valued, they can be developed.

Talent development signifies "the deliberate cultivation of ability in a specific domain."[20] The process represents a malleable view of intelligence broader than IQ, which involves cognitive and noncognitive or psychosocial factors.[21] For this reason, educators must constantly look for emerging talents and abilities in order to encourage growth.

Talent development growth plans involve students in identifying their own talents, setting goals, and engaging in activities designed with the long-term goal of creative achievement.[22] Rating scales and portfolios are useful for identifying talent, and the development process involves a plan for growth in which the students inventory and review their own talents and write personal goals.[23] Once students identify and understand their own abilities, learning activities can be designed to provide opportunities to develop talent potential.

> Students enjoy learning and do better when they are intrinsically motivated, and students who are engaged are more likely to increase their competencies—in other words, to develop their talents.

Motivate, Engage, and Develop Talent: Talent-Targeted Teaching and Learning

A new approach to teaching and learning that is "talent-targeted" puts us dead center in our WHY: to motivate and engage tomorrow's innovators today. Talent-targeted teaching and learning is a comprehensive approach that focuses on long-term aims to develop students' individual talents and the aptitudes. Transforming teaching and learning through the talent development lens begins with revisiting and re-visioning our goals for students. What is our aim, long-term? Surely, it is not just to master the content standards assessed on standardized tests. "The ability to transfer is arguably the long-term goal of education."[24] *Transfer* is learners' ability to apply the "big ideas" and enduring understandings of the discipline authentically and independently in the real world. If we aim only at content knowledge and skill acquisition, we won't develop the deep understanding that undergirds creative problem solving, or innovation.

> Transforming teaching and learning through the talent development lens begins with revisiting and re-visioning our goals for students. What is our aim, long-term?

Teach to Develop the Talent Aptitudes of Innovators

All of us have talent potential, capacities, or aptitudes that can be developed. An *aptitude* is an innate or acquired capacity, a fitness or inclination.[25] The use of *aptitude* as a synonym for talent captures its dynamic nature. In talent-targeted teaching and learning, teachers and students set "talent goals" that explicitly align the targeted aptitudes with the required content standards in STEM and the humanities. Some learners have a natural inclination to demonstrate a targeted aptitude with greater frequency, depth, and complexity. Explicitly creating goals to target this aptitude provides these students with opportunities to accelerate their talent. At the same time, talent-targeted goals encourage *all* learners' aptitudes to emerge and progress.

> The use of "aptitude" as a synonym for talent captures its dynamic nature.

Cross-Domain and Domain-Specific Talent Aptitudes

What are aptitudes of tomorrow's innovators? By studying the profiles of those who have changed our world for the better, we can identify characteristic aptitudes to target in our students. The first category consists of the seven general abilities that support high achievement across domains. I refer to these as "the seven aptitudes of innovators," which are developed in detail in Chapter 4. These seven "cross-domain aptitudes" can be further distinquished as "cognitive" and "psychosocial" aptitudes. The cognitive aptitudes are conscious ways of knowing, perceiving, and reasoning: *curiosity*, *logical reasoning*, *creativity*, and *insight*. The psychosocial aptitudes are personal ways of feeling and behaving: *perisistence*, *metacogniton*, and *leadership* (see Figure 2.0).

STEM and Humanities Aptitudes

Other aptitudes are characteristic of talent development in a specific domain. Although these domain-specific categories are not mutually exclusive, the aptitudes that typify innovators in science, technology, engineering, and mathematics (STEM) fields include *engagement in STEM*, *investigation*, *problem solving*, *spatial reasoning*, and *mathematical reasoning*. These aptitudes are defined and explained in detail in Chapter 5.

The aptitudes that are characteristic of innovators in the humanities (language, history, social sciences, the arts) include *engagement in the humanities*, *empathy*, *resourcefulness*, *verbal reasoning*, and *communication*. These are defined and explained in detail in Chapter 6.

Figure 2.0 Cross-Domain and Domain-Specific Aptitudes of Innovators

An *aptitude* is an innate capacity, a fitness or inclination that can be developed. The use of *aptitude* as a synonym for talent captures its dynamic nature.	
Cross-Domain Aptitudes	
These cognitive and psychosocial aptitudes support innovation across domains.	
Cognitive *Conscious ways of knowing, perceiving, and reasoning*	**Psychosocial** *Personal ways of feeling and behaving*
1. Curiosity 2. Logical Reasoning 3. Creativity 4. Insight	5. Persistence 6. Metacognition 7. Leadership
Domain-Specific Aptitudes	
Although not mutually exclusive categories, these aptitudes support innovation in a specific domain.	
STEM Science, Technology, Engineering, Mathematics	**Humanities** Language, Literature, Social Studies, Arts
1. Engagement in STEM 2. Investigation 3. Problem Solving 4. Spatial Reasoning 5. Mathematical Reasoning	1. Engagement in Humanities 2. Empathy 3. Resourcefulness 4. Verbal Reasoning 5. Communication

Creating, Targeting, and Assessing Talent Goals

Creating and assessing instructional goals that target these aptitudes applied in rich content is the pivotal shift in talent-targeted teaching and learning. The process is represented in a figure referred to throughout this book as the *Talent Goal Frame*. An example that develops a creativity goal for a humanities unit of study is presented in Figure 2.1. The Talent Goal Frame consists of the targeted aptitude, the required content standard and learning objective, the talent goal, performance of understanding, and student-directed goal.

> Creating and assessing instructional goals that target these aptitudes applied in rich content is the pivotal shift in talent-targeted teaching and learning.

Planning With the Talent Goal Frame

Let's walk through the goal planning process, one that will be repeated often with different examples that serve as models for your own goals. Keep in mind that the planning process, like creative thinking itself, is not always in practice this linear. Depending on your existing curriculum parameters, you might begin with the targeted aptitude, content standard, or performance of understanding.

Figure 2.1 Sample Talent Goal Frame: *Creativity in Humanities*

Talent Aptitude	Content Standard and Learning Objective	Performance of Understanding
3. Creativity Has unusual or clever ideas; enjoys divergent thinking, brainstorming, or imagining; is inventive; discovers unusual connections; initiates new projects.	**Content Standard** Demonstrate understanding of figurative language, word relationships, and nuances in word meanings. (CCSS.ELA-LITERACY.L.5.5) **Objective** Demonstrate understanding of the concept of *perspective*.	**Three-Voices Perspectives Presentation** Communicate to peers in a chosen format three different perspectives on a topic of interest.
Talent-Targeted Teaching and Learning Goal: *Perspectives in Art and Culture (4–6)* Use your *creativity* to communicate different perspectives on a topic of choice.		
Student-Directed Talent Goal: I express *creativity* through new or unusual ideas that are imaginative or inventive, making new connections, and initiating new projects.		

Choose Your Standards

Talent-targeted teaching and learning begins where your current curriculum begins: with the content standards. The examples in this book will apply national content standards currently used or adapted for use in many school systems in the United States at the time of this writing. These standards capture disciplinary core ideas that are applicable internationally: Common Core State Standards for English Language Arts and Mathematics,[26] Next Generation Science Standards (NGSS),[27] College, Career, and Civic Life (C3) Framework for Social Studies State Standards,[28] and National Core Arts Standards.[29]

Write the Learning Objective

The learning objective defines the specific application of the content standard that students will master—in this sample, understanding the "figurative language, word relationships, and nuances" of the concept of *perspective*. Once again, you can use an objective from your current curriculum. School systems often have a prescribed format for writing learning objectives, so feel free to use that here. The objective typically defines learning that occurs over a series of lessons, or an instructional module. Both the content standard and specific learning objective are incorporated into the talent goal and assessed in the performance of understanding.

Target the Talent Aptitude

Next, select the talent aptitude that you will target. You can choose from a range of possibilities—from the seven cross-domain aptitudes that can be developed in any content area to the five domain-specific humanities or STEM aptitudes (Table 2.0). You might find that the content lends itself to the expression of a particular aptitude or that your students have a particular need to develop in that area (Chapter 3 contains a pre-assessment survey). Ultimately, your goal is to provide your students with exposure to *all* the talent aptitudes so that they can discover and develop their unique abilities.

Table 2.0 presents summaries of the four talent-targeted teaching and learning studies that are sampled throughout this book. Problem scenarios for the humanities and STEM 6–8 studies can be found in the online appendix at www.resources .corwin.com/DevelopTalent.

This sample Talent Goal Planner targets *creativity*, a cross-domain aptitude that is the "DNA" of innovation but that teachers may not think they have time to

Table 2.0 Talent-Targeted Teaching and Learning Studies

Humanities 4–6	*Perspectives in Art and Culture*
	How do our perspectives shape our perceptions? In this project-based humanities unit, the core text *Shooting Kabul* by N. H. Senzai is the foundation for exploring this essential question. Students explore the Afghan immigrant family's cultural perspectives and analyze the characters' real-world conflicts and moral dilemmas. Like the young protagonist Fadi, students will use photography to express their personal perspectives by creating photo essays and artist statements to be presented at a Perspectives in Art and Culture exhibit. This cross-disciplinary study addresses content standards in English language arts, social studies, and art.
Humanities 6–8	*Creating Sustainable Communities*
	What makes communities thrive? In this project-based humanities unit, the classic novel *Watership Down* by Richard Adams is the foundation for exploring this essential question. Students analyze the four communities portrayed in the novel to determine the qualities of sustainable communities and effective leadership. They study real-life examples of community redevelopment in their own city in order to create their own community redevelopment plan for an area in their neighborhood. This cross-disciplinary study addresses content standards in English language arts, social studies, and environmental science.
STEM 4–6	*Stop Sports Injuries*
	How does data help us make good decisions? In this problem-based learning study, students explore concepts in collecting, representing, and interpreting data in order to respond to a challenge to design a product or process to prevent youth sports injuries. The call for proposals comes from a popular sportswear manufacturer, which is in search of ideas to showcase a new piece of equipment or innovative solution to protect young athletes and reduce sports injuries. Students explore the essential question "How does data help us make good decisions?" as they collect data to determine needs, conduct experiments, and analyze patterns. This cross-disciplinary STEM study develops content standards in mathematics, science, and engineering science.

STEM 6–8	*Livewell: A Healthy Community by Design*
	How does form follow function? In this problem-based learning study, students respond to a proposal from the City Department of Planning to create a plan for a healthy community based on the design principles of the Urban Land Institute. Students apply advanced mathematical concepts and skills in ratio and proportion, geometry, and statistics to create scale drawings and models for their Livewell community plan, which will be presented to local experts for review and evaluation. This cross-disciplinary STEM study develops content standards in mathematics, engineering science, and health science.

"teach" or the tools to assess. Figure 2.1 uses the "agreed-upon" definition of creativity from Chapter 4.

A learner demonstrating *creativity* . . .

Has unusual or clever ideas; enjoys divergent thinking, brainstorming, or imagining; is inventive; discovers unusual connections; initiates new projects.

To support motivation, students have a corresponding talent goal, which explicitly defines for them what it means to be creative, thus encouraging their metacognition and self-regulation:

Student-Directed Goal: I express *creativity* through new or unusual ideas that are imaginative or inventive. I start and complete new projects based on my ideas.

Design the Performance of Understanding

Talent goals are assessed in *performances of understanding*, tasks that require learners to apply knowledge and skills in order to develop and demonstrate their understanding.[30] In talent-targeted teaching and learning, these tasks are part of an ongoing process that includes formative and summative assessments of the talent aptitude. The *Perspectives Presentation* was designed to provide evidence of *creativity* as well as mastery of the content standards and learning objective through an independent performance that demonstrates transfer.

Three-Voices Perspectives Presentation: *Communicate to peers in a chosen format three different perspectives on a topic of interest.*

In what ways does this task develop *creativity*? In this open-ended task, learners have the opportunity to choose a topic that interests them, develop the perspectives, and then decide the form in which they will communicate them. They use creative thinking as they apply knowledge and skills that typically might be assessed on a short-answer test. They will use *divergent thinking* to create, looking for *new connections*, and employ *creative problem solving* to *initiate new projects*. The task opens up opportunities to *imagine and invent*.

Compose the Talent Goals

The process of creating and assessing talent goals exemplifies the core paradigm shift in talent-targeted teaching and learning. The long-term aim, *creativity*, is what drives the content and skill acquisition (short-term goal). Talent goals motivate and engage students in authentic learning with personal relevance and purpose: *I am developing my creativity*. Students are clear about what it means to "express creativity" because the student goal explicitly defines creative behaviors. Note that while the talent goal is lesson-specific, the student goals are aptitude-specific to reinforce the behaviors across time.

> Talent goals motivate and engage students in authentic learning with personal relevance and purpose.

Creativity Talent Goal: Use your *creativity* to demonstrate different perspectives on a given topic.

Creativity Student-Directed Goal: I express *creativity* through new or unusual ideas that are imaginative or inventive, making new connections and initiating new projects.

How Does This Goal Motivate, Engage, and Develop Talent?

The talent goal and performance of understanding motivate and engage learners by aiming at an authentic application of creativity, content knowledge, and skills. This answers the WHY, or purpose for learning. Students are engaged by a relevant topic of interest that is personalized through the choice of topic, perspectives, and presentation format. Overall, the task connects them to their community of peers through meaningful and diverse communication.

Assessing the Talent Goal and Performance of Understanding

Teachers have many assessment tools related to content and skills, but far fewer, if any, to assess cognitive and psychosocial aptitudes. A key resource of talent-targeted teaching and learning is provided in the Talent Aptitude Learning Progressions, which are used to compose rubrics used in formative, summative, and self-assessment (Chapter 7). Figure 2.2 displays the rubrics used to assess *creativity* in the *Perspectives in Art and Culture* performance of understanding.

> A key resource of talent-targeted teaching and learning is provided in the Talent Aptitude Learning Progressions, which are used to compose rubrics used in formative, summative, and self-assessment.

Figure 2.2 Talent Aptitude Rubrics for *Creativity*

Teacher Rubric:		
The student performance in this talent-targeted task . . .		
Emerging	**Progressing**	**Advancing**
Demonstrates typical ideas; makes literal connections.	Demonstrates some divergent thinking; makes appropriate, if expected, connections.	Demonstrates divergent thinking through unusual or clever ideas; makes unexpected or imaginative connections.
Student Rubric:		
My work on this talent-targeted task shows that . . .		
Emerging	**Progressing**	**Advancing**
I sometimes think of new ideas and how things could be improved. I prefer to follow a model or pattern that already exists.	I think of ideas for new projects and can imagine how things could be improved. I sometimes put these new ideas into practice.	I enjoy thinking of many different and unusual ideas. I often imagine what could be and discover original ideas for new projects or how to improve things.

The learning progressions develop a continuum from *emerging* to *progressing* to *advancing*. All students are considered as emerging, with potential to progress and advance. The targets affirm existing strengths while providing explicit direction for growth. For example, the *emerging* creativity target (teacher version) acknowledges that all students can "generate ideas" and "make connections." These are creative behaviors, albeit expressed at a literal level. The student version of the *emerging* level recognizes that "I can follow a pattern." The learning progressions affirm current strengths; however, their greater use is that they provide clear targets for talent development. We can use them to challenge students to *progress* into more "divergent thinking" and *advance* into generating "unusual ideas" and making "imaginative connections."

The talent goal and corresponding performance of understanding focus on developing *creativity* in the context of specific content knowledge and skills. In addition to the Talent Aptitude Rubrics, you'll develop your own formative assessments to gather evidence as to whether students have mastered the learning objective and content standard.

The Talent-Targeted Teaching and Learning Studies

The talent goals empower our long-term aim—our WHY—to develop the talents of tomorrow's innovators today. This pivotal shift in focus fortifies our efforts to deepen and transform teaching and learning. What does this look like in actual classrooms? Throughout this book, you'll explore examples and illustrations from four talent-targeted teaching and learning studies (see Table 2.0). I use the term *study* rather than the more typical *unit* because *studying* captures what learners actively do; it is their personal effort, time, and attention that are required to pursue and master knowledge in a discipline. "Studies" require motivation and engagement to develop talent.

The studies in their entirety are purposefully not included here, first and foremost because of the "teach a person to fish" principle. The goal of this book is that you will "learn to fish" and apply the methodology of talent-targeted teaching and learning to transform your own curriculum. The most effective curriculum is locally developed, and these product-based/problem-based studies were originally developed for a particular community, based on issues and resources specific to that community. Therefore, they could not be directly implemented in your school; however, the design principles they embody can be.

You'll note that the sample studies target Grades 4–8. This does not mean the talent-targeted teaching and learning is limited to these levels; we have seen applications to earlier grades, as well as to high school. The focus on the intermediate and middle grades is intentional because in the middle years, learners are beginning to differentiate their unique talent aptitudes. While the early grades are ripe for talent exploration, the middle grades are the time to begin domain-specific talent development. For this reason, all of the sample talent goals, even for cross-domain aptitudes, are rooted in content-specific standards for humanities (English language arts, social studies, art) or STEM (science, technology, mathematics, engineering).

The grade span listed for each study demonstrates their design to meet the needs of at-risk, grade-level, and advanced learners. The goal of talent-targeted teaching and learning is to develop the talents of **all students**. For example, the humanities study *Perspectives in Art and Culture* could meet the needs of advanced students in Grade 4, on-grade-level students in Grade 5, and at-risk students in Grade 6.

Challenging *Every* Student

The talent-targeted teaching and learning model can be used with at-risk students as a catalyst for identifying and developing *emerging* talent, in grade-level groups to challenge the talents of *progressing* students, and with gifted students to *advance* their identified talents. All students are motivated to face tough challenges because their aptitudes and interests are engaged. The model recognizes a broad range of talents and presents a continuum of growth so that students have clear targets for deliberate practice and improvement.

Table 2.1 presents the five stages of talent-targeted teaching and learning, as well as tools to support its implementation and assessment.

Table 2.1 The Five Stages of Talent-Targeted Teaching and Learning

	Stage	Tools
1. Prepare and Pre-Assess	Introduce the concept of talent development, survey student aptitudes, and begin using the language of talent development with students and families.	Chapter 3 • What Is Talent? quiz • Talent Aptitude Survey • Talent-Targeted Think-Alouds • Talent Aptitude Observation Scales • Parent newsletter
2. Set Goals	Create talent goals and design performances of understanding aligned with required content standards and learning objectives.	Chapters 4, 5, 6 • Talent aptitude definitions (cross-disciplinary, STEM, and humanities) • Student-directed talent goals • Sample Talent Goal Frames in STEM and humanities (goals, objectives, performances of understanding)

(Continued)

Table 2.1 (Continued)

	Stage	Tools
3. Develop Targets	Use the Talent Aptitude Learning Progressions to compose rubrics for ongoing assessment.	**Chapter 7** • Talent Aptitude Learning Progressions (teacher and student versions) • Talent Continuum Rubrics in STEM and humanities (teacher and student versions) • Teacher think-alouds for formative assessment • Kidwatching data collection protocols
4. Design Talent-Targeted Tasks	Use the seven evidence-based curriculum "design essentials" and strategies modeled in the sample studies to focus your curriculum on talent development.	**Chapter 8** • The seven Design Essentials • Examples from talent-targeted studies • Design Essential tools • Sample lesson seeds
5. Assess and Reflect	Document student progress over time to improve teaching and learning, provide opportunities to self-assess, and set growth goals.	**Chapter 7** • Talent Portfolio record-keeping and reflection protocols • Student-led portfolio conferences

The talent-targeted teaching and learning model can be used with at-risk students as a catalyst for identifying and developing *emerging* talent, in grade-level groups to challenge the talents of *progressing* students, and with gifted students to *advance* their identified talents.

Moving Into Stage 1

We've begun refocusing on our WHY to motivate, engage, and develop the talents of our students today, the innovators of tomorrow. The talent-targeted teaching and learning approach represents a paradigm shift from our current focus on short-term content and skill acquisition (often manipulated rather than motivated and measured on standardized tests) to long-term goals for talent development and transfer of learning. In the next chapter, we'll begin **Stage 1 (Prepare and Pre-Assess)** by creating a talent development mindset in our students and the school community.

Notes

1. Robinson, K., & Aronica, L. (2015). *Creative schools: The grassroots revolution that's transforming education.* Viking.
2. Schunk, D. H., Pintrich, J., & Meece, J. (2014). *Motivation in education: Theory, research, and applications* (4th ed., p. 4). Pearson Education.
3. Csiksentmihalyi, M. (1997). *Finding flow: The psychology of engagement with everyday life.* Basic Books.
4. American Psychological Association, Coalition for Psychology in Schools and Education. (2015). *Top 20 principles from psychology for preK–12 teaching and learning.* https://www.apa.org/ed/schools/teaching-learning/top-twenty-principles.pdf
5. Skinner, E. A., & Belmont, M. J. (1993). Motivation in the classroom: Reciprocal effects of teacher behavior and student engagement across the school year. *Journal of Educational Psychology, 85*(4), 571–581. https://doi.org/10.1037/0022-0663.85.4.571
6. Skinner & Belmont, 1993, p. 573.
7. Bandura, A. (1997). *Self-efficacy: The exercise of control.* W. H. Freeman.
8. The Charles A. Dana Center & Agile Mind, Inc. (n.d.). *Learning and the adolescent mind.* University of Austin. http://learningandtheadolescentmind.org
9. Skinner & Belmont, 1993, p. 572.
10. Washor, E., & Mojkowski, C. (2014). Student disengagement: It's deeper than you think. *Phi Delta Kappan, 95*(8), 8–10. https://doi.org/10.1177/003172171409500803
11. Csiksentmihalyi, 1997, p. 33.
12. Csiksentmihalyi, 1997, p. 59.
13. Csiksentmihalyi, 1997, p. 36.
14. Csiksentmihalyi, 1997, p. 77.
15. Schweizer, T. S. (2006). The psychology of novelty-seeking, creativity and innovation: Neurocognitive aspects within a work-psychological perspective. *Creativity and Innovation Management, 15*(2), 164–172.
16. Csiksentmihalyi, 1997, p. 60.
17. Csiksentmihalyi, 1997, p. 42.
18. Pink, D. (2009). *Drive: The surprising truth about what motivates us* (p. 146). Penguin Books.
19. Feldhusen, J. (1998). *Talent development expertise, and creative achievement.* Paper presented at the annual convention of the American Psychological Association. https://eric.ed.gov/?q=Feldhusen&ft=on&id=ED424555, p. 2.
20. Olszewski-Kubilius, P., & Thomson, D. (2015). Talent development as a framework for gifted education. *Gifted Child Today, 38*(1), p. 49.
21. Olszewski-Kubilius & Thomson, 2015, p. 51.
22. Feldhusen, 1998, p. 11.
23. Feldhusen, J. (2001). Talent development in gifted education. *ERIC Digest E610.* https://eric.ed.gov/
24. Wiggins, G., & McTighe, J. (2011). *The understanding by design guide to creating high-quality units.* ASCD.

25. Merriam-Webster. (n.d.). Aptitude. In *Merriam-Webster.com dictionary*. https://www.merriam-webster.com/dictionary/aptitude

26. National Governors Association Center for Best Practices and Council of Chief State School Officers. (2010.) *The Common core state standards initiative*. http://www.corestandards.org/

27. NGSS Lead States. (2013). *Next generation science standards: For states, by states*. The National Academies Press. https://www.nextgenscience.org/

28. National Council for Social Studies. (2013). *The college, career, and civic life (C3) framework for social studies state standards: Guidance for enhancing the rigor of K–12 civics, economics, geography, and history*. NCSS.

29. National Coalition for Core Arts Standards. (2014). *National core arts standards*. State Education Agency Directors of Arts Education.

30. Blythe, T. (1998). *The teaching for understanding guide*. Jossey-Bass.

Chapter
THREE

Create a Talent Development Mindset

"Schools are places for talent development."

—Dr. Joseph S. Renzulli

Talent-targeted teaching and learning begins with creating a school culture focused on our WHY: to motivate and engage tomorrow's innovators. We begin by establishing the values, beliefs, and principles that guide schools to become inspiring places for talent development. We'll walk through the process for creating and sustaining a talent development mindset in a community of learners that includes educators, students, and families.

Key Understandings

1. Talent is more than a special ability some people have. It is innate potential that must be discovered and developed.

2. Identifying and nurturing individual talents focuses effort and is the foundation of a growth mindset.

3. A three-phase process for creating a talent development mindset involves uncovering misconceptions, pre-assessing talent aptitudes, and strategically using the language of talent development in daily instruction and communication with families.

4. The process of having students identify their unique talent aptitudes and set goals for growth fosters intrinsic motivation, engagement, and achievement.

What Is a Talent Development Mindset?

A mindset is a way of thinking, a set of beliefs and convictions that predetermine how we will interpret and respond. These sets of assumptions, when activated as goals, are powerful motivators.[1] Mindsets, however, are learned and can be changed. The talent development mindset makes this shift: Our long-term goal is to see our students as tomorrow's innovators, not just today's test-takers. Our new talent-focused goals for learners will guide, facilitate, advance, and make possible our short-term goals for content and skill acquisition. In this way, the talent development mindset encompasses and exceeds the goals of "college and career readiness," which today still is being assessed through standardized tests.[2]

A talent development mindset aims at educating the world's creative problem solvers who will find unique and useful solutions to enhance our lives. But do we honestly believe that *all* of our students have the potential to become tomorrow's innovators? Do we honestly think that we can know now which of our students *don't* have the potential? Creativity expert KH Kim proposes that we can (and must) teach the creative process that leads to innovation. We do this when we cultivate creative climates, attitudes, and thinking skills.[3] Educators and families can develop a "talent scout" attitude. This is the view that talent is more than just an observed special ability some people have. It is an innate potential and capability that must be discovered and developed.

How Does the Talent Development Mindset Differ From a Growth Mindset?

Many schools today are focusing on developing a *growth mindset* in their students. Growth mindset is the belief that effort counts more than talent or ability.[4] In contrast, an emphasis on talent or ability is viewed as a "fixed mindset"—you either have it or you don't. Talent and ability are downplayed as less important than effort, "grit," hard work, or determination.[5] So if a growth mindset focused on effort is what motivates achievement, why establish a *talent development* mindset?

I believe that identifying and nurturing talent is *foundational* to a growth mindset. The talent development mindset recognizes aptitude as a *potential to excel* in a specific area. We each have unique inclinations, and to focus our effort effectively, we need to know what those are. Rather than wait for inherent aptitudes to somehow randomly emerge, a talent development mindset proactively and systematically cultivates them. As students begin to explore their talent aptitudes, they are reminded that it is only through continued "opportunities, interest, and effort" that they may discover, develop, and perform at high levels in these areas. Talent identification enables focused attention and ultimately leads to *flow*, the optimal match of skill and challenge that underlies creative achievements.[6]

> Create a talent development mindset in your school or classroom and you will as a natural by-product create a growth mindset.

Learners are more motivated to expend efforts when they experience that "optimal match."[7] Effort expended in areas that aren't natural strengths will be less productive and a potential waste of energy, leading to a loss of motivation and engagement. Create a talent development mindset in your school or classroom and you will as a natural by-product create a growth mindset.

Three Phases for Creating the Talent Development Mindset

The process for creating a talent development mindset has three phases: (1) Uncover misconceptions and "reseed" attitudes about talent; (2) pre-assess talent aptitudes as a way to focus the conversation; (3) use the language of talent development in daily instruction and communication with families. Talent development is the ethos of the classroom, as students are motivated and engaged in deep learning of content and skills.

Phase One: "What Is Talent?"—a True–False Quiz

Creating a talent development mindset begins with uncovering currently held attitudes about talent. "What Is Talent?" is a true–false quiz that helps to replace common misunderstandings such as "Talent is something you're born with—you have it or you don't" with new understandings such as "Talent must be developed" and "Effort counts as much as talent." While quiz takers mark the statements as true or false, in reality the dichotomies aren't always that distinct. Debriefing the quiz initiates a lively class discussion in which you will actually begin to see the talent aptitudes emerge: Curiosity, logical reasoning, metacognition, leadership, empathy, and communication all become evident now that you are looking for them.

Use the "What Is Talent?" quiz as professional learning for faculty and parent/community groups with the same goal of establishing the beliefs and assumptions foundational to a talent development mindset. The sample debriefing script in the next section is written for students but can be adapted for other audiences.

Figure 3.0 *What Is Talent?* Quiz

What Is Talent?
A True–False Quiz
1. Talent is something you are born with. You have it or you don't.
2. People have different talents; we are not all talented in the same way.
3. Talent can be developed.
4. Effort counts as much as, or more than, natural talent.
5. Most people know what their own talents are.
6. We discover our talents through the lessons we have in school.
7. The students in the gifted and talented/advanced classes are the talented ones.
8. "Aptitude" is another word for talent.
9. *Innovators* are persons who use their talents in new and useful ways.
10. I have new talents to discover and develop.

Debriefing the Talent Quiz: Shared Understandings About Talent Development

The following script for debriefing the "What Is Talent?" quiz communicates the shared understandings and language of talent development and introduces students to the unique features of the talent-targeted teaching and learning model.

1. **Talent is something you are born with. You either have it, or you don't.**

   The answer is YES and also NO. There is a genetic (innate) component to talent. You were born with a "predisposition" to excel in certain ways. BUT—talents can be hidden! You may not discover your talents unless you have the opportunity to express them. And talent, once discovered, must be developed!

2. **People have different talents; we are not all talented in the same way.**

YES, that is true. We all have strengths *and* areas that need development. Learn to develop your strengths to their fullest, and that will help you to grow in your weaker areas.

3. **Talent can be developed.**

YES! In fact, it *has* to be. Have you noticed? The most "talented" people are the ones who practice the most and work the hardest to improve. Talent that isn't developed, *isn't*.

4. **Effort counts as much as, or more than, natural talent.**

YES, that is true. Practice (and persistence) does makes perfect. There really isn't any other pathway to success. Those successful people you admire have failed, made mistakes, and then gotten "right back on the horse" more times than you can count.

5. **Most people know what their own talents are.**

We hope that would be true, but often it is not. We discover our talents as we have opportunities to express them. To find your talents, you must be willing to explore new things. When we find that we have a **strong interest** in an area, we develop our talents as we pursue that interest.

When we are working in our individual talent area, we might experience what is called "flow." This means that we lose track of time; we are completely engaged in the activity that we enjoy and are getting better at doing. The level of challenge is perfect! We are willing to work hard to improve.

Have this mindset: *You have talents that you haven't yet discovered!*

6. **We discover our talents through the classes we have in school.**

YES, but also, not entirely.

School provides us with many opportunities to discover and develop our talents. But many talents are discovered through activities **outside of school**. Do you have hobbies that you work on at home? Do you participate in clubs, camps, or volunteering in the community? These are places where many people have discovered what they call their *passion*: Something they are motivated to do, not for a prize or reward, but for the enjoyment and satisfaction they gain from doing it. Seek out these kinds of opportunities outside of school. Have the mindset that you might discover your true passion there!

7. **The students in the gifted and talented/advanced classes are the talented ones.**

YES, but also, not entirely.

Advanced level or "accelerated" classes in school meet the needs of students with talents in specific academic areas like language or mathematics. These students have had opportunities to express and develop their talents beyond their age and grade level. These advanced classes are necessary for them to continue to develop their talents. It's only fair that they have these opportunities to be able to learn at their depth and pace.

But *don't* have the mindset that these students are necessarily "smarter" than other students, who also have gifts and talents but in different areas. With time and effort, you may "catch up" with the GT (gifted/talented) kids!

Remember, talent can (and must) be developed!

8. *Aptitude* **is another word for talent**.

YES! According to the dictionary definition, *aptitude* is *talent potential*.

Aptitude is . . .

- An *innate or acquired* capacity for something; a readiness or quickness, talent.

- *Potential* that has not yet been tapped but can be trained.

- Latin for *fitness*.

There are *general* **aptitudes.** These "fit" us for achieving in almost any area we go into. These are *curiosity, logical reasoning, creativity, insight, persistence, metacognition*, and *leadership*. We'll begin to use these terms often in our classes.

There are subject-specific aptitudes. These fit us for achievement in particular subject areas, such as STEM (science, technology, engineering, mathematics) or the humanities (languages, social studies, arts). You might find you have strengths in multiple areas, but your interests "fit" better in one subject than another.

We are going to be using the word *aptitude* a lot in this class. We will use the term *talent aptitude* as well. Are you ready to discover more about *your* talent aptitudes?

9. *Innovators* **are persons who use their talents in new and useful ways.**

YES! An innovation is a product, idea, or service that is both unique (new) and valuable to others. Some innovations have greatly changed our lives, like the smartphone. Other innovations haven't had as great an impact but still represent unique and useful solutions that others appreciate and value. It's important for you to know that with effort and persistence *you can develop* the aptitudes of innovators. *You* could become the next Steve Jobs.

10. **I have new talents to discover and develop.**

Again, YES! How do you find them? Start looking! We discover our talents by seeking out opportunities to explore and develop new interests. Some of these you'll want to pursue further, others not. But if you aren't willing to move outside your comfort zone, you won't discover your talents. And if you aren't willing to work hard, you won't develop them. Lost talent? We can't afford that. The world needs exactly what *you* have to offer. So let's get started!

What's the point of all this talk about talent? It's about talent-targeted teaching and learning.

In the next few weeks, we're going to be doing some things differently. In our lessons, we are going to focus on developing our talent aptitudes. Each lesson will have a talent goal along with the usual content and skill mastery goal. The lessons are designed to engage you in new interests and discover and develop your talents. You will begin a Talent Development Portfolio and record your progress. This portfolio is something we will share with each other and our families to show the ways in which we are uniquely talented and the progress we are making.

Moving on to Phase Two

The "What Is Talent?" quiz and debriefing are essential to the first phase of creating a talent development mindset in your school community. By uncovering misconceptions and reseeding these with new attitudes, students are ready to explore finding out more about their own talent aptitudes in Phase Two: The Talent Aptitude Survey.

Phase Two: Pre-Assess With the Talent Aptitude Survey

As discussed in Chapter 2, we are eager to know what we can do to motivate our students and engage them more deeply in learning. We know that goals focus energy and attention, and the nature of these goals determines whether we develop our talents. The Talent Aptitude Survey introduces students to the intrinsically motivating and engaging discovery of their individual strengths and how to develop them.

How to Administer and Score the Survey

There are two versions of the Talent Aptitude Survey—one for STEM and one for humanities (visit the companion website at www.resources.corwin.com/DevelopTalent for downloadable resources). Given that students in the intermediate and secondary grades are often taught in "departmentalized" or subject-specific courses, the mathematics or science teacher might administer the STEM survey, and the language or social studies teacher, the humanities survey.

Each survey has 24 questions, with the first 14 on each quiz assessing the seven cross-disciplinary aptitudes of innovators. The remaining 10 questions on each survey assess either the five STEM or five humanities domain-specific aptitudes. If you are administering both surveys to one group of students in a non-departmentalized setting, eliminate the repeated 14 questions on the second survey (see Figures 3.1, 3.2).

Figure 3.1 Humanities Talent Aptitude Survey

Directions:

This survey helps you to identify your unique talents and aptitudes. Answer each question as honestly as you can. *There are no right or wrong answers, only what is true for you.*

	Often	Sometimes	Seldom
1. I think about how things work or why things are the way they are.			
2. I ask questions that I explore and investigate.			
3. Give me the facts, and I'll identify the problem and a solution.			
4. I come up with convincing arguments.			
5. I think of new, unusual, or imaginative ideas.			
6. I work on many different projects.			
7. I don't give up when I face a difficulty.			
8. I look for ways to improve and get better, even if it's hard.			
9. I know my strengths and how to use them to my advantage.			
10. I think about my mistakes and how I can improve next time.			
11. I'm quick to get the answer, see the pattern, or make the connection.			
12. I trust and follow my gut feelings or inner voice.			
13. I encourage and organize others to complete a project.			
14. I stick with my goals, even when others don't go along.			
15. I spend time outside of school in arts-related activities.			

	Often	Sometimes	Seldom
16. I'm interested in current events and active in social issues.			
17. I imagine what it is like to "walk in someone else's shoes."			
18. I connect to others with different cultures, interests, and ages.			
19. I know how and where to find the right information when I need it.			
20. I use the materials I already have in new and useful ways.			
21. I express myself through writing, speaking, or the arts.			
22. I use details and examples to get my point across to others.			
23. I read often on topics of interest and use what I learn.			
24. I understand and make personal connections to what I read.			

online resources   Available for download from **resources.corwin.com/DevelopTalent**

Figure 3.2 STEM Talent Aptitude Survey

Directions:

This survey helps you to identify your unique talents and aptitudes. Answer each question as honestly as you can. *There are no right or wrong answers, only what is true for you.*

	Often	Sometimes	Seldom
1. I think about how things work or why things are the way they are.			
2. I ask questions that I explore and investigate.			
3. Give me the facts, and I'll identify the problem and a solution.			
4. I come up with convincing arguments.			
5. I think of new, unusual, and imaginative ideas.			
6. I work on many different projects.			
7. I don't give up when I face a difficulty.			
8. I look for ways to improve and get better, even if it's hard.			
9. I know my strengths and how to use them to my advantage.			

(Continued)

Figure 3.2 (Continued)

10. I think about my mistakes and how I can improve next time.			
11. I'm quick to get the answer, see the pattern, or make the connection.			
12. I trust and follow my gut feelings or inner voice.			
13. I encourage and organize others to complete a project.			
14. I stick with my goals even when others don't go along.			
15. I am interested in science, technology, engineering, and math (STEM) activities.			
16. I look for ways to become involved in STEM activities.			
17. I ask questions and search out answers by collecting data.			
18. I display the data I collect and explain what it means.			
19. I solve problems accurately, using multiple strategies.			
20. I figure out why my problem-solving strategy worked or didn't.			
21. I see images and objects and remember them.			
22. I picture in my mind how objects fit together.			
23. I find the patterns in numbers or shapes and figure out the rules.			
24. I learn math concepts quickly and apply them accurately.			

online resources ☞ Available for download from **resources.corwin.com/DevelopTalent**

The survey questions are written as declarative present tense actions, crafted to elicit the most honest and accurate responses: "I come up with convincing arguments" instead of "I *can*" (but in reality, don't); and "I work on many different projects" instead of "I *like to*" (but in reality, may not). The statements are rated as *often*, *sometimes*, or *seldom* true. Student are reminded that there are no right or wrong answers, only "what is true about you."

Scoring the Talent Aptitude Surveys

To score the survey, students use the Talent Aptitude Survey Key for either STEM or humanities. Both are available in the digital appendix found online at www.resources. corwin.com/DevelopTalent. The answer key categorizes the questions according to the talent aptitude and so serves the dual purpose of defining the constructs for students as they score them (see Figure 3.3). They transcribe their responses to the

Figure 3.3 How to Score the Talent Aptitude Survey

Directions for Scoring: *Use your Talent Aptitude Survey to . . .*

1. First, record checks for questions you rated as **often** true about you. These are evident strengths.

2. Next, record checks for the questions you rated as **sometimes** true. These are areas of potential growth.

3. Finally, record the **seldom** answers. This doesn't mean you don't have the aptitude. Perhaps through new experiences you will discover and develop this talent as well.

Talent Aptitudes		Often	Sometimes	Seldom
Curiosity	1. I think about how things work or why things are the way they are.	✓		
	2. I ask questions that I explore and investigate.		✓	
Logical Reasoning	3. Give me the facts, and I'll identify the problem and a solution.		✓	
	4. I come up with convincing arguments.			✓
Creativity	5. I think of new, unusual, and imaginative ideas.	✓		
	6. I work on many different projects.	✓		
Persistence	7. I don't give up easily when I face a difficulty.		✓	
	8. I look for ways to improve and get better, even if it's hard.			✓

scoring key using the same *often*, *sometimes*, and *seldom* ratings. However, the score key directions specify that they should record all of their "often" question responses first, which focuses their attention on strengths. They are reminded in the directions that a "seldom" rating does not mean that they don't have this aptitude. Perhaps with new opportunities, they will yet discover and develop it. In scoring the survey, the pattern of strengths emerges visually as students see the areas that may be "often/often" or "often/sometimes" in contrast to "seldom/seldom or "sometimes/seldom."

Does the Survey Motivate and Engage? What the Students Say

The aim of talent-targeted teaching and learning is to increase students' intrinsic motivation, engagement, and achievement. We'll keep revisiting these concepts in order to understand how each component of the model, like the Talent Aptitude Survey, is strategically designed to accomplish those goals. This section contains student feedback from a class who completed the talent-targeted study *Perspectives in Art and Culture.*

Through the steps of completing, scoring, and reflecting upon the Talent Aptitude Survey, learners are intrinsically motivated by the *autonomy, competence*, and *involvement* inherent in the process. Autonomy—the sense of "self-power" that "I am in control"—is reinforced in each of the 24 "I statements." Students then identify their levels of competence as they rate the "I" statements as "often, sometimes, or seldom" true about them. With that information, they establish goals for growth. The survey creates a sense of involvement and belonging in a mutually respectful community of learners that recognizes, affirms, and values the diversity of each individual's talent aptitudes. It is accepted that each of us has strengths in certain areas, but not all. As one intermediate-grade student said, "By taking the Talent Aptitude Survey, I was able to learn what I am good at and what I need to get better at, which motivated me to work harder."

> "By taking the Talent Aptitude Survey, I was able to learn what I am good at and what I need to get better at, which motivated me to work harder."

Engagement

The survey process fosters the three essentials for engagement: the *optimal match, novelty*, and *purpose*. As one student said, "This survey helped me develop my talents because it showed me things about myself that I did not know . . . it revealed myself to me." Understanding one's strengths increases the likelihood that the optimal match of high skill/high challenge will occur and create *flow*, a creative state of maximum engagement. The *novelty* of taking the Talent Aptitude Survey sparks learners' interest in their own talents and the talents of others; according to another student, "I got to communicate with others and talk to people with different talents." Overall, the talent survey gives students a new sense of *purpose* by establishing personally meaningful goals, as shown by this student: "This tells me how I can get better. It shows me how I am different from the world."

> "This tells me how I can get better. It shows me how I am different from the world."

Using the Talent Aptitude Survey as Pre-Assessment

Self-report questionnaires such as the Talent Aptitude Survey are useful for providing information about psychological constructs such as aptitudes. Surveys like these are widely used by social scientists. However, some issues with self-reports are that they may elicit a response that is more "favorable" to others or that is not how the person really behaves.[8] The teacher may wonder, Do they really know enough about themselves to answer these questions?

The Talent Aptitude Survey is best used like other pre-assessments of what students know, want to know, and need to learn. As a self-report, it can provide information that the individual knows but that we might not have observed. Much like an interest survey that teachers commonly use, the Talent Aptitude Survey focuses both teachers' and learners' attention on pursuing growth in these areas and develops a community of learners as students begin to recognize, affirm, and value each other's unique contributions.

A Few Cautions

As a formative assessment, the Talent Aptitude Survey should not be used in the ways that a standardized psychometric instrument would be used. For example, the data cannot be used as summative evaluations, ability assessments, or in making "high-stakes" decisions such as eligibility for special programs. Talent-targeted teaching and learning includes opportunities to discover, develop, and advance all of the survey aptitudes. Keep the focus on developing strengths, not on remediating weaknesses. Likewise, don't allow students to use their less-developed aptitudes as excuses for avoiding these challenges (see Table 3.0).

Validating the Talent Aptitude Survey Results

How credible are the survey results? The students' self-report will be substantiated through multiple opportunities to express and apply the talent aptitudes in meaningful content-specific tasks. Assessment methods from different data sources are integrated into the talent-targeted teaching and learning process and documented in the cumulative Talent Portfolio, which shows a continuum of growth (see Chapter 7).

Table 3.0 Aptitude Survey Dos and Don'ts

Do Use the Aptitude Survey to ...	*Don't* Use the Aptitude Survey ...
1. Foster a talent development mindset	1. As summative evaluation
2. Introduce the language of talent development	2. As an ability measure
3. Focus attention on strengths	3. As data for high-stakes decisions
4. Set goals for growth	4. To remediate weaknesses
5. Develop a community of learners	5. As an excuse to avoid challenges

The Talent Aptitude Survey initiates teachers and learners into an approach to talent development that is deliberate and goal-driven. Our immediate focus is on moving students to the next level, from *emerging* to *progressing* to *advanced*, with the long-term aim of having their talent potential translated into future creative achievements.

Phase Three: Use the Language of Talent Development

The Talent Aptitude Survey introduces students to the *language of talent development*. Realistically, can we use terms like *metacognition, insight*, and *logical reasoning* with learners as young as age 10 from diverse cultures? The answer is yes, and we must! Access to authentic vocabulary is an equity issue. Compare the language of talent development with the concept of academic language. "Academic language" is defined as the discipline-specific vocabulary that students need to learn to be successful in school.[9] The talent aptitudes are that and much more; they are what students need to be successful in life. As with academic language, the language of talent development will be experienced differently across grade levels as learners deepen their understanding. It is used in both oral and written communication in the social contexts of the classroom and home environments.

> "One of the most valuable aspects was having the language of the talent aptitudes for the students to internalize their higher-order thinking. They came to use talent aptitude terms like 'creativity' and 'empathy' with ease."

In talent-targeted teaching and learning, a new type of conversation develops. As one teacher said, "One of the most valuable aspects was having the language of the talent aptitudes for the students to internalize their higher-order thinking. They came to use talent aptitude terms like 'creativity' and 'empathy' with ease." Overall, using the language of talent development builds a community of learners. Teachers become more aware of and more responsive to the whole child, and students build metacognitive awareness of how they learn.

Talent-Targeted Think-Aloud Statements

Talent-targeted teaching and learning integrates elements of explicit instruction, a research-based approach found effective for skills-based interventions to support struggling learners. However, explicit instruction is also effective for teaching higher-order thinking and inquiry learning.[10] Talent-targeted teaching and learning explicitly focuses the learners' attention on the attributes of the talent aptitude through explanations and examples. The goal is to have students recognize, understand, and reproduce those behaviors.

The teacher uses the language of talent aptitudes to explicitly name examples of the targeted aptitudes as they emerge during instruction. These teacher think-alouds verbalize thinking using scripts based on the talent aptitude definitions they'll encounter multiple times in goals and assessments. These statements can be prepared in advance and used both purposefully and extemporaneously as examples emerge. Table 3.1 presents think-aloud examples for several cross-disciplinary and domain-specific aptitudes.

Table 3.1 Sample Talent-Targeted Teacher Think-Aloud Statements

Curiosity	• We showed curiosity today because we were *open to new experiences*.
	• That *thoughtful question* showed curiosity.
	• We'll use our curiosity today as we are *observing and investigating*.
Insight	• Use your insight to *recognize the pattern*.
	• That *connection* showed insight.
	• That's an insightful idea about *how to apply this concept*.
Leadership	• That's what leaders do—they *pay attention to other people's needs*.
	• Having a *plan of action* like that shows leadership.
	• Our task requires leadership *to organize others*.
Empathy	• That *concern for others* showed empathy.
	• We'll use empathy to *see what it is like to walk in someone else's shoes*.
	• This shows an empathetic *understanding of a different group's situation*.
Problem Solving	• The explanation of *cause and effect* showed problem solving.
	• Today, we will *test and verify* our problem solutions.
	• That's another *strategy/tool* we can use in solving the problem.

Use Talent-Targeted Think-Alouds for Formative Assessment

Once you have created your talent goals, you can begin to explicitly name the talent attributes that will be used in a task: "Today, we'll use our *curiosity* when we are observing and investigating _____." This focuses students on the aptitude as it is being applied in the specific content of the lesson. As the lesson progresses, use think-alouds to point out examples of those attributes as they emerge: "That *thoughtful question* showed curiosity." Statements like these provide exemplars for the students and formative data for the teacher.

Name the Behavior, not the Person

One caution in using think-alouds is to remember to name the behavior—for example, "That was an *insightful* comment"—and not the person: "Antoine is insightful," or "*You* showed insight when *you* made that connection." Of course, the students will know who made the comment, but we don't need to reinforce it by saying the name or pronoun reference. Having a talent development mindset means that in this community of learners, we focus on the work, not the worker; we recognize the quality of others' performances, but believe in our own capabilities to perform at high levels with additional opportunities, interest, and effort.

Capturing Observational Data

Talent-Targeted Think-Alouds provide rich opportunities to systematically capture and document an individual student's talent development. Teachers in secondary grades typically are not as familiar as their early childhood peers with the process of making observational or "anecdotal records."[11] These brief narrative notes help teachers to record information about a student's behavior and classroom performance. The notes are easy to maintain when using targeted behavioral checklists or note-making sheets prepared in advance with students' names. Not only do the records track progress over time, but the notes assist the teacher in assessing the effectiveness of the lesson and plan changes. Anecdotal records capture qualitative data that gives new insights into student learning. The notes can be shared with parents and with the students themselves at one-on-one conferences. Strategies and tools for keeping and using anecdotal records will be discussed further in Chapter 7.

Using the Talent Aptitude Observation Scales

A behavior observation scale is a structured way to capture student data observed over time. These scales are completed by teachers or other adults who know the child well. The Talent Aptitude Observation Scales in the humanities and STEM use the talent aptitude constructs as prompts to observe and rate the targeted behaviors on a 1–4 Likert scale from *not evident* to *clearly evident*. Ratings are based on the *frequency*, *intensity*, and *complexity* of the observations. The scales can be used periodically for identifying students' emerging strengths that can be nurtured. However, the same cautions exist as were presented earlier in regard to the

Talent Aptitude Survey (see Table 3.0). In addition, adults who complete the scales should become familiar with observable expressions of the aptitudes, such as those descriptions on the Talent Aptitude Survey.

The Talent Aptitude Behavioral Scales in STEM and humanities can be found at www.resources.corwin.com/DevelopTalent.

Create a Talent Development Mindset at Home

The talent development mindset and language provide new ways to communicate information about student learning to parents and families. The three phases implemented in the classroom represented by the "What Is Talent?" quiz, Talent Aptitude Survey, and talent-targeted anecdotal notes all present opportunities for home–school connections. While the Talent Development Portfolio is the main tool for home–school communication, preferably shared through student-led conferences (see Chapter 7), more frequent "talent communication" through school newsletters or websites is useful in building shared understandings and a common language.

Through the language of talent development, parents/guardians can begin to observe their children's behaviors in a new light. Children may express each aptitude in ways that we might perceive as "negative," particularly when that aptitude differs from that of our own children. A child with a strong *creative* aptitude might appear disorganized, unfocused, "outrageous," and a day dreamer, with many projects started and fewer finished. Children with an aptitude for *leadership* might show their latent ability to motivate others in ways that appear bossy or controlling. When we begin to see these "negative" characteristics as manifestations of latent but immature talent potential instead of as a behavior problem, we can take steps to channel strengths into productive pursuits. When both parents and teachers begin to *recognize*, *affirm*, and *value* a child's strengths, then we are educating with a talent development mindset.

Talent Aptitude of the Month

Most schools maintain websites and parent/community newsletters. Consider how you might create an *Aptitude of the Month* newsletter with tips as to how families can recognize and nurture that aptitude at home. This is an opportunity to inform the school community about how the talent aptitude is being integrated into the current curriculum, specifying how the aptitude facilitates content and skill acquisition—for example, "We'll use *curiosity* to help us learn the mathematics concept of random sampling" (see Table 3.2). Being explicit about the disciplinary concepts being taught will allay any parent concerns about the talent-targeted approach: "I want my children learning *math* and not this

Table 3.2 Sample Parent Newsletter Item

Talent Aptitude of the Month: *Curiosity*

What is *curiosity?*

Curiosity is the desire to know and learn. To observe *curiosity* in your child, ask these questions:

Does my child . . .

- Ask thoughtful, searching questions?
- Like to observe, explore, investigate?
- Seek out new ideas, experiences, and environments?

Why is it important to develop *curiosity*?

- Curiosity is the basis for learning, motivation, creativity, and achievement.
- Curiosity sparks interest, and interest leads to developing one's talents and discovering one's passion and life's work.
- Tomorrow's innovators must be curious.

***Curiosity* in Our Curriculum:** Grade 7 STEM *Healthy Community by Design*

- We are developing *curiosity* by surveying different groups in our community to find out what outdoor recreational activities they prefer.
- We'll use *curiosity* by being open to new ideas and experiences, asking thoughtful questions, observing, and investigating.
- We'll use *curiosity* to help us learn the mathematics content of using random sampling to draw inferences about a population.
- This lesson is part of the *Healthy Community by Design* problem-based learning study in which students will create scale drawings and models for their *Livewell* healthy community proposals.

How do I encourage *curiosity* in my child?

- Seek out a variety of experiences that can spark new interests. Visit libraries, museums, and historical sites in the community, most of which are free.
- Observe your child's interests and look for ways to encourage him or her.
- Allow for "unscheduled" time with freedom to explore. Too many structured activities are curiosity killers.
- Cultivate your own curiosity! Start by asking questions that you and your child can explore and investigate together.

talent aptitude stuff!" As we'll explore in upcoming chapters, talent goals are always grounded in disciplinary concepts and aim at deep learning of content. Innovators first must become experts!

Summary

In this chapter, we saw how to focus on our WHY by creating a talent development mindset. We challenged beliefs about talent being an inherent act of birth and adopted a strategic process that begins with taking on the role of talent scouts. Using a three-phase process with practical tools for implementation, we can create a talent development mindset.

In Chapter 4, we begin the work of integrating the talent-targeted approach into our curriculum by creating long-term goals for talent development.

Notes

1. Gollweitzer, P. M., & Keller, L. R. (2016). Mindset theory. In V. Zeigler-Hill & T. K. Shackelford (Eds.), *Encyclopedia of personality and individual differences.* Springer International.
2. Achieve. (2018). *States must build assessment of college and career readiness into their high school assessment systems to determine whether students are on track for credit-bearing post-secondary courses and careers before their senior year.* https://www.achieve.org/assessments
3. Kim, KH. (2016). *The creativity challenge: How we can recapture American innovation.* Prometheus Books.
4. Dweck, C. S. (2006). *Mindset: The new psychology of success.* Random House.
5. Duckworth, A. (2016). *Grit: The power of passion and perseverance.* Scribner.
6. Csiksentmihalyi, M. (1997). *Finding flow: The psychology of engagement with everyday life.* Basic Books.
7. Whalen, S. P. (n.d.). Revisiting the problem of match: Contributions of flow theory to talent development. In *Talent Development IV* (pp. 317–328). Great Potential Press. http://www.davidsongifted.org/search-database/entry/a10012
8. McDonald, J. D. (2008). Measuring personality constructs: The advantages and disadvantages of self-reports, informant reports and behavioural assessments. *Enquire, 1*(1), 75–94.
9. Gottlieb, M., & Ernst-Slavit, G. (2013). *Academic language in diverse classrooms: Promoting content and language learning.* Corwin Press.
10. Zohar, A., & Peled, B. (2008). The effects of explicit teaching of metastrategic knowledge on low- and high-achieving students. *Learning and Instruction, 18,* 337–353.
11. Beaty, J. J. (2013). *Observing the development of the young child.* (8th ed.). Pearson Education.

Chapter
FOUR

Teach the Seven Aptitudes of Innovators

If critical and creative thinking is the goal long term, then when we go to plan, week in and week out, we are focusing on critical and creative uses of content.

—Grant Wiggins

Y ou can begin today to transform your current curriculum into one focused on educating innovators, our future creative problem solvers who will change our world for the better. There is no need to wait for a board policy revision or new content standards, assessments, or resources. Whether you have a standardized curriculum or a more personalized one, you can shift the focus from short-term content knowledge and skill acquisition to long-term aims for *talent development*, the process by which learners gain content expertise as they develop their individual talent aptitudes.

We have measured achievement using standardized test scores for so long that we have lost sight of the long-term goals of education. Grant Wiggins, co-creator of the *Understanding by Design* (UbD) curriculum planning framework, concludes that regardless of what our 21st-century-skills-focused mission statements proclaim, "it is possible to get straight A's at every school in America without [developing] critical and creative thinking."[1] If this is the case, we are not equitably preparing *all* students for the innovation economy. We need to frame our goals around—plan, teach, and assess—the aptitudes of innovators.

> Whether you have a standardized curriculum or a more personalized one, you can shift the focus from short-term content knowledge and skill acquisition to long-term aims for *talent development*.

Key Understandings

1. We can identify the aptitudes of innovators by studying their real-life achievements that demonstrate their *curiosity, logical reasoning, creativity, insight, persistence, metacognition,* and *leadership*.

2. By explicitly creating goals to target these aptitudes, we provide our students with opportunities to discover and develop their unique talent potential to become tomorrow's innovators.

3. The Talent Goal Frame planning process is used to create goals and performances of understanding aimed at the expression of talent aptitudes in the context of rich content.

4. Talent-targeted goals and performances of understanding are explicitly designed to support students' intrinsic motivation, engagement, and achievement.

5. The Talent Aptitude Learning Progressions can be used to create rubrics that assess students' demonstration of the targeted aptitudes as emerging, progressing, or advancing.

The Seven Aptitudes of Innovators

This chapter focuses on seven aptitudes that are seminal to expert achievement and innovation across talent domains (see Table 4.0). As stated earlier, *aptitude*, a synonym for talent, connotes a natural inclination or potential that can be developed. The seven general, or "cross-domain," aptitudes represent cognitive and psychosocial skills, all of which can be explicitly taught and developed over time. Cognitive aptitudes are ways of learning and understanding information, reasoning, and making judgments. These include *curiosity*, *logical reasoning*, *creativity*, and *insight*. The psychosocial aptitudes, sometimes referred to as "soft skills" by employers or as "social and emotional skills" in schools, include *persistence*, *metacognition*, and *leadership*. In the process of talent development, the cognitive and psychosocial aptitudes are interdependent, with psychosocial skills differentiating those who reach the highest levels of achievement.[2]

All seven aptitudes are worthy, long-term aims for teaching and learning because they undergird the process of creative problem solving, or innovation. Research shows that as children approach adolescence, their talent development becomes more domain-specific.[3] Therefore, talent goals in the cross-domain aptitudes must be grounded in challenging, domain-specific content. For example, you would create a goal for students to develop *curiosity* in the context of mastering essential content in STEM or humanities.

> Talent goals in the cross-domain aptitudes must be grounded in challenging, domain-specific content.

Learning to Create Talent-Targeted Goals

The process of creating talent goals shifts the focus of teaching and learning from short-term objectives assessed on standardized tests to long-term aims to educate innovators. The good news is that you can begin this transformation NOW with your *existing curriculum standards*. The starting place is gaining a common understanding of the seven aptitudes and the research documenting their key role in educating innovators.

Next, using the Talent Goal Frame introduced earlier in Chapter 2, we'll walk through the same process of creating a goal by identifying the content standard, targeting an aptitude, and developing a performance of understanding that requires learners to apply the content in an authentic, personalized task. For each of the seven aptitudes, a sample Talent Goal Frame presents an example from one of the four talent-targeted teaching and learning humanities and STEM studies (see Table 4.1).

Table 4.0 The Seven Aptitudes of Innovators (Cross-Domain)

1. **Curiosity**	Seeks new ideas; asks thoughtful, searching questions; is inquisitive; observes, explores, and investigates keenly and alertly in any environment.
2. **Logical Reasoning**	Draws conclusions from facts or premises; observes patterns and infers rules; hypothesizes and tests; uses a systematic process to make sound judgments and form sensible arguments.
3. **Creativity**	Has unusual or clever ideas; enjoys brainstorming, imagining, or divergent thinking; is inventive; discovers unusual connections; initiates new projects.
4. **Insight**	Is keenly observant and aware; is intuitive; perceives new patterns and relationships; readily grasps concepts and applies them to new situations.
5. **Persistence**	Focuses time and energy on a topic of interest; looks for more than one way to accomplish a task; continues in spite of difficulty; strives to improve and refine; tests and verifies; may resist closure.
6. **Metacognition**	Understands own thought processes; self-selects appropriate problem-solving strategies; plans; self-monitors, reflects, assesses, and corrects; learns from mistakes.
7. **Leadership**	Motivates others to achieve a goal; initiates ideas and listens to concerns of others; influences others to adopt and participate in a plan of action; organizes others to implement a plan.

Table 4.1 Seven Sample Talent Goals Categorized by Domain

STEM Studies		Humanities Studies	
Stop Sports Injuries (Grades 4–6)	*Healthy Community by Design* (Grades 6–8)	*Perspectives in Art and Culture* (Grades 4–6)	*Creating Sustainable Communities* (Grades 6–8)
3. Creativity	1. Curiosity	6. Metacognition	4. Insight
5. Persistence	2. Logical Reasoning		7. Leadership

How to Use This Chapter

This chapter may become your most dog-eared, underlined, and bookmarked one. Use it as you would a "how-to" book or reference manual. Although the following sections are numbered 1 through 7, according to the talent aptitudes (see Table 4.0), there is no need to read or work sequentially (although you may). To identify a starting place (which aptitude?), consult your current curriculum, which is the content and skills you are required to teach. You may have little more than a list of standards, or maybe you have a well-developed or scripted curriculum guide. Perhaps you have a favorite, successful lesson module or unit that you'd like to transform with talent-targeted goals and assessments. You might begin by asking, "Which talent aptitudes would be a natural focus for this lesson?" Keep in mind that these are cross-domain talents that can be developed in any content area.

> You might begin by asking, "Which talent aptitudes would be a natural focus for this lesson?"

Each of the seven sections is "self-contained" in that it reiterates the goal development process using that specific aptitude. This repetition is intentional and allows you to explore one aptitude at a time. For example, if you decide to target *persistence* in a talent goal, you can turn to its section (see "5. Persistence"), which provides you with a complete description of the goal development and assessment process.

I. Curiosity

Curiosity is the essential prerequisite for creativity and innovation, and it must be cultivated through opportunities to explore and engage new interests. Our attention is limited, so where we choose to focus it is crucial to developing our creative potential.[4] A curious attitude is one of childlike openness—seeking, expecting, and motivated by a strong desire to learn. Curiosity opens up new possibilities and fuels inquiry and persistence. A rigid learning environment is the enemy of curiosity.[5]

Innovators Are Curious

Innovators approach learning with childlike, open minds and curious attitudes that have been nurtured early in life. Steve Jobs's parents encouraged his love of reading, and his father involved him in a love of all things mechanical. At a young age, Steve was exploring electronics with his neighbor, an engineer at Hewlett Packard. The curious young Albert Einstein's constant questions in school resulted in him being labeled a troublemaker.[6]

In a sense, curiosity is the molecular basis for "the innovator's DNA."[7] The innovator's skills of associating (making new connections), questioning, observing, networking, and experimenting are all driven by an insatiable curiosity. While as educators we don't have control over all learning environments, we can create a talent-targeted culture that supports and rewards curiosity.

How to Create a *Curiosity* Talent Goal

Learners demonstrate curiosity as they seek new ideas; ask thoughtful, searching questions; and observe, explore, and investigate in different environments. Some learners will have a natural inclination to be curious with a greater frequency, depth, or complexity. Explicitly creating goals to target this aptitude provides opportunities to accelerate their talent. At the same time, talent-targeted goals encourage all learners' curiosity to emerge and progress.

> Learners demonstrate curiosity as they seek new ideas; ask thoughtful, searching questions; and observe, explore, and investigate in different environments.

Table 4.2 Student-Directed Talent Goals: Seven Aptitudes of Innovators

1. **Curiosity**	I demonstrate *curiosity* by being open to explore new ideas and experiences, asking thoughtful questions, observing, and investigating.
2. **Logical Reasoning**	I use *logical reasoning* to draw conclusions and make arguments that are based on facts and premises. I follow a systematic process to solve problems in a clear and sensible way.
3. **Creativity**	I express *creativity* through new or unusual ideas that are imaginative or inventive. I start and complete new projects based on my ideas.
4. **Insight**	I use *insight* to recognize patterns, make connections, and understand relationships. I can apply what I have learned in new situations.
5. **Persistence**	I demonstrate *persistence* when I focus energy and effort on a task; I continue working even when it is difficult, trying different methods to improve and refine.
6. **Metacognition**	I use *metacognition* to understand how I think, learn, and solve problems and use that knowledge to complete tasks, improve my work, and learn from my mistakes.
7. **Leadership**	I demonstrate *leadership* when I pay attention to people's needs and concerns, develop a positive plan of action, and organize others to achieve a goal.

Using the Talent Goal Frame

You can use the Talent Goal Frames to create a talent-targeted teaching and learning goal for *curiosity* (see Figure 4.0). Typically, begin in the center cell of the frame, filling in your required content standards and specific objectives. Next, select the talent aptitude you want to target—in this instance, *curiosity*—keeping in mind that the seven cross-domain aptitudes can become goals in any content area. You can keep track of the aptitudes you have targeted using the Talent Aptitude Unit Planners (available in the online appendix at www.resources.corwin.com/DevelopTalent).

> Keep in mind that, in practice, the talent goal planning process is not always linear.

If your lesson module is already part of a problem-based study such as *Healthy Community by Design*, you will have an authentic context for the talent goal and performance of understanding. If not, the next step is to consider authentic applications of the content knowledge and skills. Keep in mind that, in practice, the talent goal planning process is not always linear. Depending on your existing curriculum parameters, you might begin with any cell in the frame.

Sample *Curiosity* Talent-Targeted Goal

The *curiosity* Talent Goal Frame develops a goal from the STEM study, *Healthy Community by Design*. The corresponding student-directed goal explicitly defines *curious* behaviors and supports self-efficacy (see Table 4.2).

Figure 4.0 Sample Talent Goal Frame: *Curiosity* in STEM

Talent Aptitude	Content Standard Learning Objective	Performance of Understanding
1. Curiosity Seeks new ideas; asks thoughtful, searching questions; is inquisitive; observes, explores, and investigates keenly and alertly in any environment.	**Content Standard** Use random sampling to draw inferences about a population. (CCSS.MATH.CONTENT. 7.SP.1.) **Objective** Survey a stratified random sample that is representative of your community.	**Outdoor Recreation Survey** Design and conduct a survey for a stratified random sample of your community in order to draw conclusions about which recreational activities to include in your *Healthy Community by Design* plan to attract different groups.

Talent Aptitude	Content Standard Learning Objective	Performance of Understanding
Talent-Targeted Teaching and Learning Goal: STEM *Healthy Community by Design* (Grades 6–8) Demonstrate *curiosity* by surveying your community to draw conclusions about the recreational behavior of distinct populations.		
Student-Directed Talent Goal: I demonstrate *curiosity* by being open to explore new ideas and experiences, asking thoughtful questions, observing, and investigating.		

Curiosity Goal

Demonstrate curiosity by surveying your community to draw conclusions about the recreational behavior of distinct populations.

The *Curiosity* Performance of Understanding

The performance of understanding is an authentic task that provides both evidence of curiosity and mastery of the content standards through an independent application that demonstrates transfer of learning.

Outdoor Recreation Survey

Design and conduct a survey for a stratified random sample of your community in order to draw conclusions about which recreational activities to include in your Healthy Community by Design *plan that would attract different groups.*

In what ways does this performance of understanding develop *curiosity*? To design, conduct, and interpret their surveys, students must be open to *seek new ideas* and *investigate possibilities* for different types of outdoor activities. They must *observe* and *explore* which activities might be enjoyed by different groups and which would bring groups together. Finally, they will *compose thoughtful, searching questions* in order to obtain the most accurate and useful data.

How This Motivates and Engages Learners

The *curiosity* talent goal and performance of understanding support intrinsic motivation and student engagement through autonomy, competence, novelty, and involvement. The talent goal motivates learners by aiming at an authentic and novel application of STEM content and skills in the context of community planning. The goal answers the "why" for learning the skills of random sampling and data analysis by making real-life connections to the needs and interests of diverse people in the learners' own community. Students exercise autonomy through the choices they make in design of survey topics and questions, and they develop competence through the challenge of analyzing data and drawing conclusions. Overall, the tasks foster involvement by connecting them to their local community and the meaningful purpose of designing healthy outdoor activities that bring diverse persons together. Throughout the lesson module, learners are motivated by a self-directed talent goal that explicitly defines and describes *curiosity*.

How to Create a Talent Cluster Goal

The curiosity-focused performance of understanding could just as appropriately target other cross-domain talent aptitudes such as *logical reasoning, insight,* or *persistence.* Clustering several aptitudes in a goal provides more opportunities for learners to discover and develop their aptitudes as innovators. To challenge students, write a cluster goal that integrates domain-specific STEM aptitudes (see Chapter 5).

Curiosity Cluster Goal

Students will use curiosity, persistence, *and* mathematical reasoning *to draw conclusions about the recreational behavior of distinct populations.*

This cluster goal models how to integrate the cross-domain aptitudes of curiosity and persistence with the domain-specific aptitude, *mathematical reasoning.* As you become more adept at designing talent goals, begin to use cluster goals to provide more opportunities for learners to discover their areas of strength.

Assessing the Aptitude of *Curiosity*

Your talent-targeted goal and corresponding performance of understanding focus on developing curiosity in the context of mastering specific knowledge and skills. You can assess evidence of curiosity using the Talent Aptitude Learning Progressions to compose rubrics (Figure 4.1). This assessment process is discussed in detail in Chapter 7.

In addition to assessing the talent aptitudes, use your own formative assessments to collect evidence of mastery of content knowledge and skills in the standards and objectives.

Figure 4.1 *Curiosity* Learning Progressions

Curiosity	Emerging	Progressing	Advancing
Teacher Rubric	Asks questions on topics of interest; observes, explores, and investigates when prompted.	Shows interest in new ideas; asks questions; observes, explores, and investigates.	Seeks out new ideas; asks searching questions; observes intently; widely explores and investigates.
Student Rubric	I am mostly interested in ideas and environments that are familiar to me.	I am interested in new ideas and environments, and I ask questions that I can explore.	I am eager to learn new ideas, and I investigate new environments to find answers to my questions.

2. Logical Reasoning

Reasoning is the process by which we think, learn, and make decisions. However, not all reasoning is *logical*. Logical reasoning is a type of critical thinking that helps us to see the relationships among facts, deduce patterns and rules, and apply them to make sensible judgments removed from emotion. While logic is important in understanding abstract subjects such as mathematics, the principles of logic are universal and can be used to reason across all disciplines. Logic improves our critical thinking by helping us to identify sound from fallacious reasoning, to discern truth from lies. Its universal principles can be taught.[8]

Logical reasoning is one aptitude of innovators that can be assessed on intelligence (IQ) tests. Young children who are intellectually gifted will question, argue, and defend their arguments "logically."[9] While some have an advanced aptitude for logical reasoning, all of us can learn strategies to improve.

Innovators Use Logical Reasoning

Innovators use logical reasoning to decide which ideas to pursue to completion. They must hypothesize consequences, evaluate them, and know when to delay a decision. They use logical reasoning to systematically evaluate their ideas and "prune out" those with little chance for success. Within their optimistic risk-taking, they make "educated inferences." Innovators also use logic to sell their ideas to others: "If you expect people to accept your own conclusions, then it's your responsibility to give them reasons they can appreciate."[10] Successful innovators use logical reasoning to find and define the "real problem" that needs to be solved. For example, when Jeff Bezos started Amazon, he wasn't solving the problem of how to sell more books but rather answering the question "What are people likely to buy over the Internet?"[11]

> Successful innovators use logical reasoning to find and define the "real problem" that needs to be solved.

How to Create a *Logical Reasoning* Talent-Targeted Goal

Learners demonstrate logical reasoning when they draw conclusions from facts or premises; observe patterns and infer rules; use a systematic process to make sound judgments and form sensible arguments; and hypothesize and test. Some learners will have a natural inclination to use logical reasoning at a greater frequency, depth, or complexity. Explicitly creating goals to target this aptitude provides opportunities to accelerate talent. At the same time, talent-targeted goals encourage all learners' logical reasoning to emerge and progress.

Using the Talent Goal Frame

You can use the Talent Goal Frame to create a talent-targeted goal for *logical reasoning* (see Figure 4.2). Typically, begin in the center cell of the frame, filling in your required content standards and specific objectives. Next, select the talent aptitude you want to target—in this instance, *logical reasoning*—keeping in mind that the seven cross-domain aptitudes can become goals in any content area. If your lesson module is part of a problem-based study such as *Healthy Community by Design*, you will already have an authentic context for the talent goal and performance of understanding. If not, the next step is to consider authentic applications of the content knowledge and skills. Keep in mind that, in practice, the Talent Goal Frame planning process is not always linear. Depending on your existing curriculum parameters, you might begin with any cell in the frame.

Figure 4.2 Sample Talent Goal Frame: *Logical Reasoning*

Talent Aptitude	Content Standard Learning Objective	Performance of Understanding
2. Logical Reasoning Draws conclusions from facts or premises; observes patterns and infers rules; hypothesizes and tests; uses a systematic process to make sound judgments and form sensible arguments.	**Content Standards** Analyze proportional relationships and use them to solve real-world problems. (CCSS.MATH. CONTENT.7.RP.A.) Draw, construct, and describe geometrical figures and describe the relationships between them. (CCSS.MATH. CONTENT.7.G.A) **Objective** Use the actual lengths and areas of geometric figures to produce a scale drawing.	**Scale Model** Apply *Healthy Community by Design* principles to determine the actual dimensions for the buildings in your plan. Choose one rectangular building and determine a reasonable scale factor to use in making a 3D scale model. Prove mathematically that your model is proportional to the original.

Talent-Targeted Teaching and Learning Goal: STEM *Healthy Community by Design* (Grades 6–8)

Use *logical reasoning* to recognize patterns and implied relationships in order to determine a proportional scale for a model building in your *Healthy Community by Design* plan.

Student-Directed Talent Goal:

I use *logical reasoning* to draw conclusions and make arguments that are based on facts and premises. I follow a systematic process to solve problems in a clear and sensible way.

Sample *Logical Reasoning* Talent-Targeted Goal

The *logical reasoning* Talent Goal Frame develops a goal from the STEM study *Healthy Community by Design*. The corresponding student-directed goal explicitly defines *logical reasoning* behaviors and supports self-efficacy.

Logical Reasoning Goal

Use logical reasoning *to recognize patterns and implied relationships in order to determine a proportional scale for a model building in your healthy community plan.*

In what ways does this goal develop *logical reasoning*? Students must *draw conclusions* about proportional relationships, *observe patterns* and *infer relationships* between similar figures, use a *systematic process* to produce a scale drawing and model, *make sound judgments* regarding a reasonable scale factor, and *test and verify* that the model is proportional.

The *Logical Reasoning* Performance of Understanding

The performance of understanding is an authentic task that provides evidence of logical reasoning and mastery of the content knowledge and skills through an independent application that demonstrates transfer of learning.

Scale Model

Apply Healthy Community by Design *principles to determine the actual dimensions for the buildings in your plan. Choose one rectangular building and determine a reasonable scale factor to use in making a 3D scale model. Prove mathematically that your model is proportional to the original.*

How This Motivates and Engages Learners

The *logical reasoning* talent goal and performance of understanding support intrinsic motivation and student engagement through autonomy, competence, novelty, and involvement. The talent goal motivates learners by aiming at an authentic and novel application of STEM content knowledge and skills in the context of community planning. The goal answers the "why" for learning the concepts of proportional relationships and scale factor in the context of the real-life needs of diverse groups. Students exercise autonomy through the choices they make in the "healthy" design of the buildings and develop competence in applying mathematics to the task of making a 3D model. Overall, students become involved in their community and the meaningful purpose of designing living spaces that encourage healthy living. Throughout the lesson module, learners are motivated by a self-directed talent goal that explicitly defines and describes *logical reasoning*.

Create a *Logical Reasoning* Cluster Goal

This *logical reasoning* goal and performance of understanding could just as appropriately target other cross-domain aptitudes such as *insight* or domain-specific talent aptitudes such as *problem solving* (see Chapter 5). Clustering several aptitudes in a goal provides more opportunities for learners to discover and develop their aptitudes as innovators. To challenge students, write a talent cluster goal.

Logical Reasoning Cluster Goal

Use logical reasoning, insight, *and* problem solving *to determine an appropriate proportional scale for a model building in your* Healthy Community by Design *plan.*

The cluster goal shows how to integrate the cross-domain aptitudes of *logical reasoning* and *insight* with the STEM aptitude *problem solving*. As you become more adept at designing talent goals, begin to use cluster goals to provide more opportunities for learners to discover their strengths.

Assessing the Aptitude of *Logical Reasoning*

The talent goal and corresponding performance of understanding focus on developing logical reasoning in the context of mastering specific knowledge and skills. You can assess evidence of logical reasoning using the Talent Aptitude Learning Progressions to compose rubrics (see Figure 4.3). The complete assessment process is discussed in detail in Chapter 7.

In addition to using the rubrics to assess the talent aptitudes, use your own formative assessments to collect evidence as to student mastery of the specific content knowledge and skills in the standards and objectives.

Figure 4.3 *Logical Reasoning* Learning Progressions

Logical Reasoning	Emerging	Progressing	Advancing
Teacher Rubric	With guidance and modeling, can draw conclusions from evidence to make sound judgments and arguments.	Applies systematic thinking to draw conclusions from evidence in order to make sound judgments and sensible arguments.	Consciously selects a systematic process to form a hypothesis, draw conclusions from evidence, make sound judgments, and develop sensible arguments.
Student Rubric	I use evidence to draw conclusions and form arguments.	I draw conclusions and form sensible arguments based on evidence.	I use evidence to make convincing arguments and justify sensible solutions.

3. Creativity

Creativity is one talent aptitude that many people openly will claim *not* to have. Those who say "I'm not creative" are most likely referring to what Abraham Maslow named "Big C"—the artistic genius of creatives like Van Gogh or Martha Graham. In contrast, "little c" creativity is the kind that is essential to our humanness. Maslow applied the term "creative" not only to products but to people, activities, attitudes, and organizations.[12] In our homes and classrooms, children exhibit *creativity* when they express new or unusual ideas and connections; enjoy imagining, inventing, and divergent thinking; and initiate new projects based on their ideas.

Creativity researcher E. Paul Torrance, known as the "Father of Modern Creativity," derived four creative thinking abilities from studying the real-life creative achievements of famous scientists and inventors as well as from examples of everyday creativity. He maintained that the creative thinking skills of *fluency, flexibility, originality*, and *elaboration* can be taught.[13] Moreover, Torrance's research using his tests of creative thinking showed that creativity is a separate construct from intelligence as measured by IQ. Nor do creativity test scores manifest the "achievement gaps" among groups that are characteristic of other ability/achievement tests.[14] Creativity, it seems, is culture-fair.

Innovators Use Creativity

Innovation occurs when the creative process is applied in a product, idea, or service that is unique and useful. Creativity expert KH Kim explains that the term *unique* is preferable to *new* because most innovations build on existing ideas that have been combined in unique ways. All types of innovations must be useful to society, and the impact on populations over time determines whether the innovation is considered "Big I," such as the telephone, or "small i," such as your unique use of duct tape to fashion a costume for the school play.[15]

> Children exhibit *creativity* when they express new or unusual ideas and connections; enjoy imagining, inventing, and divergent thinking; and initiate new projects based on their ideas.

Innovators apply the creative process to solve problems. The creative problem-solving (CPS) method developed by Alex Osbourne, Sidney Parnes, Donald Treffinger, and others uses *divergent thinking* to explore broad possibilities and *convergent thinking* to focus on a single answer.[16] Both types of thinking are integral to the innovation process. While the creative person must be open to new ideas and willing to take risks, the creative product requires focus and discipline.

How to Develop a *Creativity* Talent-Targeted Goal

Some learners will have a natural inclination to demonstrate *creativity* with greater frequency, depth, and complexity. Explicitly creating goals to target this aptitude provides these students with opportunities to accelerate their talent. At the same time, talent-targeted goals encourage all learners' aptitudes for *creativity* to emerge and progress.

Using the Talent Goal Frame

You can use the Talent Goal Frame to develop a talent-targeted goal for *creativity* (see Figure 4.4). Generally, begin in the center cell of the frame, filling in the required content standards and specific learning objective. Next, select the talent aptitude, keeping in mind that the seven cross-domain aptitudes can be developed in any content area. If this lesson is part of a problem-based study, such as *Stop Sports Injuries*, you already have an authentic context for the talent goal and performance of understanding. If not, the next step is to consider authentic applications of this content. Keep in mind that the Talent Goal Frame process, like creative thinking itself, is not always this linear in practice. Depending on your existing curriculum parameters, you might begin with any cell in the frame.

Figure 4.4 Sample Talent Goal Frame: *Creativity*

Talent Aptitude	Content Standard Learning Objective	Performance of Understanding
3. Creativity Has unusual or clever ideas; enjoys divergent thinking, brainstorming, or imagining; is inventive; discovers unusual connections; initiates new projects.	**Content Standard** Understand ratio concepts and use ratio reasoning to solve problems. (CCSS.MATH. CONTENT.6RP.1) **Objective** Collect, graph, and analyze data to interpret ratio relationships.	**Sports Injuries Prevention** We are planning our responses to the call for proposals to Stop Youth Sports Injuries. Collect and analyze data on classmates' sports injuries to identify the greatest areas of need and propose a new product or process to reduce youth sports injuries.

Talent-Targeted Teaching and Learning Goal: STEM *Stop Sports Injuries (Grades 4–6)*

Use *creativity* to collect, graph, and interpret data on classmates' sports injuries to identify needs and propose an idea for a new youth sports injury prevention.

Student-Directed Talent Goal:

I express *creativity* through new or unusual ideas that are imaginative or inventive, making new connections, and initiating new projects.

Sample *Creativity* Talent-Targeted Goal

The *creativity* Talent Goal Frame develops a goal from the STEM study *Stop Sports Injuries* (see Chapter 2). The corresponding student-directed goal explicitly defines creative behaviors and supports self-efficacy.

Creativity Goal

Use creativity to collect, graph, and analyze data on classmates' sports injuries in order to identify needs and propose an idea for a new youth sports injury prevention.

In what ways does this goal develop *creativity*? Learners use creative thinking as they apply knowledge and skills that typically might be assessed on a short-answer test. They will use *divergent thinking* to create a variety of ratio interpretations, looking for *new connections* in sports injury statistics, using *creative problem solving* to determine the greatest need and *initiate new projects*. The task opens up opportunities to *imagine* and *invent*.

The *Creativity* Performance of Understanding

The performance of understanding is an authentic task that provides evidence of *creativity* and mastery of the mathematics content standards through an independent performance that demonstrates transfer.

Sports Injuries Prevention

We are planning our responses to the call for proposals to Stop Youth Sports Injuries. Collect and analyze data on classmates' sports injuries to identify the greatest areas of need and propose a new product or process to reduce sports injuries in young athletes.

How This Motivates and Engages Learners

The *creativity* goal and performance of understanding support intrinsic motivation and engagement through autonomy, competence, novelty, and involvement. The talent goal motivates learners by aiming at an authentic and novel application of creativity, math content knowledge, and skills. The performance of understanding answers the "why" for learning the concepts of ratio reasoning and the skills of graphing and analyzing data. Students are engaged by a relevant topic of interest, exercising autonomy through the choice of what sport or injury they might pursue and developing competence in analyzing and interpreting data to propose a new product or process. Overall, the task connects them to their community of peers through the meaningful purpose to reduce youth sports injuries. Throughout the lesson module, learners are motivated by a self-directed goal that explicitly defines and describes *creativity*.

Develop a *Creativity* Cluster Goal

The complexity of the creativity-targeted goal and performance of understanding could just as appropriately target other cross-domain aptitudes such as *logical reasoning*, *insight*, or *persistence* or domain-specific aptitudes. Clustering several talents in a goal provides more opportunities for learners to discover and develop their aptitudes as innovators. To challenge students, write a talent cluster goal for *creativity*.

Throughout the lesson module, learners are motivated by a self-directed goal that explicitly defines and describes *creativity*.

Creativity Cluster Goal

Students will use their creativity, insight, *and* persistence *to collect, graph, and analyze data on classmates' sports injuries in order to identify needs and propose an idea for a new youth sports injury prevention.*

As you become more adept at designing talent goals, begin to use cluster goals to provide more opportunities for learners to discover and develop specific strengths.

Assessing the *Creativity* Aptitude

Your talent goal and corresponding performance of understanding focus on developing *creativity* in the context of mastering specific knowledge and skills. You can assess evidence of creativity using the developmental Talent Aptitude Learning Progressions to compose rubrics (see Figure 4.5). The assessment process is described in detail in Chapter 7.

Figure 4.5 *Creativity* **Learning Progressions**

Creativity	Emerging	Progressing	Advancing
Teacher Rubric	Demonstrates typical ideas; makes literal connections; works on assigned projects.	Demonstrates divergent thinking when prompted; makes appropriate connections; is open to new projects.	Demonstrates divergent thinking through unusual or clever ideas; makes unexpected or imaginative connections; initiates new projects.
Student Rubric	I sometimes think of ideas about how things could be improved. I like to follow a model or pattern that already exists.	I think of ideas for new projects and can imagine how things could be improved. I sometimes put these new ideas into practice.	I enjoy thinking of different and unusual ideas. I often imagine what could be improved and discover new ideas for projects.

In addition to the aptitude rubrics, you'll develop your own formative assessments for evidence as to whether students have mastered the specific knowledge and skills in the content standard and learning objective.

4. Insight

Insight, the deep intuitive understanding that gives us new vision, is an important element in creative thinking and the innovation process. Because insight comes as a feeling or emotion from within, it conjures images of miraculous meditations or mad scientists running from the lab shrieking, "Eureka! I've got it!" We observe learners demonstrate insight when they are keenly observant and aware, intuitive, perceptive of patterns and relationships, and can readily grasp concepts to apply them in new situations.

Innovators Use *Insight*

While it may seem like a bolt from the blue, insight favors the prepared mind. In the Wallas four-stage creative process, insight is the illumination, or "aha" breakthrough, that follows a period of incubation and intense preparation in the domain.[17] Howard Gardner theorized that it takes 10 years of preparation to develop the expertise needed for innovation.[18] Malcom Gladwell in *Outliers* documents the 10,000 hours that prepared Steve Jobs as he was growing up in Silicon Valley.[19]

Learners demonstrate insight when they are keenly observant and aware, intuitive, perceptive of patterns and relationships, and can readily grasp concepts to apply them in new situations.

If insight follows preparation, then we can prepare future innovators today by targeting the aptitude of *insight* along with our goals to develop content expertise. According to Wallas, insight can't be consciously willed, but we can support learners' development of insight as they move through the creative process of *preparation* (conscious pursuit of knowledge), *incubation* (unconscious process of free association), and *verification* (testing through application).

How to Create an *Insight* Talent Goal

Some learners will have a natural inclination or potential to demonstrate *insight* with greater frequency, depth, and complexity.

Some learners will have a natural inclination or potential to demonstrate *insight* with greater frequency, depth, and complexity. Explicitly creating goals to target this aptitude provides them with opportunities to accelerate their talent. At the same time, talent-targeted goals encourage all learners' aptitude for *insight* to emerge and progress.

Using the Talent Goal Frame

You can use the Talent Goal Frame to create a goal for learners to develop *insight*. Typically, begin in the center cell of the frame, filling in your required content standards and specific objectives. Next, select the aptitude you want to target—in this instance, *insight*—keeping in mind that the seven cross-domain aptitudes can become a goal in any content area.

If the lesson module you're planning is part of a problem-based study, such as *Creating Sustainable Communities*, you will already have an authentic context for the talent goal and performance of understanding. If not, the next step is to consider authentic applications of the content knowledge and skills. Keep in mind that, in practice, the Talent Goal Frame process is not necessarily linear. Depending on your existing curriculum parameters, you might begin with any cell in the frame (see Figure 4.6).

Figure 4.6 Sample Talent Goal Frame: *Insight*

Talent Aptitude	Content Standard Learning Objective	Performance of Understanding
4. Insight Is keenly observant and aware; is intuitive; perceives new patterns and relationships; readily understands concepts and applies them to new situations.	**Content Standard** Determine a theme or central idea of a text and analyze its development over the course of the text, including its relationship to the characters, setting, and plot. (CCSS.ELA-LITERACY. RL.8.2) **Objective** Analyze the characters in *Watership Down* and people in your own community to infer how their needs motivate actions that impact the community.	**Multi-Voice Poem** Compose a multi-voice poem to communicate the insights you have gained from characters in the text and from community members about how people's needs motivate their actions that impact the community. Perform your poem with a partner at our school's poetry café.
Talent-Targeted Teaching and Learning Goal: Humanities *Creating Sustainable Communities* (Grades 6–8) Use *insight* to determine how people's needs motivate actions that impact the community.		
Student-Directed Talent Goal: I use *insight* to recognize patterns, make connections, and understand relationships. I can apply what I have learned to new situations.		

Sample *Insight* Talent-Targeted Goal

The *insight* Talent Goal Frame develops a goal from the humanities study *Creating Sustainable Communities*. The corresponding student-directed goal explicitly defines *insight* behaviors.

Insight Goal

Use insight *to determine how people's needs motivate their actions that impact the community.*

In what ways does this goal develop *insight*? Learners need to *keenly observe* the character traits in the novel; use their *intuition* to sense needs and infer motivations; *perceive patterns and relationships* among needs, actions, and impacts; *understand the concepts* of needs and motivations; and *apply concepts in new ways* to real-life situations in their communities.

The *Insight* Performance of Understanding

The performance of understanding is an authentic task that provides evidence of the talent aptitude and mastery of the content standards and objectives through an independent application that promotes transfer of learning.

Multi-Voice Insights Poem

Compose a multi-voice poem to communicate the insights you have gained from the characters in the text and from community members about how people's needs motivate their actions that impact the community. Perform your poem with a partner at our school's poetry café.

How This Motivates and Engages Learners

The *insight* goal and performance of understanding support intrinsic motivation and student engagement through autonomy, competence, novelty, and involvement. The talent goal motivates learners by aiming at an authentic and novel application of English language arts content and skills. The goal answers the "why" for learning by connecting the literary skill of analyzing characters in a text to the real-life skill of understanding the needs, motivations, and actions of people and their impact on community. Students exercise autonomy when choosing which "voices" to include, and they develop competence through the challenges of analyzing human motivations and composing and performing poetry. Overall, the goal connects them with others in their community and the meaningful purpose of understanding our interdependence. Throughout the lesson module, learners are motivated by a self-directed goal that explicitly defines and describes *insight*.

Create an *Insight* Talent Cluster Goal

The complexity of this *insight*-focused performance of understanding could just as appropriately target other cross-domain aptitudes such as *creativity*, *metacognition*, or *leadership*. Clustering several talents in a goal provides more opportunities for learners to discover and develop their aptitudes as innovators. To challenge students, write a cluster goal.

Insight Talent Cluster Goal

Students will use their insight, empathy, *and* communication *skills to determine how people's needs motivate their actions that impact the community.*

This goal models how to integrate the cross-domain aptitude of *insight* with two domain-specific humanities aptitudes, *empathy* and *communication*.

Assessing the *Insight* Aptitude

Your talent goal and corresponding performance of understanding focus on developing *insight* in the context of mastering specific knowledge and skills. You can assess evidence of *insight* using the developmental Talent Aptitude Learning Progressions (teacher and student versions) to compose rubrics (see Figure 4.7). The assessment process is described in detail in Chapter 7. In addition to the aptitude rubrics, you'll develop your own formative assessments for evidence as to whether students have mastered the specific knowledge and skills in the content standard and learning objective.

Figure 4.7 *Insight* Learning Progressions

Insight	Emerging	Progressing	Advancing
Teacher Rubric	Sees patterns and relationships when modeled; acquires concepts through experience and applies them to new situations with practice.	Observes patterns and relationships; acquires concepts through examples and applies them to new situations with modeling.	Grasps patterns and relationships quickly and easily transfers them to new situations; applies concepts independently in novel ways.
Student Rubric	I recognize patterns and relationships when given examples. I understand by following models.	I recognize patterns and relationships and understand ways to apply these to new situations.	I look for and quickly recognize patterns and relationships. I think of ways to apply understandings in new situations.

5. Persistence

We learned in childhood that *persistence* undergirds all achievement. The persistent tortoise won the race with the hare, and the "little engine that could," did. Persistence may be referred to as task commitment, perseverance, hard work, effort, or "grit." It's a personal trait or psychosocial skill that can be taught and developed. Learners persist when they focus effort and energy on a task, trying one more way to accomplish it when the previous way fails. Persistence empowers us to test and verify, improve and refine. It is fueled by a "growth mindset," or belief that achievement outcomes are not "fixed" and that effort produces results.[20] Many now believe that persistence is more crucial to success than talent.[21]

Innovators Are Persistent

Attaining expertise requires persistence, but innovators persist uniquely. Their persistence morphs into an intrinsically motivated passion that sustains them through the ups and downs of the creative problem-solving process. In his interviews with young innovators, their parents, and teachers, Tony Wagner found that *passion* was the most frequently mentioned word.[22] When young innovators discover an interest that kindles to passion, their zeal may cause them to resist closure and pursue that interest to the exclusion of others. Our well-meaning attempts to develop a "well-rounded" child with a variety of balanced interests may be stubbornly resisted. What we may not realize is that they are on their path to the 10,000 hours of deliberate practice that, theoretically, they need to become innovators.[23]

> Learners persist when they focus effort and energy on a task, trying one more way to accomplish it when the previous way fails.

How to Create a *Persistence* Talent Goal

Some learners will have a natural inclination to demonstrate *persistence* with greater frequency, depth, and complexity. Explicitly creating goals to target this aptitude provides these students with opportunities to accelerate their talent. At the same time, talent-targeted goals encourage all learners' aptitudes for *persistence* to emerge and progress.

Using the Talent Goal Frame

You can use the Talent Goal Frames to develop a talent-targeted goal for *persistence* (see Figure 4.8). Generally, you'll begin in the center cell of the frame, filling in the required content standards and specific learning objective. Next, select the talent aptitude, keeping in mind that the seven cross-domain aptitudes can be developed in any content area. If this lesson module is part of a problem-based study such as *Stop Sports Injuries*, you already have an authentic context for the talent goal and performance of understanding. If not, the next step is to consider authentic applications of this content. Keep in mind that the Talent Goal Frame process, in practice, is not always this linear. Depending on your existing curriculum parameters, you might begin with any cell in the frame.

Sample *Persistence* Talent-Targeted Goal

The *persistence* Talent Goal Frame develops a goal from the STEM study *Stop Sports Injuries*. The corresponding student-directed goal explicitly defines *persistent* behaviors and supports self-efficacy.

Figure 4.8 Sample Talent Goal Frame: *Persistence*

Talent Aptitude	Content Standard / Learning Objective	Performance of Understanding
5. Persistence Focuses time and energy on a topic of interest; looks for more than one way to accomplish a task; continues in spite of difficulty; strives to improve and refine; tests and verifies; may resist closure.	**Content Standards** Represent and interpret data. (CCSS.MATH.CONTENT.5.MD.B.2) **Objective** Collect data and make a line plot to calculate the average.	**Better Shoe Sizing** Poorly fitting athletic shoes can lead to sports injuries. Therefore, a popular sports apparel manufacturer is sponsoring a contest to determine the best way to designate shoe sizes. Gather data about the lengths of people's feet to determine a new way to designate shoe sizes and help the designers decide on a better, safer way to size shoes.
Talent-Targeted Teaching and Learning Goal: STEM *Stop Sports Injuries (Grades 4–6)* Use *persistence* to collect, display, and describe data to determine a new way to designate athletic shoe sizes.		
Student-Directed Talent Goal: I demonstrate *persistence* when I focus energy and effort on a task. I continue working even when it is difficult, trying different methods to improve and refine.		

Persistence Goal

Use persistence *to collect, display, and describe data to determine a new way to designate athletic shoe sizes.*

In what ways does this goal target *persistence*? Learners will need to *focus time and energy* on collecting and displaying the data. The data collection process must *continue despite difficulty*. As they *test and verify* measures, they look for patterns that enable them *to improve and refine* the shoe sizing process.

The *Persistence* Performance of Understanding

The performance of understanding is an authentic task that provides evidence of *persistence* and mastery of the mathematics content standards through an independent performance that demonstrates transfer.

Better Shoe Sizing

Poorly fitting athletic shoes can lead to sports injuries. Therefore, a popular sports apparel manufacturer is sponsoring a contest to determine the best way to designate shoe sizes. Gather data on the lengths of people's feet to determine a new way to designate shoes sizes and help the designers decide on a better, safer way to size shoes.

How This Motivates and Engages Learners

The *persistence* talent goal and performance of understanding support intrinsic motivation and student engagement through autonomy, competence, novelty, and involvement. The goal motivates learners by aiming at an authentic and novel application of *persistence*, content knowledge, and skills. It answers the "why" for learning the concepts of representing and interpreting data. Students are engaged by a relevant topic of interest (sports apparel) and exercise autonomy though the opportunity to submit their ideas to a contest. The challenging, creative, and open-ended task promotes mathematical competence. Overall, the task connects them to their community and to peers through the meaningful purpose to improve shoe sizing and prevent sports injuries. Throughout the lesson module, learners are motivated by a self-directed goal that explicitly defines and describes *persistence*, and they get frequent feedback throughout the study.

> The goal motivates learners by aiming at an authentic and novel application of *persistence*, content knowledge, and skills. It answers the "why" for learning the concepts.

Create a *Persistence* Cluster Goal

The complexity of the *persistence*-targeted goal and performance of understanding could just as appropriately target other cross-domain aptitudes such as *curiosity*, *insight*, or *logical reasoning*. Cluster goals may also integrate domain-specific apti-tudes such as *engagement in STEM* or *investigation*. Clustering several talents in a goal provides more opportunities for learners to discover and develop their apti-tudes. To challenge students, write a talent cluster goal.

Persistence Cluster Goal

Use curiosity, persistence, *and* insight *to collect, display, and describe data to determine a new way to designate athletic shoe sizes.*

As you become more adept at designing talent goals, begin to use cluster goals to provide more opportunities for learners to discover and develop specific strengths.

Assessing the *Persistence* Aptitude

Your talent goal and corresponding performance of understanding focus on devel-oping *persistence* in the context of mastering specific knowledge and skills. You can assess evidence of *persistence* using the developmental Talent Aptitude Learning Progressions (teacher and student version) to compose rubrics (see Figure 4.9). The assessment process is described in detail in Chapter 7. In addition to using the aptitude rubrics, you'll develop your own formative assessments for evidence as to whether students have mastered the specific knowledge and skills in the con-tent standard and learning objective.

> You can assess evidence of *persistence* using the developmental Talent Aptitude Learning Progressions (teacher and student version) to compose rubrics.

Figure 4.9 *Persistence* Learning Progressions

Persistence	Emerging	Progressing	Advancing
Teacher Rubric	Stays on task for a reasonable period of time, if not bringing it to completion.	Continues in a task with sufficient time and energy to bring it to completion, if not refinement.	Focuses energy and time to accomplish a task in spite of difficulty; examines alternatives; strives to test, refine, and improve.
Student Rubric	I work on a task for what I think is enough time and then stop, even if I am not finished.	I continue working on a task with enough time and energy to complete it, unless it's too difficult.	I focus my energy and time on a task and keep working when it is difficult, trying different ways to improve and refine.

6. Metacognition

Metacognition literally means "thinking about thinking." We use metacognition when we ponder the following questions: "What is the best way to solve this problem? Am I being successful with this strategy, or do I need to make modifications? What goals motivate and engage me? What are my strengths and weaknesses as a learner?" These reflective questions are part of the process of analyzing one's own knowledge and learning processes. Effective metacognitive skills help learners to become more confident and successful, and these skills can be taught.[24]

Innovators Use Metacognition

Innovators use their well-developed metacognitive skills to bring their unique visions into practical reality. They follow their interests, try out new things, experiment, and make modifications. They understand and expect that their experiments won't often succeed but provide necessary new learning. Edison said, "I haven't failed. . . . I've just found 10,000 ways that do not work."[25] Innovators use their metacognition to know when to shift strategies. Amazon founder Jeff Bezos shocked shareholders when he shifted from his completely "no bricks and mortar" online bookstore to his current discount retail warehouse model: "When one way doesn't work, you have to regroup and try a different approach."[26]

How to Create a *Metacognition* Teaching and Learning Goal

We don't know which of our students will develop into "disruptive innovators" like Edison or Bezos, but we can create a classroom that develops their metacognition. Learners use metacognition to understand their own thought processes, self-select appropriate problem-solving strategies; plan; self-monitor, reflect, assess, and correct; and learn from mistakes. Some students will show a natural inclination toward expressing metacognition with greater frequency depth, or complexity. Explicitly creating goals to target this aptitude provides opportunities to accelerate their talent. At the same time, talent-targeted goals encourage all learners' potential for metacognition to emerge and progress.

> Learners use metacognition to understand their own thought processes, self-select appropriate problem-solving strategies; plan; self-monitor, reflect, assess, and correct; and learn from mistakes.

Using the Talent Goal Frame

You can use the Talent Goal Frame to create a talent-targeted teaching and learning goal for *metacognition* (see Figure 4.10). Typically, begin in the center cell of the frame, filling in the required content standards and specific learning objective. Next, select the talent aptitude, keeping in mind that the seven cross-domain aptitudes can be developed in any content area. If this lesson module is part of a problem-based study, such as *Perspectives in Art and Culture*, you already have an authentic context for the talent-targeted teaching goal and performance of understanding. If not, the next step is to consider authentic applications of this content. Keep in mind that the Talent Goal Frame process is not, in practice, always linear. Depending on your existing curriculum parameters, you might begin with any cell in the frame.

Figure 4.10 Sample Talent Goal Frame: *Metacognition*

Talent Aptitude	Content Standard Learning Objective	Performance of Understanding
6. Metacognition Understands own thought processes; self-selects appropriate problem-solving strategies; plans; self-monitors, reflects, assesses, and corrects; learns from mistakes.	**Content Standards** Determine theme from details in the text, including how characters respond to challenges. (CCSS.ELA-LITERACY. RL.5.2) Interpret art to identify ideas and mood conveyed. (NATIONAL CORE ARTS STANDARDS: Visual Arts) **Objective** Demonstrate understanding of the concept of perspective in art and literature.	**Perspective Photo Essay** In the novel *Shooting Kabul*, Fadi expresses his personal perspective through photography, which also helped him work through problems. Express yourself like Fadi and create an original photo essay and artist's statement that illustrates your perspective, conveys your values, and may help others work through problems.
Talent-Targeted Teaching and Learning Goal: Humanities *Perspectives in Art and Culture* Demonstrate *metacognition* by creating a personal perspective photo essay and compose an artist's statement to interpret the photo essay.		
Student-Directed Talent Goal: I use *metacognition* to understand how I think, learn, and solve problems. I use that knowledge to complete tasks, improve my work, and learn from my mistakes.		

Sample *Metacognition* Talent Goal

The *metacognition* Talent Goal Frame develops a goal from the humanities study *Perspectives in Art and Culture*. The corresponding student-directed goal explicitly defines *metacognitive* behaviors and supports self-efficacy.

Demonstrate metacognition *by creating a personal perspective photo essay that reflects your interests and values and compose an artist's statement to interpret the photo essay.*

How does this goal develop *metacognition*? The goal encourages students to explore their personal interests and values, *self-select strategies* to develop the photo essay, *monitor* and *assess* the photographs' effectiveness at conveying ideas (modifying as needed), and *understand their thought processes* in order to express these in the artist's statement.

The *Metacognition* Performance of Understanding

The performance of understanding is an authentic task that provides evidence of metacognition and mastery of the humanities content standards through an independent performance that demonstrates transfer of learning.

Personal Perspective Photo Essay

In the novel Shooting Kabul, *Fadi expresses his personal perspective through his hobby of photography, which also helped him work through problems. Express yourself like Fadi and create an original photo essay and artist's statement that illustrates a personal perspective, conveys your values, and may help you or others work through problems.*

How This Motivates and Engages Learners

The *metacognition* goal and performance of understanding support intrinsic motivation and student engagement through autonomy, competence, novelty, and involvement. The goal motivates learners by aiming at a novel and authentic application of the required humanities content and skills, a photo essay and artist's statement. It answers the "why" for analyzing the overarching theme of perspective by making real-life connections to the students' personal perspectives.

> The performance of understanding encourages student engagement through its appeal to individual interests and emotions.

The performance of understanding encourages student engagement through its appeal to individual interests and emotions. In the study's core text, *Shooting Kabul* by N. H. Senzai, the main character Fadi uses his talent for photography to work out his grief and guilt over the disappearance of his sister when the family escaped Kabul. Students will need to reflect on their own experiences, use creative problem solving, and put time and effort into planning, organizing, and implementing their photo essays. Overall, the task connects them to their community through the meaningful purpose to communicate a personal perspective that may help others work through their problems. Throughout the lesson module, learners are motivated by a self-directed goal that explicitly defines and describes *metacognition*.

Create a *Metacognition* Cluster Goal

The complexity of the *metacognition* talent goal and performance of understanding could just as appropriately target other cross-domain aptitudes such as *curiosity* or *persistence* or domain-specific aptitudes such as *humanities engagement*. As you become more adept at designing talent goals, begin to use cluster goals to provide more opportunities for learners to discover and develop specific strengths. To challenge students, write a cluster goal.

Metacognition Cluster Goal

Demonstrate metacognition, persistence, *and* humanities engagement *by creating a personal photo essay and composing an artist's statement to interpret it.*

Assessing the *Metacognition* Aptitude

Your talent goal and corresponding performance of understanding focus on developing *metacognition* in the context of mastering specific knowledge and skills. You can assess evidence of metacognition using the developmental Talent Aptitude Learning Progressions (teacher and student versions) to compose rubrics (see Figure 4.11). The assessment process is described in detail in Chapter 7.

Figure 4.11 *Metacognition* **Learning Progressions**

Metacognition	Emerging	Progressing	Advancing
Teacher Rubric	Can identify own thinking when prompted; uses problem-solving strategies as provided; may correct mistakes if asked; typically acts before deliberating.	Is aware of own thought processes; chooses a problem-solving strategy from those provided; applies feedback to correct mistakes when prompted; considers own thoughts and actions.	Understands own thought processes; self-selects appropriate problem-solving strategies; self-monitors, assesses and corrects; learns from mistakes; is deliberate, reflective.
Student Rubric	I start working on a task or solving a problem before thinking about the best way for me to complete it. I'm not sure how to use the feedback I'm given to improve my work.	I think about the best way for me to solve a problem or complete a task before I start it. I can use the feedback I'm given to improve my work and learn from my mistakes.	I understand how I think, learn, and solve problems, and I use that knowledge to complete tasks. I think about how I can improve and learn from my mistakes.

In addition to the aptitude rubrics, you'll develop your own formative assessments for evidence as to whether students have mastered the specific knowledge and skills in the content standard and learning objective.

7. Leadership

All of us have leadership potential that can be developed. According to Howard Gardner, the cognitive abilities of leaders—awareness of self and others, understanding dynamics of social settings, personal wants and goals—are all observable in five-year-olds! What talent aptitudes differentiate gifted leaders from others? Leaders have uncanny social and communication skills, or "personal and linguistic intelligences." They take risks, are confident, seek power for self and others, and often feel, from a young age, a sense of destiny or being special.[27]

Innovators Become Leaders

Regardless of talent domain, all innovators will likely become leaders, either directly or indirectly. Indirect leaders influence through their "disruptive innovations" and expertise in a particular domain. Gardner explains that neither Albert Einstein nor Margaret Mead sought to become leaders but became so through the innovative impact they made in their fields. In contrast, direct leaders are "leaders by choice" who have a desire to effect change and seek to influence the broader community. Eleanor Roosevelt and Dr. Martin Luther King Jr. were visionary direct leaders who advocated for change to improve the lives of "invisible" Americans.[28]

How to Create a *Leadership* Talent Development Goal

We have direct and indirect future leaders in our classrooms today, although we may not know who they are or which type of leader they will become. Leaders listen to the concerns of others; set goals and initiate plans; and they influence, motivate, and organize people to adopt a plan of action.

> Leaders listen to the concerns of others; set goals and initiate plans; and they influence, motivate, and organize people to adopt a plan of action.

Some learners will have a natural inclination to demonstrate *leadership* with greater frequency, depth, and complexity. Explicitly creating goals to target this aptitude provides these students with opportunities to accelerate their talent. At the same time, talent-targeted goals encourage all learners' aptitudes for *leadership* to emerge and progress.

Using the Talent Goal Frame

You can use the Talent Goal Frames to develop a talent-targeted teaching and learning goal for *leadership* (see Figure 4.12). Typically, begin in the center cell of the frame, filling in the required content standards and specific learning objective. Next, select the talent aptitude, keeping in mind that the seven cross-domain aptitudes can be developed in any content area. If this lesson module is part of a problem-based study, such as *Creating Sustainable Communities*, you already have an authentic context for the goal and performance of understanding. If not, the next step is to consider authentic applications of this content. Keep in mind that the Talent Goal Frame process is not, in practice, always this linear. Depending on your existing curriculum parameters, you might begin with any cell in the frame.

Figure 4.12 Sample Talent Goal Frame: *Leadership*

Talent Aptitude	Content Standard Learning Objective	Performance of Understanding
7. **Leadership** Motivates others to achieve a goal; initiates ideas and listens to concerns of others; influences others to adopt and participate in a plan of action; organizes others to implement a plan.	**Content Standards** Analyze how dialogue or incidents propel the action, reveal character, or provoke a decision. (CCSS.ELA-LITERACY. RL.8.3) Write arguments to support claims with clear reasons and relevant evidence. (CCCS.ELA-LITERACY.W.8) **Objective** Identify, analyze, and apply the leadership qualities of characters in the novel *Watership Down*.	**Defend Your Plan** Apply analysis of characters in the novel and research on local community leaders to compose a speech or blog that defends how your community redevelopment plan will succeed and motivates others to adopt your plan.
Talent-Targeted Teaching and Learning Goal: Humanities *Creating Sustainable Communities* (Grades 6–8) Demonstrate *leadership* by influencing others to adopt and implement a plan for community redevelopment.		
Student-Directed Talent Goal: I demonstrate *leadership* when I pay attention to people's needs and concerns, develop a positive plan of action, and organize others to achieve a goal.		

Sample *Leadership* Talent-Targeted Goal

The *leadership* Talent Goal Frame develops a goal from the humanities study *Creating Sustainable Communities*. The corresponding student-directed goal explicitly defines *leadership* behaviors and supports self-efficacy.

Demonstrate leadership *by influencing others to adopt and implement a plan for community redevelopment.*

In what ways does this goal develop *leadership*? In order for students to *initiate their ideas* and formulate a plan, they must *consider the concerns of others*. This helps them to gain *influence* and eventually *organize others* to adopt and implement the plan.

The *Leadership* Performance of Understanding

The performance of understanding is an authentic task that provides evidence of the aptitude of *leadership* and mastery of the English language arts content standards through an independent application that demonstrates transfer.

Defend Your Plan

Apply analysis of characters in the novel and research on local community leaders to compose a speech or blog that defends how your community redevelopment plan will succeed and motivates others to adopt your plan.

How This Motivates and Engages Learners

The talent-targeted goal and performance of understanding support intrinsic motivation and student engagement though autonomy, competence, novelty, and involvement. The goal motivates learners by aiming at a novel and authentic application of the humanities content and skills, motivating others to develop and support a community redevelopment plan. The goal answers the "why" for mastering the skills of analyzing character development and writing arguments to support claims. In this example, the classic novel *Watership Down* by Richard Adams develops four different rabbit communities and leadership styles, only one of which is "sustainable." These principles are applied in an engaging and challenging task to identify a local area in need of redevelopment and create a plan that they persuade others to adopt. Students are emotionally connected to spend the time and effort on defense of their community development plan, supporting autonomy through choice and competence through authentic challenge. Overall, the task connects them to the meaningful purpose to redevelop and reclaim an area in their neighborhood for the good of the community. Throughout the study, learners are motivated by the self-directed goal that explicitly defines and describes *leadership* behaviors.

Create a *Leadership* Cluster Goal

The complexity of the *leadership* talent goal and performance of understanding could just as appropriately target other cross-domain aptitudes such as *creativity* or *insight* and domain-specific humanities aptitudes such as *resourcefulness* or *communication*. Clustering several aptitudes in a goal provides more opportunities for learners to discover and develop their talents. To challenge students, write a cluster goal.

Leadership Cluster Goal

Demonstrate leadership, insight, *and* communication *by influencing others to adopt and implement a plan for community redevelopment.*

Assessing the *Leadership* Aptitude

The talent goal and corresponding performance of understanding focus on developing *leadership* in the context of mastering specific knowledge and skills. You can assess evidence of leadership using the developmental Talent Aptitude Learning Progressions (teacher and student versions) to compose rubrics (see Figure 4.13). The assessment process is described in detail in Chapter 7.

In addition to the aptitude rubrics, you'll develop your own formative assessments for evidence as to whether students have mastered the specific knowledge and skills in the content standard and learning objective.

In addition to the aptitude rubrics, you'll develop your own formative assessments for evidence as to whether students have mastered the specific knowledge and skills in the content standard and learning objective.

Figure 4.13 *Leadership* Learning Progressions

Leadership	Emerging	Progressing	Advancing
Teacher Rubric	When provided with the goals, can follow a plan of action and work with others to achieve it.	Sets goals and creates a plan of action to achieve them; influences others to participate in the plan.	Casts a vision and develops a plan of action; motivates and organizes others to participate and bring the vision into reality.
Student Rubric	I can work with others to follow a plan of action to achieve a goal.	I can set goals and work with others to achieve a plan of action.	I have a vision for what I want to achieve and can persuade others to participate in my plan of action.

Notes

1. Wiggins, G. (2013, March 7). *Understanding by design part 1*. AVENUESdotORG. https://www.youtube.com/watch?v=4isSHf3SBuQ

2. Subotnik, R. J. (2009). Developmental transitions in giftedness and talent: Adolescence into adulthood. In F. D. Horowitz, R. F. Subotnik, & D. J. Matthews (Eds.), *The development of giftedness and talent across the lifespan* (pp. 155–170). American Psychological Association.

3. Matthews, D. J. (2009). Developmental transitions in giftedness and talent: Childhood into adolescence. In F. D. Horowitz, R. F. Subotnik, & D. J. Matthews (Eds.), *The development of giftedness and talent across the lifespan* (pp. 89–107). American Psychological Association.

4. Csiksentmihalyi, M. (1997). *Finding flow: The psychology of engagement with everyday life*. Basic Books.

5. Kim, KH. (2016). *The creativity challenge: How we can recapture American innovation*. Prometheus Books.

6. Kim, 2016.

7. Dyer, J., Gregersen, H., & Christensen, C. M. (2011). *The innovator's DNA: Mastering the five skills of disruptive innovators*. Harvard Business Review Press.

8. Dowden, B. H. (2011/2017). *Logical reasoning*. California State University.

9. Rimm, S. B., Siegle, D., & Davis, G.A. (2018). *Education of the gifted and talented* (7th ed.). Pearson Education.

10. Dowden, 2011/2017.

11. Dyer, Gregersen, & Christensen, 2011.

12. Maslow, A. (1962). *Toward a psychology of being*. D. Van Nostrand Co.

13. Torrance, E. P., & Myers, R. E. (1970). *Creative teaching and learning*. Dodd Mead.

14. Cramond, B., Mathews-Morgan, J., Bandalos, D., & Zuo, L. (2005). A report on the 40-year follow-up of the Torrance tests of creative thinking: Alive and well in the new millennium. *Gifted Child Quarterly, 49*(4), 283–291.

15. Kim, 2016.

16. Treffinger, D. J., & Firestien, R. L. (1989). *Handbook of creative learning*. Center for Creative Learning.

17. Wallas, G. (1926/2014). *The art of thought*. Solis Press.

18. Gardner, H. (1993/2011). *Creating minds: An anatomy of creativity*. Basic Books.

19. Gladwell, M. (2008). *Outliers: The story of success*. Little, Brown, & Co.

20. Dweck, C. S. (2006). *Mindset: The new psychology of success*. Random House.

21. Duckworth, A. (2016). *Grit: The power of passion and perseverance*. Scribner.

22. Wagner, T. (2012). *Creating innovators: The making of young people that will change the world*. Scribner.

23. Gardner, 1993/2011.

24. Donovan, M. S., & Brandsford, J. D. (Eds). (2005). *How students learn: History, mathematics, and science in the classroom*. The National Academies Press.

25. Dyer, Gregersen, & Christensen, 2011.

26. Dyer, Gregersen, & Christensen, 2011.

27. Gardner, H. (1995). *Leading minds: An anatomy of leadership*. Basic Books.

28. Gardner, 1995.

Chapter
FIVE

Teach to Develop STEM Talent

Many students are convinced they are not and cannot be good at STEM by the time they are in high school. As educators, we must not confirm this belief. We must instead encourage students of all ages to see themselves in STEM.

—Dr. Freeman Hrabowski

While the seven aptitudes of innovators promote achievement across domains, each of the talent goals developed in Chapter 4 were rooted in rich, domain-specific content. In this chapter, we'll explore the role of STEM-specific aptitudes in talent development. As learners enter the middle grades, it becomes increasingly important to "talent spot" for their natural inclinations in a domain and to provide opportunities to discover and extend domain-specific interests. The STEM and humanities-specific talent aptitudes are not mutually exclusive, but when clusters of the traits are observed in a learner, it may indicate domain-specific potential that can be explicitly targeted. By creating STEM talent goals, we activate the possibility that learners will discover and pursue their passions to one day become tomorrow's STEM innovators.

> By creating STEM talent goals, we activate the possibility that learners will discover and pursue their passions to one day become tomorrow's STEM innovators.

Key Understandings

1. As learners enter the middle grades, it becomes increasingly important to identify and nurture "at promise" talent in a specific domain, such as STEM or humanities.

2. There are five STEM-specific talent aptitudes that undergird innovation: STEM engagement, investigation, problem solving, spatial reasoning, and mathematical reasoning.

3. We have a STEM talent gap based on incorrect beliefs about STEM, inconsistent educational opportunities, and lack of access due to geographical and demographic factors.

4. Creating and assessing STEM-targeted talent goals and performances of understanding is a strategy for increasing access for all learners to develop the skills they need for success in the innovation economy.

STEM Talent Is Domain-Specific

A talent development mindset focuses on the ways in which students are "at promise" for talents to emerge. We know that talent develops over time from a broad expression to a narrow focus and that domains have different trajectories across the lifespan.[1] Research shows that academic strengths are not necessarily consistent across domains. Studies of eminent adults reveal that they are often "uneven" in their areas of giftedness. Additionally, among high-performing adolescents, scores of mathematical and verbal abilities are not highly correlated.[2]

As we teach to develop talent, it is important that we are identifying the specific ways that learners are motivated and engaged.

The STEM Talent Aptitudes

What is STEM talent? We know that the acronym stands for science, technology, engineering, and mathematics, yet STEM is more than the content of these disciplines. It includes "the set of knowledge and skills and mindsets that all students and workers need to succeed in both middle- and high-skill jobs in the modern economy."[3] The emphasis here is on "all students and workers." Yet we have evidence that the average K–12 American student does not meet the competencies demanded in the STEM-driven labor market.[4] The number of STEM jobs outnumber the qualified candidates. Through its focus on developing STEM-specific aptitudes, the talent-targeted teaching and learning model is one solution to the causes of the STEM talent gap.

Filling the STEM Talent Gap

The 2018 report *State of STEM* explains that there are multiple root causes for the STEM talent gap, which lie in six different areas: skills, beliefs, K–12 and postsecondary education, geography, and demographics.[5] As you create STEM-specific talent goals aligned with rich content and assessed in performances of understanding, you are working to fill the gaps in each of these areas.

> The "skills" in STEM go beyond content acquisition to include higher-order thinking and problem solving, the focus of the five STEM talent aptitudes.

To begin, the "skills" in STEM go beyond content acquisition to include higher-order thinking and problem solving, the focus of the five STEM talent aptitudes: *engagement in STEM*, *investigation*, *problem solving*, *spatial reasoning*, and *mathematical reasoning* (see Table 5.0).

Table 5.0 Five Aptitudes of STEM Innovators

1. Engagement in STEM	Exhibits high interest in science, technology, engineering, or mathematics content; is enthusiastic, observant, and involved in STEM activities; is self-motivated to pursue STEM knowledge and skills.
2. Investigation	Uses a systematic approach to explore natural phenomenon; collects, examines, analyzes, and summarizes data; offers logical explanations; interprets and communicates findings.
3. Problem Solving	Identifies and frames problems; analyzes causes and effects to generate solutions; selects appropriate strategies and technologies; develops a plan of action; tests and verifies.

(Continued)

Table 5.0 (Continued)

4. Spatial Reasoning	Visualizes and interprets images; understands and remembers relationships among objects; can construct and manipulate mental models.
5. Mathematical Reasoning	Perceives patterns and relationships; quickly and accurately applies mathematical knowledge to solve problems; selects appropriate strategies; analyzes and evaluates results; proposes alternate solutions.

> As you cultivate a talent development mindset and create goals that stimulate STEM aptitudes, you are replacing these incorrect beliefs with newfound confidence.

Incorrect beliefs about what it takes to succeed in STEM careers cause students (and the adults around them) to lack confidence in their abilities: They think "STEM is too hard," and when they don't have the highest grades and test scores, they disqualify themselves. However, STEM is not for the "top few": "Innovation is not solely within the realm of PhDs. It takes ten technicians at the middle skill level to contribute to any single engineering breakthrough."[6] As you cultivate a talent development mindset and create goals that stimulate STEM aptitudes, you are replacing these incorrect beliefs with newfound confidence.

Another root cause of the STEM talent gap is the failure of K–12 and postsecondary education to fully implement the curricular shifts needed to prepare tomorrow's STEM innovators. Project-based learning and community-based internships are two strategies for engaging students in STEM. These opportunities exist but have not been implemented to scale across all populations. In this book, the two sample STEM talent-targeted teaching and learning studies, *Stop Sports Injuries* and *Healthy Community by Design*, demonstrate how students can develop and apply their STEM aptitudes in solving local community problems. Chapter 8 presents the 5P Planner, a design strategy for developing project-based/problem-based studies.

Both geography and demographics influence the STEM talent gap. Increasingly, we see the development of "STEM hubs," economic centers where the culture of STEM abounds to support students' interest and opportunities. What happens if your students do not live in such a community? Similarly, there is a lack of STEM participation among demographic groups, with women and minorities underrepresented in STEM education and careers.[7] Talent-targeted teaching and learning promotes STEM access for all students.

Teach to Develop the Five STEM Aptitudes

To close the STEM talent gaps, we must teach to develop STEM talent aptitudes. While the five aptitudes are not an exhaustive or mutually exclusive list, these traits are useful for talent scouting and identifying a learner's natural inclinations that can be developed.

How to Use This Chapter

In the following chapter, each of the five STEM aptitudes is defined and explained as it relates to real-world achievement and to developing STEM talent, our long-term goal for students. You'll review examples of goals from the two STEM talent-targeted studies, *Stop Sports Injuries* and *Healthy Community by Design*, already introduced in Chapters 2 and 4.

Each section will continue to emphasize how the STEM talent goal is designed to motivate and engage learners and develop their talent along a continuum. The Talent Goal Frames provide examples of how to cultivate the aptitudes in the context of STEM content standards and learning objectives. The student-directed goals explicitly target the behaviors associated with each aptitude (see Table 5.1). Use these sample Talent Goal Frames not as "prescriptions" but as models for transforming your existing curriculum.

Table 5.1 Student-Directed Goals in STEM Aptitudes

1. Engagement in STEM	I demonstrate *engagement in STEM* by showing interest in science, engineering, or mathematics activities and looking for more ways to become involved in them.
2. Investigation	I conduct an *investigation* by asking questions that can be explained by systematically collecting, displaying, and interpreting data.
3. Problem Solving	I use *problem solving* to identify problems, analyze cause and effect, and propose solutions to test and verify using appropriate methods.
4. Spatial Reasoning	I use *spatial reasoning* to visualize, remember, and understand relationships among objects.
5. Mathematical Reasoning	I use *mathematical reasoning* to recognize the patterns in numbers or shapes, determine the rules, and apply mathematical knowledge to solve problems.

1. Engagement in STEM

Children have a natural curiosity, which is the foundation for learning. We saw earlier that *curiosity*, one of the cross-disciplinary aptitudes, is "the innovator's DNA."[8]

(Continued)

(Continued)

This inquisitive, searching, exploring aptitude is also the foundation for engagement in STEM. Mario Livio, an astrophysicist and author of *Why: What Makes Us Curious*, believes that curiosity drives all scientific research and creativity in all disciplines. He posits that Leonardo Da Vinci and Richard Feynman (both scientists) exemplify the most curious minds in history. This "epistemic curiosity," the drive to learn something new, evokes a pleasurable reward and fosters our love of learning. Children are curious in this way; however, epistemic curiosity remains constant across the lifespan.[9]

While we aim to provide opportunities to create STEM interest in all students, the fact is that some will show a natural inclination that causes them to gravitate to STEM activities. All creative behavior begins with interest, an openness to experience, accompanied by access to the domain.[10] Whether it is genetically or experientially originated, learners with an aptitude for STEM will exhibit high interest in science, technology, engineering, or mathematics content; be enthusiastic, observant, and involved in STEM activities; and self-motivate to pursue STEM knowledge and skills. For these students, and all others, the teacher can motivate, strengthen, and document STEM engagement through the phases of the talent-targeted teaching and learning process.

Create a Talent Goal for *STEM Engagement*

The sample talent-targeted teaching and learning goal is for students to demonstrate *engagement in STEM* by analyzing and framing the problem presented in a popular sports apparel company's call for proposals to develop a "mathematically sound" product to prevent youth sports injuries (see Figure 5.0). In a problem-based learning (PBL) format, this lesson would introduce the open-ended problem that drives the study, with the objective to craft the PBL problem statement.[11] In the discussion of the problem scenario, the students have multiple opportunities to demonstrate interest, enthusiasm, background knowledge, and motivation to pursue STEM.

This *engagement in STEM* talent goal could just as effectively target a different STEM aptitude, such as problem solving, and can be expanded to become a cluster goal. Clustering several aptitudes in a goal provides more opportunities for students to discover and develop their aptitudes as innovators.

While we aim to provide opportunities to create STEM interest in all students, the fact is that some will show a natural inclination that causes them to gravitate to STEM activities.

Clustering several aptitudes in a goal provides more opportunities for students to discover and develop their aptitudes as innovators.

TEACH TO DEVELOP TALENT

Figure 5.0 Sample Talent Goal Frame: *Engagement in STEM*

Talent Aptitude	Content Standard Learning Objective	Performance of Understanding
1. Engagement in STEM Exhibits high interest in science, technology, engineering, or mathematics content; is enthusiastic, observant and involved in STEM activities; is self-motivated to pursue STEM knowledge and skills.	**Content Standards** Make sense of problems and persevere in solving them. (CCSS.Math.Practice.MP1) Model with mathematics. (CCSS.Math.Practice.MP4) **Objective** Identify the mathematical knowledge and skills that are needed to solve the problem to propose a new piece of equipment to stop youth sports injuries.	***Stop Sports Injuries* Problem Statement** Respond to the call for proposals to stop sports injuries by creating a know/need-to-know/need-to-do (KNN) chart and using it to craft a problem statement with criteria for success.

Talent-Targeted Teaching and Learning Goal: STEM *Stop Sports Injuries (Grades 4–6)*

Students will demonstrate *engagement in STEM* by analyzing and framing the problem presented in the call for proposals to develop a product to stop youth sports injuries.

Student-Directed Talent Goal:

I demonstrate *engagement in STEM* by showing interest in science, technology, engineering, or mathematics activities and looking for ways to become more involved in them.

Engagement in STEM Cluster Goal

Students will demonstrate *engagement in STEM*, *logical reasoning*, and *problem solving* by analyzing and framing the problem presented in the call for proposals to develop a product to stop youth sports injuries.

Motivate, Engage, and Develop STEM Engagement

By crafting a goal in which the aptitude of STEM engagement drives the mathematics standards to "make sense of problems and persevere in solving them" and "model with mathematics," you focus students' attention on the essence of what motivates scientists and engineers to create and innovate. Students take on the role of innovators, solving a problem that promotes autonomy through choice, competence through challenge, and involvement in the local community. The task engages through a novel topic of high interest (sports injuries) and a sense of purpose in working to reduce injuries. The *Stop Sports Injuries* study was originally developed for students living in a city of a popular sports apparel designer's headquarters (making the problem "local"), and representatives from the company were invited (and came!) to review their final products. Because the most motivating and engaging curriculum is locally developed, you will generate your own community-based PBL scenarios using local issues and connections.

Assessing *Engagement in STEM*

You can assess students' ongoing demonstration of STEM engagement using the Talent Aptitude Learning Progressions (see Figure 5.1). These stages of development provide a systematic way to describe and document evidence and provide feedback. Chapter 7 provides a detailed process for assessing talent aptitudes.

Figure 5.1 *STEM Engagement* **Learning Progressions**

STEM Engagement	Emerging	Progressing	Advancing
Teacher Rubric	Demonstrates some interest in STEM activities; completes the required STEM activities with external prompting.	Demonstrates interest in STEM through involvement in class activities; is self-motivated to complete the required activities without external prompting.	Demonstrates high interest in and enthusiasm for STEM through active and focused involvement; initiates new tasks beyond requirements.
Student Rubric	I have some interest in science, technology, engineering, and mathematics (STEM) topics, and I am sometimes engaged by the activities.	I am interested in science, technology, engineering, and mathematics (STEM) topics and motivated to complete the activities.	I am very interested and engaged in science, technology, engineering, and mathematics (STEM) topics. I am self-motivated to engage in STEM activities.

2. Investigation

When we teach to develop STEM talent aptitudes, we cultivate what Howard Gardner calls "the disciplined mind." He concludes that schools have focused more on instilling the *subject matter* of science rather than on the *discipline*, which consists of the particular ways that scientists think and view the world.[12] Scientists are *investigators*; they observe, question, make hypotheses about cause and effect, test, collect and analyze data, and verify. Investigation teaches students how knowledge is produced. It is "the interaction of content and process."

Investigation is a habit of mind and a process that can be modeled and learned; it is also a talent aptitude that must be identified and nurtured if our students are to become disciplinary experts with the potential to become tomorrow's innovators. While there is a renewed emphasis in teaching science processes,[13] an explicit talent-scouting process is required. Writes Gardner, "The training of disciplinarians takes place through the identification of mutual interests and gifts ('You have the talent to become a scientist/historian/literary critic/engineer/executive')."[14]

Create a Talent Goal for *Investigation*

The sample Talent Goal Frame for the *investigation* aptitude continues to develop the core problem posed in the goal for STEM engagement. Here, students practice the discipline of collecting and graphing data on class sports injuries in order to explain the various ratio relationships.

Both the subject matter of ratio relationships and the aptitude for investigation are applied in a performance of understanding that demonstrates transfer of learning and the creation of new knowledge rather than recall (see Figure 5.2).

> Investigation is a habit of mind and a process that can be modeled and learned; it is also a talent aptitude that must be identified and nurtured.

The *investigation*-focused goal and performance of understanding could appropriately target another STEM aptitude such as *mathematical reasoning* or target cross-domain aptitudes such as *curiosity* and *persistence*. Clustering several aptitudes in a goal provides more opportunities for students to discover and develop their aptitudes as innovators.

Investigation Cluster Goal

Students will use *curiosity*, *persistence*, and *investigation* to explore the ratio relationships among sports injuries.

Motivate, Engage, and Develop *Investigation* Talent

Investigations begin with questions, and these should be of interest and importance to the learners. The question of how we can better understand data on sports injuries in order to prevent them is intrinsically motivating through an authentic and novel application of STEM content. The goal answers the "why" for learning the skills and concepts of ratio relationships applied to a situation that greatly affects them and their peers. Students exercise autonomy as they interpret the data through different scenarios and competence as they use data to help them identify the best directions for their sports injury prevention product. The meaningful tasks foster involvement with their peers and the greater community.

> Investigations begin with questions, and these should be of interest and importance to the learners.

Figure 5.2 Sample Talent Goal Frame: *Investigation*

Talent Aptitude	Content Standard Learning Objective	Performance of Understanding
2. Investigation Uses a systematic approach to explore natural phenomenon; collects, examines, analyzes, and summarizes data; offers logical explanations; interprets and communicates findings.	**Content Standard** Understand ratio concepts and use ratio reasoning to solve problems. (CCSS.MATH. CONTENT.6.RP.) **Objective** Collect and graph data on class sports injuries and explain the ratio relationship.	**Sports Injuries Scenarios** Collect data on sports injuries among classmates and create your choice of graph that reflects class data. Using the data and the graphs, create a variety of ratio scenarios. Present these to the class, discuss your reasoning, and use these data to propose which sports have the greatest need for a new *Stop Sports Injuries* product.

Talent-Targeted Teaching and Learning Goal: STEM *Stop Sports Injuries (Grades 4–6)*

Conduct an *investigation* into the ratio relationships among sports injuries.

Student-Directed Talent Goal:

I conduct an *investigation* by asking questions that can be explained by systematically collecting, displaying, and interpreting data.

Assessing *Investigation*

You can assess students' ongoing demonstration of the *investigation* aptitude using the Talent Aptitude Learning Progressions (see Figure 5.3). These stages of development provide a systematic way to describe and document evidence and provide feedback. Chapter 7 provides a detailed process for assessing talent aptitudes.

Figure 5.3 *Investigation* **Learning Progressions**

Investigation	Emerging	Progressing	Advancing
Teacher Rubric	Implements methods to explore natural phenomenon; uses prescribed procedures to collect, analyze, and summarize data.	Selects appropriate procedures to explore natural phenomenon and methods to collect, analyze, and summarize data to communicate findings.	Develops procedures to explore natural phenomenon and methods to collect, analyze, and summarize data; explains and interprets findings.
Student Rubric	I follow the procedures that are provided to explore and find answers to questions, collect data, and summarize findings.	I explore and search out answers to questions. I select appropriate strategies to collect and display data and summarize findings.	I propose questions and search out answers, developing a system to accurately collect, display, analyze, and interpret findings.

3. Problem Solving

Problem solving is widely accepted as an essential 21st-century skill. Simply defined, problem solving is "the process of finding solutions to difficult or complex issues."[15] We have known for more than a decade that we need to teach problem solving, particularly in the context of engineering and design, two themes with high priority on every nation's agenda.[16] We now have national standards for engineering practices; yet, as we learned earlier, employers still do not find enough qualified STEM problem solvers to fill the demand. We need to create and assess talent-targeted goals for problem solving.

The crucial first step in problem solving is having students ask questions to define the problem to be solved. Albert Einstein once said, "If I were given one hour to save the planet, I would spend 59 minutes defining the problem and one minute resolving it." There are various problem-solving models, such as creative problem solving (CPS) and the Wallas model (see Chapter 4). The National Aeronautics and Space Administration (NASA) developed the BEST Engineering Design Model, which consists of six stages: ask, imagine, plan, create, test, and improve.[17] Key elements across models include identifying problems, analyzing cause and effect, generating solutions, testing and verifying, and developing a plan of action. These are the STEM disciplinary habits of mind that we want to develop in our students.

Create a Talent Goal for *Problem Solving*

The sample talent-targeted teaching and learning goal is for students to demonstrate their problem-solving aptitude by conducting an experiment to determine which running shoe best reduces foot strike impact (see Figure 5.4). This study develops the engineering concept of fair tests in which variables are controlled in order to determine aspects of a model that can be improved. The talent goal for *problem solving* prepares students to generate a solution to the *Stop Sports Injuries* call for proposals to develop a new product. The experiment provides opportunities for them to identify and frame problems, analyze cause and effect, generate solutions, use technology, test and verify, and develop a plan of action. As a performance of understanding, the experiment applies in a new context the mathematics and engineering skills and understandings that have been introduced and practiced in other more structured tasks.

The problem-solving talent goal could appropriately target a different STEM aptitude such as *investigation* or *mathematical reasoning*, or target cross-domain aptitudes such as *insight* or even *leadership*, if working in teams. Clustering several aptitudes in a goal provides more opportunities for students to discover and develop their STEM aptitudes. To challenge students, write a cluster goal.

Problem Solving Cluster Goal

Students will use *problem solving, mathematical reasoning*, and *insight* to conduct an experiment to determine which running shoe best reduces foot strike impact.

Motivate, Engage, and Develop *Problem Solving*

The talent goal makes it explicit that students are first and foremost *problem solvers* who happen to be conducting a fair test, and the students' attention is focused on the process of the experiment, which is transferrable. The problem-solving talent goal and performance of understanding motivate by focusing energy on an authentic task, testing the foot strike impact among different running shoes. Students are engaged by the novelty of measuring foot strike with an impact accelerometer. Answering the question of which shoe best reduces foot strike impact serves the meaningful purpose to potentially reduce running injuries.

Figure 5.4 Sample Talent Goal Frame: *Problem Solving*

Talent Aptitude	Content Standard Learning Objective	Performance of Understanding
3. Problem Solving Identifies and frames problems; analyzes causes and effects to generate solutions; selects appropriate strategies and technologies; develops a plan of action; tests and verifies.	**Content Standards** Represent and interpret data. (CSSS.MATH. CONTENT.5.MD) Plan and carry out fair tests in which variables are controlled and failure points are considered to identify aspects of a model or prototype that can be improved. (NGSS Engineering Design 3-5-ETS1-3) **Objective** Collect, display, and describe data on foot strike impact.	**Safest Running Shoe?** Each year 30% of runners experience foot, ankle, shin, or knee injuries due to foot strike impact. Design and conduct an experiment to determine which running shoe best reduces foot strike impact.
Talent-Targeted Teaching and Learning Goal: STEM *Stop Sports Injuries (Grades 4–6)* Use *problem solving* to design an experiment to determine which running shoe best reduces foot strike impact.		
Student-Directed Talent Goal: I use *problem solving* to identify problems, analyze cause and effect, and propose solutions to test and verify using appropriate tools and methods.		

Assessing *Problem Solving*

You can assess students' ongoing demonstration of the *problem solving* aptitude using the Talent Aptitude Learning Progressions. These stages of development provide a systematic way to describe and document evidence and provide feedback. Chapter 7 provides a detailed process for assessing talent aptitudes.

Figure 5.5 *Problem Solving* Learning Progressions

Problem Solving	Emerging	Progressing	Advancing
Teacher Rubric	Solves problems with guidance and modeling of cause and effect; uses the tools and strategies provided to follow a plan of action.	Identifies problems and applies strategies to analyze causes and effects; selects appropriate tools and processes to find solutions.	Frames new problems and determines appropriate strategies, tools, and processes to generate verifiable solutions.
Student Rubric	I solve problems using the strategies and tools that are provided for me to use.	I solve problems selecting from the strategies and tools I have learned and test my solutions for accuracy.	I identify new problems to solve and select appropriate strategies and tools to find solutions that I test and verify.

4. Spatial Reasoning

The research is clear that spatial ability is a predictor of success in STEM careers. It is also evident that we miss spatial reasoning ability when we test only with mathematical and verbal measures.[18] We are failing to identify spatial aptitude and thereby contributing to the STEM talent gap. What is spatial ability, or reasoning? There are several definitions, but the dominant factor across these is *visualization*—in particular, the ability to mentally rotate three-dimensional objects and solve problems using rotation. Spatial ability includes visual memory, complex image recognition, and the abilities to recognize partially visible objects and to estimate lengths. It is what we use to find our way out of a maze.[19]

Spatial reasoning is both an innate aptitude and a learned ability. A study conducted among engineering students scoring "low" in spatial ability showed that, with intervention, spatial reasoning can be acquired.[20] Training in spatial skills among younger students has shown promise in helping them learn new mathematical concepts.[21] These findings strongly support the practice of creating and assessing *spatial reasoning* talent-targeted teaching and learning goals.

> We are failing to identify spatial aptitude and thereby contributing to the STEM talent gap.

Create a *Spatial Reasoning* Talent Goal

The sample talent goal for *spatial reasoning* is for students to create a scale drawing or three-dimensional model for a building in their *Healthy Community by Design* plan (see Figure 5.6). The performance of understanding requires them to use their spatial skills of visualization as they apply the mathematical concept of scale factor and the engineering process of designing according to criteria and constraints.

The spatial reasoning talent goal could appropriately target a different STEM aptitude, such as *mathematical reasoning*, or one of the cross-disciplinary aptitudes, such as *logical reasoning* or *persistence*. Clustering several aptitudes in a goal provides more opportunities for students to discover and develop their aptitudes as innovators. To challenge students, write a talent cluster goal.

Spatial Reasoning Cluster Goal

Students will use *spatial reasoning*, *mathematical reasoning*, and *persistence* to create a scale drawing or three-dimensional model of a building.

Motivate, Engage, and Develop *Spatial Reasoning*

The spatial reasoning goal and performance of understanding provide authentic applications of content that are motivating and engaging for students. The scale model is not an isolated task, but it focuses students' attention and energy on the larger project, their *Livewell* community proposal. Students have autonomy through the choices they make in deciding on the scale factor, and their competence is challenged in making the scale drawing or 3D model. The novelty of the task involves students as they continue to work toward the meaningful goal of a healthier community for all. You can develop your students' spatial reasoning talent by applying these same principles in your teaching.

Figure 5.6 Sample Talent Goal Frame: *Spatial Reasoning*

Talent Aptitude	Content Standard Learning Objective	Performance of Understanding
4. Spatial Reasoning Visualizes and interprets images; understands and remembers relationships among three-dimensional objects; mentally manipulates objects to solve problems.	**Content Standards** Solve problems involving scale drawings of geometric figures. (CSSS.MATH. CONTENT.7.G.1) Define the criteria and constraints of a design problem with sufficient precision to ensure a successful solution. (NGSS Engineering Design MS-ETS1-1) **Objective** Determine an appropriate scale factor to use in making a scale drawing or 3D model.	**Building to Scale** Your *Livewell* community plan requires you to build a scale model for a mixed-use building. A local architect has provided us with actual dimensions for several such buildings in our community. Choose one and determine an appropriate scale factor to use in making a scale drawing or 3D model. Draw or build your scale model and prove that your model is similar to the original.
Talent-Targeted Teaching and Learning Goal: STEM *Healthy Community by Design (Grades 6–8)* Use *spatial reasoning* to create a scale drawing or three-dimensional model of a building.		
Student-Directed Talent Goal: I use *spatial reasoning* to visualize, remember, and understand relationships among three-dimensional objects.		

Assessing *Spatial Reasoning*

You can assess students' ongoing demonstration of *spatial reasoning* using the Talent Aptitude Learning Progressions. These stages of development provide a systematic way to describe and document evidence and provide feedback. Chapter 7 provides a detailed process for assessing talent aptitudes.

Figure 5.7 *Spatial Reasoning* Learning Progressions

Spatial Reasoning	Emerging	Progressing	Advancing
Teacher Rubric	Recognizes and remembers simple images; visualizes three-dimensional objects and identifies relationships.	Recognizes and remembers complex images; visualizes and manipulates three-dimensional objects to solve problems.	Mentally manipulates, constructs, and interprets relationships among three-dimensional objects to solve problems.
Student Rubric	I recognize and remember images and three-dimensional objects.	I visualize, remember, and understand relationships among three-dimensional objects.	I understand the relationships among three-dimensional objects and mentally manipulate them to solve problems.

5. Mathematical Reasoning

When people react negatively to the subject of mathematics, the reason is usually based on the way that it was taught: We learned the rules without the reasoning.[22] Mathematical reasoning is sensemaking—the critical thinking that enables us to recognize patterns; develop arguments; explore, explain, and evaluate mathematical arguments; and communicate insights.[23] While procedural understanding is important, we must link it to conceptual understanding in order to solve problems. Advanced mathematical reasoning is a key aptitude of STEM innovators, but it is not the only factor. Research shows that young people with high mathematical aptitude who also had engaged in rich and varied STEM experiences were more likely to achieve at high levels in STEM careers.[24]

> Mathematical reasoning is sensemaking—the critical thinking that enables us to recognize patterns; develop arguments; explore, explain, and evaluate mathematical arguments; and communicate insights.

All learners can develop their mathematical reasoning, beginning with the process of engaging their preconceptions about learning mathematics (i.e., it's just about

(Continued)

(Continued)

computing and following rules). We can allow them to begin problem solving with their own informal strategies, followed by making thinking visible through "math talk." Learners develop mathematical conceptual understanding by making real-world connections and using metacognitive strategies such as self-monitoring and reflection.[25]

Learners with a natural aptitude for mathematical reasoning use their unschooled "fluid intelligence" to intuitively see relationships and solve problems for which they have not had any formal instruction, and this can emerge at an early age. They develop their own number sense and may be stronger in conceptual understanding than computation. These students will need instructional adaptations, including acceleration and enrichment.[26]

By creating and assessing *mathematical reasoning* talent-targeted teaching and learning goals, all learners have focused opportunities for this aptitude to emerge, progress, and advance.

Create a *Mathematical Reasoning* Talent Goal

The sample talent goal for mathematical reasoning requires students to solve a real-world problem related to their *Healthy Community by Design* proposal (see Figure 5.8). Students must accurately apply mathematical knowledge and select strategies to calculate the surface area of a building in order to determine the amount and cost of ecofriendly material needed to cover the exterior. Once they have researched sustainable materials, they will choose two of these and calculate their costs based on the surface area estimates. Finally, students will analyze and evaluate the results to suggest the best exterior covering for their *Livewell* community proposal.

This *mathematical reasoning* goal and performance of understanding could appropriately target a different STEM aptitude, such as *investigation*, or a cross-disciplinary aptitude, such as *curiosity* or *insight*. Clustering several aptitudes in a goal provides more opportunities for students to discover and develop their talents. To challenge students, write a mathematical reasoning cluster goal.

Mathematical Reasoning Cluster Goal

Students will use *curiosity*, *mathematical reasoning*, and *insight* to calculate the surface area of a building and the cost to cover the exterior using sustainable materials.

Motivate, Engage, and Develop *Mathematical Reasoning*

The mathematical reasoning talent goal and performance of understanding are intrinsically motivating through the choices students must make in researching and selecting sustainable materials. Taking on the role of professional builders and doing what they actually do fosters learners' competence and self-efficacy. The novelty and complexity of making a recommendation for the best exterior building material provides the optimal match of challenge and skill. Finally, the task involves students in an important moral cause: environmental sustainability. While your curriculum context may differ, you can apply these same design principles to develop mathematical reasoning aptitude in your students.

Figure 5.8 Sample Talent Goal Frame: *Mathematical Reasoning*

Talent Aptitude	Content Standard Learning Objective	Performance of Understanding
5. Mathematical Reasoning Perceives patterns and relationships; quickly and accurately applies mathematical knowledge to solve problems; selects appropriate strategies; analyzes and evaluates results; proposes alternate solutions.	**Content Standard** Solve real-world and mathematical problems involving area, volume, and surface area of two- and three-dimensional objects. (CSSS.MATH. CONTENT.7.G.6.) **Objective** Calculate the surface area to determine how much material will be needed to cover a given structure.	**Sustainable Materials Recommendation** Your *Livewell* proposal requires that all structures are covered using sustainable materials such as the ones we have researched. Using the dimensions from buildings in our community, select two ecofriendly materials and calculate the amounts needed and the costs based on current rates. Propose a recommendation for which material to use for the exteriors of your community buildings.

Talent-Targeted Teaching and Learning Goal: STEM *Healthy Community by Design* (Grades 6–8)

Use *mathematical reasoning* to calculate surface area of a building and the cost to cover the exterior using sustainable materials.

Student-Directed Talent Goal:

I use *mathematical reasoning* to recognize patterns in numbers or shapes, determine the rules, and apply mathematical knowledge to solve problems.

Assessing *Mathematical Reasoning*

You can assess students' ongoing demonstration of *mathematical reasoning* using the Talent Aptitude Learning Progressions. These stages of development provide a systematic way to describe and document evidence and provide feedback. Chapter 7 provides a detailed process for assessing talent aptitudes.

Figure 5.9 *Mathematical Reasoning* Learning Progressions

Mathematical Reasoning	Emerging	Progressing	Advancing
Teacher Rubric	Recognizes patterns and relationships from multiple examples; uses strategies to solve mathematical problems with modeling and practice.	Recognizes patterns and relationships after a few examples; selects strategies to accurately solve mathematical problems.	Readily perceives patterns and relationships; proposes, implements, and evaluates multiple strategies to accurately solve problems.
Student Rubric	I see how the patterns in numbers or shapes follow rules when these are modeled for me. I follow the strategy provided to solve mathematical problems.	I see the rules in patterns of numbers or shapes that I apply to select strategies to accurately solve mathematical problems.	I find new patterns in numbers or shapes, propose rules, and use multiple strategies to accurately solve mathematical problems.

Notes

1. Subotnik, R. J. (2009). Developmental transitions in giftedness and talent: Adolescence into adulthood. In F. D. Horowitz, R. F. Subotnik, & D. J. Matthews (Eds.), *The development of giftedness and talent across the lifespan* (pp. 155–170). American Psychological Association.
2. Winner, E. (2009). Toward broadening our understanding of giftedness: The spatial domain. In F. S. Horowitz, R. F. Subotnik, & D. J. Matthews (Eds.), *The development of giftedness and talent across the life span* (pp. 75–85). American Psychological Association.
3. White, E. S. (2018). *State of STEM. Defining the landscape to determine high-impact pathways for the future workforce.* STEMconnector. https://www.stemconnector.com/state-stem-report/
4. White, 2018.
5. White, 2018.
6. Smith, N. (2018). In E. S. White (Ed.), *State of STEM: Defining the landscape to determine high-impact pathways for the future workforce* (p. 16). https://www.stemconnector.com/state-stem-report/
7. White, 2018.
8. Dyer, J., Gregersen, H., & Christensen, C. M. (2011). *The innovator's DNA: Mastering the five skills of disruptive innovators.* Harvard Business Review Press.
9. Livio, M. (2017). *Why: What makes us curious.* Simon & Schuster.
10. Csikszentmihalyi, M. (1997). *Finding flow: The psychology of engagement with everyday life* (pp. 53–54). Basic Books.
11. Torp, L., & Sage, S. (2002). *Problems as possibilities: Problem-based learning for K–16 education* (2nd ed.). ASCD.
12. Gardner, H. (2006). *Five minds for the future.* Harvard Business School Press.
13. The National Academy of Sciences. (2012). *A framework for K–12 science education: Pratices, crosscutting concepts, and core ideas.* The National Academies Press.
14. Gardner, 2006, p. 31.

15. Problem solving. (n.d.). https://www.lucidchart.com/blog/problem-solving-definition

16. Bybee, R. W. (2010, August 27). What is STEM education? *Science*, p. 996.

17. National Aeronatics and Space Administration. (2018). *Engineering design model.* NASA. https://www.nasa.gov/audience/foreducators/best/edp.html

18. Wai, J., Lubinski, D., & Benbow, C. (2009). Spatial ability for STEM domains: Aligning over 50 years of cumulative psychological knowledge solidifies its importance. *Journal of Educational Psychology*, *101*(4), 817–835.

19. Jeffey Buckley, N. S. (2018, September). A heuristic framework of spatial ability: A review and synthesis of spatial factor literature to support its translation into STEM education. *Educational Psychology Review, 30*(3), 947–972.

20. Sorby, S. (1999). Developing 3-D spatial visualization skills. *Engineering Design Graphics Journal*, *63*(2), 21–32.

21. Young, C. J., Levine, S. C., & Mix, K. S. (2018, June 4). The connection between spatial ability and mathematical ability across development. *Frontiers in Psychology*, *9*, 755.

22. Fusion, K., Kalchman, M., & Bransford, J. D. (2005). Mathematical understanding: An introduction. In National Research Council (Ed.), *How students learn: Mathematics in the classroom* (pp. 217–256). National Academies Press.

23. National Council of Teachers of Mathematics. (2000). *Principles and standards for school mathematics*. National Council of Teachers of Mathematics.

24. Wai, J., Lubinski, D., Benbow, C., & Steiger, J. H. (2010). Accomplishment in science, technology, engineering, and mathematics (STEM) and its relation to STEM educational dose: A 25-year longitudinal study. *Journal of Educational Psychology*, *102*(4), 860–871.

25. Fusion, Kalchman, & Bransford, 2005.

26. Rutigo, J. V., & Fello, S. (2004). Mathematically gifted students: How can we meet their needs? *Gifted Child Today, 27*(4), 46–51.

●

Chapter
SIX

Teach to Develop Humanities Talent

Not everything that counts can be counted, and not everything that can be counted counts.

—attributed to Albert Einstein

arly in the 21st century, a *New York Times* best-seller placed the humanities on equal footing with STEM as essential 21st-century skills. In his book *A Whole New Mind: Why Right-Brainers Will Rule the Future*, Daniel Pink identified six humanities-related aptitudes necessary for success in the "conceptual age of creators and empathizers."[1] We must master what he calls "the new six senses," which value *design* over function, *story* over argument, *symphony* or *synthesis* over focus, *empathy* over logic, *play* over seriousness, and *meaning* over accumulation.[2] Pink describes the new "high concept/high touch" economy where computers or low-cost workers replace routinized jobs and what we now produce must be "physically beautiful and emotionally appealing."[3] In the conceptual age, our work must have purpose and meaning. Based on this view, the humanities, the study of what *it means to be human*, are exactly what is needed to educate tomorrow's innovators.

Key Understandings

1. Social innovators often come from a humanities or liberal arts background, where they have developed their aptitudes for *humanities engagement, empathy, resourcefulness, verbal reasoning,* and *communication.*

2. Creating and assessing humanities-targeted goals and performances of understanding prepares students for successful citizenship and careers in the conceptual age.

3. Humanities talent goals foster intrinsic motivation and engagement through choice, challenge, personal relevance, involvement, and authentic application.

4. Teachers and students can assess humanities talent goals using learning progressions that define the levels of expression from emerging to progressing to advancing.

The humanities include history, philosophy, religion, languages, literature, arts, media, and all cultural studies. These subjects always have been considered essential to the "well-rounded curriculum." The humanities develop the critical thinking and questioning that are essential for creative problem solving because, as writer George Santayana said, "Those who cannot remember the past are condemned to repeat it." In K–12 education, the humanities curriculum typically includes language arts, arts integration, and social studies. The National Council for Social Studies (NCSS) defines "social studies" as "the integrated study of the social sciences and humanities to promote civic competence" and draws upon "such disciplines as anthropology, archaeology, economics, geography, history, law, philosophy, political science, psychology, religion, and sociology, as well as appropriate content from the humanities, mathematics, and natural sciences."[4]

Despite the crucial importance of the humanities in the conceptual age, today many students in universities are drawn to majors that are perceived as directly vocational in nature. The humanities, however, have a broader purpose to cultivate the individual citizen.[5] Social innovators often come from a humanities or "liberal arts" educational background. As Tony Wagner states in his book *Creating Innovators,*

"STEM innovators want to *make things* that will change the world.... Social innovators, on the other hand, want to *make change*."[6] Wagner goes on to report that the humanities-oriented social innovator often shows an early interest in community service projects, local community engagement, and pursuing interdisciplinary studies in college.[7]

The key roles that the humanities play in our personal lives, citizenship, and social and cultural innovation are important reasons to identify and develop our students' humanities aptitudes that are keys to success in the conceptual age: *engagement in the humanities*, *empathy*, *resourcefulness*, *verbal reasoning*, and *communication*. While these are not mutually exclusive to the humanities, a student who consistently displays a cluster of these aptitudes may possess this domain-specific talent, which can be nurtured (see Table 6.0).

Table 6.0 Five Aptitudes of Humanities Innovators

1. Engagement in the Humanities	Shows active interest in human society and culture, contemporary and historical issues, academic disciplines, languages, or the arts; is self-motivated to expand knowledge and experiences in these areas.
2. Empathy	Readily makes personal associations; understands and shares the feelings of others; identifies with human concerns beyond one's own cultural group.
3. Resourcefulness	When presented with a problem, can locate and effectively use a variety of resources to extract relevant information and significant ideas; uses existing materials effectively and in new ways.
4. Verbal Reasoning	Demonstrates depth and complexity of comprehension by making inferences and forming interpretations; integrates prior knowledge and monitors comprehension; synthesizes and applies reading in creative problem solving.
5. Communication	Expresses ideas fluently and effectively in written, oral, or visual forms; expands and elaborates on ideas in ways that others understand; conveys meaning through symbol and emotion; develops a personal voice or style.

How to Use This Chapter

As in Chapter 4 and Chapter 5, this chapter is organized into five self-contained sections for each of the humanities aptitudes. Each is defined and explained as it relates to real-world achievement, our long-term goal for students. The sample

> The key roles that the humanities play in our personal lives, citizenship, and social and cultural innovation are important reasons to identify and develop our students' humanities aptitudes.

Talent Goal Frames provide examples of how to cultivate the aptitudes in the context of humanities content standards and learning objectives. The student-directed goals explicitly target the behaviors associated with each aptitude (see Table 6.1). Both the aptitudes and content standards are demonstrated in performances of understanding with authentic contexts for transfer of learning. The "Motivate and Engage" section highlights the design principles that you can apply to creating your own authentic talent-targeted tasks. You can assess the goals and performances of understanding using the Talent Aptitude Learning Progressions, a process discussed in detail in Chapter 7. Use these sample Talent Goal Frames not as "prescriptions" but as models for teaching to develop humanities talent.

Table 6.1 Student-Directed Goals in Humanities Aptitudes

1. Engagement in the Humanities	I demonstrate *engagement in the humanities* by showing interest in literature, language, social studies, or arts-related activities and look for more ways to become involved in them.
2. Empathy	I show *empathy* when I connect to others from different groups and cultures and imagine what it is like to walk in their shoes.
3. Resourcefulness	I demonstrate *resourcefulness* by knowing where to find and how to use information and materials to solve problems.
4. Verbal Reasoning	I use *verbal reasoning* to interpret what I read, make connections, and apply reading to solve problems.
5. Communication	I use *communication* to express and expand upon ideas and effectively convey my meaning to others.

1. Engagement in the Humanities

Learners demonstrate engagement in the humanities when they show active interest in society and culture, contemporary and historical issues, academic disciplines, languages, and the arts. They are self-motivated to expand their knowledge and experiences in these areas. While we aim to provide opportunities to encourage humanities engagement in all learners, some will show a natural inclination or aptitude that causes them to gravitate to these activities. Creating a talent goal for humanities engagement serves to advance their involvement as well as to cultivate it in those who are less inclined, possibly due to lack of opportunities.

Create a Talent Goal for *Humanities Engagement*

The sample talent-targeted teaching and learning goal for *humanities engagement* is from the study *Perspectives in Art and Culture* (see Figure 6.0). In the core novel

Shooting Kabul by N. H. Senzai, the main character Fadi uses his favorite and only book *From the Mixed-Up Files of Mrs. Basil E. Frankweiler* as a source of comfort and inspiration in dealing with the challenge of having his younger sister Miriam left behind when the family was fleeing from Afghanistan. In this way, the book is Fadi's "bibliotherapy," the practice of using targeted reading materials to find solutions to personal problems.[8] The talent-targeted goal for students to demonstrate *engagement in the humanities* is to explain how a book they read is a source of comfort and inspiration to them in dealing with their own life challenges (the teacher could modify this goal to include the choices of movie, TV show, or song). This goal and performance of understanding provide students with opportunities to demonstrate their interest and prior experiences in literature, social studies, or arts-related activities.

Figure 6.0 Sample Talent Goal Frame: *Engagement in Humanities*

Talent Aptitude	Content Standard Learning Objective	Performance of Understanding
1. Engagement in Humanities Shows active interest in human society and culture, contemporary and historical issues, academic disciplines, languages, or the arts; is self-motivated to expand knowledge and experiences in these areas.	**Content Standards** Determine a theme of a story from details in the text, including how characters in a story respond to challenges; summarize the text. (CCSS.ELA-LITERACY. RL.5.2) **Objective** Summarize the text of a book that is personally meaningful and explain why and how you connect with it.	**Book Talk: Take It With You** In the novel *Shooting Kabul*, Fadi's favorite book, which he brought with him from Afghanistan, is a source of comfort and inspiration in dealing with his own challenges. Imagine that you must leave your home quickly and can only take one book. What would you choose? Compose a book talk for your peers that explains why and how you connect with the book you chose.

Talent-Targeted Teaching and Learning Goal: Humanities *Perspectives in Art and Culture (Grades 4–6)*

Demonstrate *engagement in the humanities* by explaining how a book you read is a source of comfort and inspiration to you in dealing with challenges.

Student-Directed Talent Goal:

I demonstrate *engagement in the humanities* by showing interest in literature, language, social studies, or arts-related activities and look for more ways to become involved in them.

Motivate, Engage, and Develop *Humanities Engagement*

In the sample talent goal, the long-term purpose of fostering learners' humanities engagement also accomplishes the language arts skill of summarizing a text. Both will be assessed in the performance of understanding, the "Take It With You" book talk for peers. The task is intrinsically motivating and engaging through student choice and personal reflection on their own reading/viewing/listening experiences.

Learners are challenged through the higher-order thinking skills of analyzing, synthesizing, and evaluation. Overall, students can see this: The task matters to me, and I am emotionally involved. My effort is rewarded as I make authentic connections to text, applying the outer world of humanities studies to solving problems in my inner, personal world.

This *humanities engagement* goal and performance of understanding could just as effectively target a different humanities aptitude, such as *empathy* or *verbal reasoning*, and can be expanded to a cluster goal using cross-disciplinary aptitudes such as *metacognition* or *insight*. To challenge students and provide more opportunities for them to discover and develop their talents, create a talent cluster goal.

Engagement in Humanities Cluster Goal

Demonstrate *metacognition, insight,* and *engagement in the humanities* by explaining how a book you read is a source of comfort and inspiration to you in dealing with challenges.

Assessing *Humanities Engagement*

You can assess students' ongoing levels of humanities engagement and provide formative feedback using the humanities Talent Aptitude Learning Progressions (see Figure 6.1). The talent development assessment process is described in detail in Chapter 7.

Figure 6.1 *Humanities Engagement* **Learning Progressions**

Humanities Engagement	Emerging	Progressing	Advancing
Teacher Rubric	Demonstrates some interest in humanities activities; completes required humanities activities with external prompting.	Demonstrates interest in humanities through involvement in class activities; is self-motivated to complete the required activities with external prompting.	Demonstrates high interest in and enthusiasm for the humanities through active and focused involvement; initiates new tasks beyond requirements.
Student Rubric	I have some interest in humanities topics, but I am not always motivated by the activities.	I am interested in humanities and am usually motivated to complete the activities.	I am very interested in humanities and am self-motivated to complete the activities.

2. Empathy

Empathy can be defined as the ability to "walk in someone else's shoes." You feel what they feel, see what they see. While empathy could have been included as a cross-disciplinary aptitude, it is core to the humanities because empathy is essential to understanding and creating in the arts, political, and social arenas.[9] Persons who express empathy readily make personal associations, understand and share the feelings of others, and identify with the concerns of others from different cultural groups.

Empathy is one of the five components of emotional intelligence that Daniel Goleman refers to as "recognizing the emotions in others."[10] It is an intuitive "knowing" what others need and the desire to bring them comfort. In the field of social and emotional learning (SEL), empathy is included under the category of "positive social relationships." Research in SEL shows that it contributes to overall academic success.[11]

> Empathy is how we understand and get along with others, and as such, it is an aptitude that undergirds social innovation.

Empathy is how we understand and get along with others, and as such, it is an aptitude that undergirds social innovation. It is fundamental to success in the caring professions—teaching, medicine, sales, and leadership.

Create a Talent Goal for *Empathy*

The sample Talent Goal Frame for *empathy* is from the study *Perspectives in Art and Culture* and continues to develop the main conflict in the novel *Shooting Kabul* (see Figure 6.2). Students use empathy to communicate the perspective and emotions of one family member regarding the loss of Miriam. They will each play the role of that member in a Kiva discussion. The Kiva was an underground round chamber used by Pueblo Indians as a ceremonial room where the leaders of the tribe met to discuss business. The performance of understanding requires them to use empathy to connect to others from different cultural groups and, in this case, age groups. Students demonstrate mastery of the language arts objective to compare and contrast characters using specific details from the text as they show their talent aptitude for perspective taking and empathy. Perspective, or point of view, is objective, but empathy is when they must imagine what it is like to "walk in that person's shoes."

Figure 6.2 Sample Talent Goal Frame: *Empathy*

Talent Aptitude	Content Standard Learning Objective	Performance of Understanding
2. Empathy Readily makes personal associations; understands and shares the feelings of others; identifies with human concerns beyond one's own cultural group.	**Content Standards** Compare and contrast two or more characters, settings, or events in a story or drama, drawing on specific details in the text. (CCSS.ELA.LITERACY. RL.5.5) Come to discussions prepared, having read or studied required material; explicitly draw on that preparation and other information known about the topic to explore ideas under discussion. (CCSS.ELA.LITERACY. SL.5.1) **Objective** Analyze and communicate in a discussion one character's perspective on the loss of Miriam in *Shooting Kabul*.	**Kiva Discussion*** In the novel *Shooting Kabul*, each family member takes a different perspective on Miriam's loss. Take the role of one member and analyze the text for that character's thoughts, actions, and dialogue. Come to the Kiva prepared to express your character's perspective on and emotions about the loss of Miriam. **A Kiva was an underground round chamber used by Pueblo Indians as a ceremonial room where the men of the tribe met to discuss business.*

Talent-Targeted Teaching and Learning Goal: Humanities *Perspectives in Art and Culture (Grades 4–6)*

Use *empathy* to communicate the perspective and emotions of a family member on the loss of Miriam.

Student-Directed Talent Goal:

I show *empathy* when I connect to others from different groups and cultures and imagine what it is like to walk in their shoes.

Develop an *Empathy* Cluster Goal

The *empathy* talent goal and performance of understanding could appropriately develop other humanities aptitudes, such as *communication* or *verbal reasoning*, and cross-domain aptitudes, such as *curiosity* or *leadership*. To challenge students and provide more opportunities for them to discover and develop their aptitudes, create an *empathy* cluster goal.

Empathy Cluster Goal

Use *empathy, communication,* and *leadership* to discuss the perspective and emotions of a family member on the loss of Miriam.

Motivate, Engage, and Develop *Empathy*

The *empathy* talent goal uses a familiar strategy of role-playing or simulation in which students take the role of a family member of a different age and culture. The goal is for them to prepare their roles for the Kiva discussion, and the novelty of the task focuses their attention and energy, motivating them with an authentic reason to analyze the text, inferring the character's perspective and emotions. The Kiva discussion represents the family coming together to communicate openly and honestly (a discussion that actually doesn't happen in the novel, causing additional conflicts). Thus, the performance of understanding is personally meaningful, supporting social and emotional learning about how empathy contributes to improving the interpersonal relationships in their own lives.

Assessing the Aptitude of *Empathy*

You can assess students' ongoing expressions of *empathy* and provide formative feedback using the humanities Talent Aptitude Learning Progressions (see Figure 6.3). The talent development assessment process is described in detail in Chapter 7.

Figure 6.3 *Empathy* Learning Progressions

Empathy	Emerging	Progressing	Advancing
Teacher Rubric	Recognizes that others' feelings and circumstances differ from their own.	Recognizes and identifies with others' feelings and circumstances, including those from different groups and cultures.	Readily identifies with others' feelings and circumstances outside of own group or culture; shows concern by meeting needs.
Student Rubric	I recognize that other people have feelings and circumstances that are different from my own.	I recognize and make connections to other people's feelings and circumstances, including those who are very different from me.	I understand and identify with other people's feelings and circumstances; I reach out to others who are very different from me.

3. Resourcefulness

Resourcefulness is the ability to come up with clever or ingenious solutions to problems using existing materials or assets. It is often associated with creativity, but while resourceful solutions may not be always new, original, or imaginative, they are always practical, efficient, and effective. Resourcefulness enables us to persist in difficulty

(Continued)

(Continued)

and achieve our goals, whether great or small.[12] "Life hacks," those clever tricks that make everyday tasks more efficient and productive, are simply ways to be more resourceful.

Like the creative person, resourceful people are curious and open to learning. Resourcefulness could have been included as a cross-disciplinary aptitude because of its key role in the creative problem-solving process. While resourcefulness is a talent aptitude that may not be limited to the humanities, the humanities provide ample opportunities to develop it in real-world situations. Resourcefulness is a talent aptitude that is necessary for success in the arts, all areas of leadership, and in entrepreneurship. Resourceful artists use found objects in their work (Picasso used newspapers and matchboxes in his cubist designs).[13] Leaders often need to make bold moves when resources are limited, using their resourcefulness to decide "How do I leverage my assets?"[14] History's greatest social reform movements were led by resourceful leaders like Martin Luther King Jr. and Mohandas Gandhi, who used their most basic resource—their bodies—in sit-ins and hunger strikes to further their goals for freedom and equality.[15]

> Resourcefulness is a talent aptitude that is necessary for success in the arts, all areas of leadership, and in entrepreneurship.

Learners use resourcefulness to solve problems by locating and using a variety of sources of relevant information and ideas and by using existing materials effectively and in new ways. Some learners will demonstrate a natural inclination for resourcefulness; creating a talent goal advances their aptitude while supporting all students in discovering and developing the resourcefulness they will need as tomorrow's innovators.

Create a *Resourcefulness* Talent Goal

The sample Talent Goal Frame for *resourcefulness* is from the humanities study *Creating Sustainable Communities* (see Figure 6.4). This project-based study uses the classic novel *Watership Down* by Richard Adams to explore the overarching concept of sustainability. Early in their reading of the novel, students are introduced to the authentic application of the novel's themes: They will identify an area in their neighborhood and propose a redevelopment plan based on national standards for sustainable communities *and* the lessons learned from the four rabbit warrens in *Watership Down*.[16] The talent goal is for students to demonstrate *resourcefulness* by brainstorming ideas for information and materials they can apply to developing a sustainable community redevelopment plan for an area in their neighborhood. The performance of understanding is to create a "resources mind map," including ideas from *Watership Down* as one source.

Figure 6.4 Sample Talent Goal Frame: *Resourcefulness*

Talent Aptitude	Content Standard Learning Objective	Performance of Understanding
3. Resourcefulness When presented with a problem, can locate and effectively use a variety of resources to extract relevant information and significant ideas; uses existing materials effectively and in new ways.	**Content Standards** Determine or clarify the meaning of unknown and multiple-meaning words or phrases, choosing flexibly from a range of strategies. (CCSS.ELA.LITERACY.7.4) Determine the kinds of resources that will be helpful in answering compelling and supporting questions, taking into consideration multiple points of views represented in the sources. (C3 Framework for Social Studies D1.5.6–8) **Objective** Develop a shared definition of community and sustainability in order to determine local resources on these topics.	**Resources Mind Map** Create a resources mind map around the concepts of "community" and "sustainability." Add to your map resources you could use to learn more about these concepts as they apply to creating a community redevelopment plan for your neighborhood. Note: *Watership Down* is one source.

Talent-Targeted Teaching and Learning Goal: Humanities *Creating Sustainable Communities (Grades 6–8)*

Demonstrate *resourcefulness* by brainstorming ideas for information and materials you can apply to developing a sustainable community redevelopment plan for your neighborhood.

Student-Directed Talent Goal:

I demonstrate *resourcefulness* by knowing where to find and how to use information and materials to solve problems.

The goal and performance of understanding could effectively target other humanities aptitudes such as *engagement in the humanities* or cross-domain aptitudes such as *curiosity* or *persistence*. To challenge students and provide more opportunities to discover and develop their talent aptitudes, create a talent cluster goal.

Resourcefulness Cluster Goal

Use *curiosity, resourcefulness,* and *persistence* to brainstorm ideas for information and materials you can apply to developing a sustainable community redevelopment plan for your neighborhood.

Motivate, Engage, Develop *Resourcefulness*

The *resourcefulness* goal and performance of understanding from the *Creating Sustainable Communities* humanities study provide students with an authentic purpose for meeting the challenge of reading a lengthy classic text like *Watership Down*. They are motivated to apply the sustainability principles (or lack thereof) from the fictional rabbit warrens to their own communities. Regardless of where they live, their communities have areas to be developed or redeveloped, and they begin to see how they can have a stake in whether or not this is done sustainably. The goal engages their interest and involvement and warrants the investment of time and effort. They see the relevance of literature to their own lives, and this may transfer to greater humanities engagement and overall higher achievement.

Assessing the Aptitude of *Resourcefulness*

You can assess students' ongoing levels of *resourcefulness* and provide formative feedback using the humanities Talent Aptitude Learning Progressions (see Figure 6.5). The talent development assessment process is described in detail in Chapter 7.

Figure 6.5 *Resourcefulness* **Learning Progressions**

Resourcefulness	Emerging	Progressing	Advancing
Teacher Rubric	Uses existing resources and materials to find facts and ideas to solve a problem.	Uses and adapts existing resources and materials to extract information and ideas that are effective in solving a problem.	Searches for new and relevant resources to solve a problem; experiments with and adapts existing resources; extracts and applies significant information and ideas.
Student Rubric	I use the resources and materials that are provided and available to solve a problem.	I use, adapt, and obtain new resources and materials to find information and ideas that are effective in problem solving.	I experiment with using existing resources to solve a problem; I search for suitable resources to gain and apply important information and ideas.

4. Verbal Reasoning

Verbal reasoning is the ability to comprehend, interpret, and make inferences about what is read, synthesizing prior knowledge in order to apply it in new contexts to solve problems. We use verbal reasoning to think critically, reflect, listen, remember, analyze, and problem solve. Certainly, proficiency in verbal reasoning is a competency goal for all students across domains. Furthermore, we know that some STEM innovators—Albert Einstein and Steve Jobs, for example—as children were voracious readers on a wide variety of topics. Why then is verbal reasoning categorized here as a domain-specific humanities aptitude?

Research shows that verbal reasoning and mathematical reasoning are different abilities or separate intelligences. Learners with high verbal potential may not have high mathematical ability. As we learned earlier, developing domain-specific talent involves acquiring the habits of mind specific to a discipline.[17] Studies of exceptional talent show that students who build on their particular strength, be it mathematical or verbal,

> We use verbal reasoning to think critically, reflect, listen, remember, analyze, and problem solve.

are more likely to become successful in that discipline. For example, students with high verbal aptitude preferred humanities courses in college and pursued verbally demanding disciplines, and 65% went on to earn awards in the arts, humanities, or social sciences.[18]

While maintaining our goal to develop verbal reasoning among all learners, we recognize that some will have a natural inclination or aptitude in this area that should be cultivated. Creating and assessing goals that target verbal reasoning supports these students as they advance their talent, while furthering the verbal reasoning of all learners.

Create a Talent Goal for *Verbal Reasoning*

The sample talent goal for *verbal reasoning* is from the humanities study *Creating Sustainable Communities* (see Figure 6.6). Students analyze the core novel *Watership Down* by Richard Adams in order to infer principles of community sustainability among the four rabbit warrens and apply these to the students' community redevelopment plans. The talent goal is to use verbal reasoning to analyze and evaluate the sustainability features of each *Watership Down* community in order to suggest changes that would improve its sustainability. The goal accomplishes the language arts content objective of analyzing the development of theme over the course of a text. In the performance of understanding, students engage in a "meeting of the minds" sustainability conference in which they role-play members from the four different warrens in order to arrive at a consensus about the ways that their communities could change to become more sustainable. The students are using verbal reasoning to solve problems and accomplish goals.

Figure 6.6 Sample Talent Goal Frame: *Verbal Reasoning*

Talent Aptitude	Content Standard Learning Objective	Performance of Understanding
4. Verbal Reasoning Demonstrates depth and complexity of comprehension by making inferences and forming interpretations; integrates prior knowledge and monitors comprehension; synthesizes and applies reading in creative problem solving.	**Content Standards** Determine a theme or central idea of a text and analyze its development over the course of the text, including its relationship to the characters, setting, and plot; provide an objective summary of the text. (CCSS.ELA-LITERACY. RL.8.2) Pose questions that connect the ideas of several speakers and respond to others' questions and comments with relevant evidence, observations, and ideas. (CCSS.ELA-LITERACY. SL.8.1.C) **Objective** Analyze and evaluate the sustainability features of each of four rabbit warrens in *Watership Down*.	**Sustainable Communities Meeting of the Minds** Participate in a "meeting of the minds" discussion in which you represent one of the four rabbit warrens in *Watership Down*. Be prepared to ask and answer questions about community sustainability in order for the four warrens to arrive at a meeting of the minds about how their communities can become more sustainable.

Talent-Targeted Teaching and Learning Goal: Humanities *Creating Sustainable Communities (Grades 6–8)*

Use *verbal reasoning* to analyze and evaluate sustainability features of different communities in order to reach consensus about how to improve community sustainability.

Student-Directed Talent Goal:

I use *verbal reasoning* to interpret what I read, make connections, and apply reading to solve problems.

The *verbal reasoning* goal and performance of understanding could target other humanities aptitudes such as *communication* or *empathy*, as well as cross-disciplinary aptitudes such as *insight* or *leadership*. To challenge students and provide more opportunities for them to discover and develop their talent aptitudes, create a talent cluster goal.

Verbal Reasoning Cluster Goal

Use *verbal reasoning, insight,* and *leadership* to analyze and evaluate the sustainability features of each *Watership Down* community in order to suggest changes that would improve its sustainability.

Motivate, Engage, and Develop *Verbal Reasoning*

The *verbal reasoning* goal and performance of understanding motivate students by involving them, through role-playing, in a novel task with a clear and challenging goal: Arrive at a consensus. The Meeting of the Minds Summit is, at present, an actual event held by the Meeting of the Minds organization, "focused on the future of environmentally, socially, and economically sustainable cities. Meeting of the Minds brings together urban sustainability and technology leaders to share knowledge and build lasting alliances."[19] For the students, the summit simulation engages their higher-order thinking as they analyze evidence of sustainability and critically reflect on the areas in which their community needs to improve. Students are engaged on a personal level as they persuasively represent their communities. The intense and challenging task of coming to a consensus warrants their time and effort.

Assessing the *Verbal Reasoning* Aptitude

You can assess students' ongoing levels of *verbal reasoning* and provide formative feedback using the humanities Talent Aptitude Learning Progressions (see Figure 6.7). The talent development assessment process is described in detail in Chapter 7.

Figure 6.7 *Verbal Reasoning* Learning Progressions

Verbal Reasoning	Emerging	Progressing	Advancing
Teacher Rubric	Attains literal comprehension of facts and ideas; with prompting, makes connections and applications.	Makes inferences and forms interpretations by integrating prior knowledge; suggests applications.	Demonstrates depth of understanding by synthesizing and applying what is read to solve problems.
Student Rubric	I understand what I read and make connections between reading and real life. I read the materials that are required.	I interpret what I read based on my prior knowledge and apply reading in real life to solve problems. I select reading based on interest.	I compare and contrast things I have read and apply my interpretations to solve problems. I select reading that is interesting and challenging.

5. Communication

The dictionary defines *communication* as a process by which information is exchanged between individuals through a common system of symbols, signs, or behavior.[20]

(Continued)

(Continued)

It is how we convey meaning. Communication has been identified as an essential 21st-century skill and is integrated into content standards across disciplines.[21] The visual arts communicate using symbol, color, composition, and so on to convey ideas without words.

Communication is how we understand and connect with others. Therefore, active listening is essential to communication. Unfortunately, many of us are not as effective communicators as we believe. "The single biggest problem in communication," wrote George Bernard Shaw, "is the illusion that it has taken place." Communication is included here as a humanities-specific aptitude because the humanities present so many opportunities to develop it.

> Communication is how we understand and connect with others.

Communication requires empathy and is essential for leaders in any realm. Great communicators use *story*, one of Daniel Pink's six aptitudes for the conceptual age. Stories are how we understand ourselves and others, how we remember, and how we gain deeper meaning. As Pink reminds us, "There are only so many stories." The stories we tell resonate with others because they are told and retold.[22]

Communication is how we know what we know. In his article "Why Communication Is Today's Most Important Skill," Greg Satell explains it this way:

> In order to innovate, it's not enough to come up with big ideas, you also need to work hard to communicate them clearly.... In truth, we can't really know anything that we can't communicate. To assert that we can possess knowledge, but are unable to designate what it is, is nonsensical.[23]

Some learners will have a natural inclination or aptitude for *communication*. These learners express ideas fluently and effectively in written, oral, or visual forms; expand and elaborate on ideas in ways that others understand; convey meaning through symbol and emotion; and develop a personal voice or style. Creating a talent goal that targets *communication* allows these learners to advance their talent while encouraging others to discover and develop their communication skills.

Create a *Communication* Talent Goal

The sample Talent Goal Frame for *communication* is from the humanities study *Creating Sustainable Communities* (see Figure 6.8). The goal is for students to use communication to express understandings gained from the core text *Watership Down* about how a character's individual needs impact the community as a whole. Developing the aptitude of *communication* facilitates acquisition of the language arts skills of making inferences and using language to convey experiences and events. The performance of understanding presents students with the task of composing a "multi-voice" poem to perform at a school-based poetry café. The poem communicates two different views of the same situation: the character's needs and the community's. Multi-voice poems are meant to be read aloud by two persons, sometimes alternating voices and sometimes simultaneous.

Figure 6.8 Sample Talent Goal Frame: *Communication*

Talent Aptitude	Content Standards Learning Objective	Performance of Understanding
5. **Communication** Expresses ideas fluently and effectively in written, oral, or visual forms; expands and elaborates on ideas in ways that others understand; conveys meaning through symbol and emotion; develops a personal voice or style.	**Content Standards** Cite several pieces of textual evidence to support analysis of what the text says explicitly and draw inferences from the text. (CCSS.ELA-LITERACY. RL.7.1.) Use precise words and phrases, relevant descriptive details, and sensory language to capture the action and convey experiences and events. (CCSS.ELA-LITERACY. W.7.3.d) **Objective** Analyze the text to infer the characters' individual needs and the impact of individual needs on the community as whole.	**Poetry Café** Compose a multi-voice poem to communicate your understandings about how different characters' individual needs impact the community as a whole. Perform your poem with a partner at your school's poetry café.
Talent-Targeted Teaching and Learning Goal: Humanities *Creating Sustainable Communities (Grades 6–8)* Use *communication* to express understandings gained from the text about how an individual's needs impact the community as a whole.		
Student-Directed Talent Goal: I use *communication* to express and expand upon ideas and effectively convey my meaning to others.		

The *communication* goal and performance of understanding could effectively target other humanities aptitudes such as *empathy* or *verbal reasoning*, as well as cross-disciplinary aptitudes such as *creativity* or *insight*. To challenge students and provide more opportunities to develop their talent aptitudes, write a talent cluster goal.

Communication Cluster Goal

Use *insight, creativity*, and *communication* to express understandings gained from the text about how a character's needs impact the community as a whole.

Motivate, Engage, and Develop *Communication*

The *communication* goal and performance of understanding motivate and engage learners through creativity, challenge, emotional involvement, and real-world application. The skill of analyzing characters rarely is applied in an authentic product or performance such as the multi-voice poem presents. Poetry cafés are prevalent in cities today and provide a purpose and audience for this form of communication. The opportunity to perform with and for peers engages students' attention and rewards their efforts. The task is personalized through their individual choice of a character with whom they can empathize, whose story resonates with their own, so that the character's needs become their needs. To build students' competency in composing poetry, the teacher can find examples of multi-voice poems performed on the Internet and graphic organizers to scaffold the multi-voice poem composition process.

> The opportunity to perform with and for peers engages students' attention and rewards their efforts.

Assessing the Aptitude of *Communication*

You can assess students' ongoing levels of *communication* and provide formative feedback using the humanities Talent Aptitude Learning Progressions (see Figure 6.9). The talent development assessment process is described in detail in Chapter 7.

Figure 6.9 *Communication* Learning Progressions

Communication	Emerging	Progressing	Advancing
Teacher Rubric	Expresses ideas in written, oral, or visual forms in ways that others can understand.	Expresses ideas in written, oral, or visual forms; expands and elaborates on ideas to convey meaning.	Expresses ideas in written, oral, or visual forms using elaboration, symbol, and emotion to convey a personal voice or style.
Student Rubric	I express my ideas to others using writing, speaking, or art.	I express my ideas and develop them with details so that others understand my meaning.	I develop my ideas with emotion and imagery to engage others with my personal style.

Notes

1. Pink, D. (2006). *A whole new mind: Why right-brainers will rule the future* (p. 49). Penguin Books.
2. Pink, 2006, pp. 65–66.

3. Pink, 2006, p. 53.
4. National Council for Social Studies. (2010). *Executive summary: National curriculum standards for social studies*. https://www.socialstudies.org/standards/execsummary
5. Aspen Ideas Festival. (2016, July 6). *Do we need to rescue the humanities?* https://www.youtube.com/watch?v=OQy5Y4FxYEo
6. Wagner, T. (2012). *Creating innovators: The making of young people who will change the world* (p. 102). Scribner.
7. Wagner, 2012.
8 American Library Association. (2012). *Bibliotherapy*. http://www.ala.org/tools/atoz/bibliotherapy
9. Koss, J. (2006). On the limits of empathy. *Art Bulletin, 88*(1), 139–157. http://www.jstor.org/stable/25067229
10. Goleman, D. (2006/1995). *Emotional intellgence.* Bantam Dell.
11. Goleman, 2006/1995.
12. Baldoni, J. (2010). The importance of resourcefulness. *Harvard Business Review.* https://hbr.org/2010/01/leaders-can-learn-to-make-do-a
13. Tate Museum. (n.d.). *Found object.* https://www.tate.org.uk/art/art-terms/f/found-object
14. Murphy, B. (2014). 7 things really resourceful people do.
15. Gardner, H. (2011/1995). *Leading minds: An anatomy of leadership.* Basic Books.
16. STAR Communities. (2012). *STAR community rating system.* US Green Building Council. http://www.starcommunities.org/about/framework/
17. Gardner, H. (2006). *Five minds for the future.* Harvard Business School Press.
18. Lubinski, D., Webb, R. M., Morelock, M. J., & Benbow, C. P. (2001). Top 1 in 10,000: A 10-year follow-up of the profoundly gifted. *Journal of Applied Psychology, 86*(4), 718–729.
19. Meeting of the Minds. (n.d.). https://meetingoftheminds.org/
20. Merriam Webster. (2020). Communication. *Merriam-Webster.com dictionary.* https://www.merriam-webster.com/dictionary/communication
21. P21 Partnership for 21st Century Learning. (2019). *P21 framework definitions.* https://www.battelleforkids.org/networks/p21
22. Pink, 2006, p. 105.
23. Satell, G. (2015). Why communication is today's most important skill. https://www.forbes.com/sites/gregsatell/2015/02/06/why-communication-is-todays-most-important-skill/#7c7b4bdb1100

Chapter
SEVEN

Teach to Assess Talent

If we do not change our direction, we are likely to end up where we are headed.

—Lao Tzu

Assessment dominates the educational conversation today, which typically focuses on accountability for schools to produce students who are "college and career ready," a complex outcome that, at the time of this writing, is still narrowly captured in standardized test scores. The overarching purpose of assessment is to evaluate whether students are learning what we intend for them to learn. Once again, it is the nature of our goals that is most important.

Also present in the assessment conversation today, however, is a call for change of direction, a new approach: What does it look like when students are learning higher-order processes like problem solving? What are the stages of development? How can we assess their growth over time?[1]

> What does it look like when students are learning higher-order processes like problem solving? What are the stages of development? How can we assess their growth over time?

Talent-targeted teaching and learning answers these new assessment questions by defining complex higher-order processes, the aptitudes of innovators, and delineating how we should expect students to develop these over time. The Talent Aptitude Learning Progressions provide shared understandings for formative feedback, reflection, and improving teaching and learning.

Key Understandings

1. Talent-targeted teaching and learning is a formative assessment model in which teachers and students gradually internalize the learning targets for advancing long-term goals for talent development.

2. The Talent Aptitude Learning Progressions are statements of ability that provide shared understandings about the stages of development for each aptitude.

3. Analytic rubrics composed from the learning progressions are useful for targeted feedback, student self-reflection, and improvements in teaching and learning.

4. Talent-Targeted Think-Aloud statements and question prompts focus and extend the expression of the talent aptitudes during instruction.

5. Kidwatching is a structured process for capturing moment-in-time talent development data using anecdotal records.

6. The Talent Development Portfolio documents patterns of student strengths and a talent development journey that is shared at student-led conferences.

Talent-Targeted Teaching and Learning as Formative Assessment

Talent-targeted teaching and learning is essentially a formative assessment model with the focus on setting learning goals, documenting progress, and providing feedback primarily as assessment "for learning" rather than an assessment "of learning." This involves both students and teachers in a continuous process that begins with the teacher, and "gradually students internalize the learning goals and become able to see the target themselves. They begin to be able to decide how close they are to it."[2] The practice of formative assessment is now widely used, and research shows evidence of its positive impact on student achievement.[3] "Formative assessment—while not a 'silver bullet' that can solve all educational challenges—offers a powerful means for meeting goals for high-performance, high-equity of student outcomes, and for providing students with knowledge and skills for lifelong learning."[4] In talent-targeted teaching and learning, formative assessments are integrated into the learning process and focus on communicating clear feedback about what is needed to improve so that students take ownership of their learning.

> Formative assessments are integrated into the learning process and focus on communicating clear feedback about what is needed to improve so that students take ownership of their learning.

Not Used for Grades

Because talent development is a lifelong process, talent goal assessments cannot be considered as summative. Formative assessment focuses the teacher and student on the intrinsic value of learning rather than extrinsic rewards such as grades. Therefore, the Talent Continuum Rubrics should not be used in traditional ways for grading, unless it is to give a "completion" credit in the grade book.

Formative Assessment Tools in This Chapter

This chapter presents practical tools for assessing talent goals, methods that you can integrate with your existing assessment protocols. The foundational, most unique, and useful tools are the *Talent Aptitude Learning Progressions*, written in both teacher and student versions. You will use these learning progressions to create customized assessment rubrics for the seven aptitudes of innovators and the domain-specific STEM and humanities aptitudes. Using the student versions of the rubrics, learners self-assess their student-directed goals, reflect, set growth goals, and record their progress in their Talent Development Portfolios. Throughout the talent-targeted teaching and learning process, you'll model the aptitudes through teacher think-alouds and capture moment-in-time student performance data through anecdotal records.

The formative assessment tools in this chapter are designed to create and communicate talent development feedback in practical and effective ways. Each of these tools is modeled with explanations and examples:

1. Talent Aptitude Learning Progressions (teacher and student versions)

2. Talent Continuum Rubrics (teacher and student versions)

3. Task Prompt and Student Self-Assessment

4. Talent-Targeted Teacher Think-Alouds

5. Talent-Targeted Kidwatching Protocols

6. The Talent Development Portfolio and Portfolio Review Process

Part I. Assess Talent Using the Talent Aptitude Learning Progressions

The term *learning progression* is typically used to describe stages of development in the sequence of mastery for content standards. Any learning pathway is "inferential or hypothetical."[5] Experts agree that while learning progressions represent an approximation of student learning and that educators may differ in their interpretations of the stages, learning progressions provide a systematic way to collect evidence of student progress and provide formative feedback.[6]

Why Talent Aptitude Learning Progressions Transform Assessment

The Talent Aptitude Learning Progressions capture the essence of the talent aptitude as expressed in broad developmental stages: *emerging, developing*, and *advancing*. These dynamic stages are backmapped from the aptitude constructs. While talent does not necessarily develop in such a linear way, the Talent Aptitude Learning Progressions describe how the aptitudes might be demonstrated at various stages of development. "We don't know a great deal about the 'typical development' of many of these 21st century skills in which society is currently interested . . . therefore we don't currently have roadmaps for guiding teachers in what might be expected of students at different levels of skills, and how they might move students from one level to the next."[7] The good news is that the Talent Aptitude Learning Progressions provide those road maps.

Now You Have the Assessment Rubrics You Need!

I have heard from many educators who would like to target higher-level cognitive skills like *creativity* and *logical reasoning* or psychosocial skills like *metacognition* and *persistence*. They just aren't sure how they can assess these, and what isn't assessed just "doesn't count" in their schools. Now, you have the assessment tools that you need! The Talent Aptitude Learning Progressions represent the developmental trajectory of the talent aptitudes, and while they are "approximations," as stated earlier, they are research-based constructs that are likely to benefit students. We can say now that we do have the "road maps" for guiding teachers and students in the development of the essential 21st-century aptitudes of innovators: the Talent Aptitude Learning Progressions, which can be used to compose assessment rubrics.

Composing Analytic Rubrics

Rubrics, generally speaking, are simply evaluation tools presenting the guidelines for measuring the achievement of goals. Scoring work with rubrics provides learners with information about the quality of their performance. In education today, we see many styles, but the *analytic rubric* can effectively integrate instruction and assessment when used at the beginning to convey expectations. As an evaluation tool, the analytic rubric provides targeted feedback on performance that is useful for reflection, goal-setting, and instructional improvement. To compose analytic rubrics, use the Talent Aptitude Learning Progressions (teacher and student versions), structured with the aptitude criteria on the left followed by levels of performance (emerging, progressing, advancing) in columns to the right (see examples in Tables 7.0–7.7).

Common Definition = Shared Vision

The breakthrough advantage of the Talent Aptitude Learning Progressions is that we now have shared understandings about what we mean by talent aptitudes such as *creativity*, *logical reasoning*, or *communication* and what accelerating levels of performance look like. Now, a consistent purpose and vision unites us across content areas, grade levels, schools, and districts. This shared understanding is a powerful tool for achieving our WHY to motivate and engage tomorrow's innovators.

Composing Rubrics to Assess Talent
Goals and Performances of Understanding

Now that we have clear direction and targets, make the Talent Aptitude Learning Progressions work for you! Use them to plan instruction, explicitly model through think-alouds, capture observational data, provide ongoing feedback, and communicate progress. In this next section, we'll learn step-by-step how to use the learning progressions to create Talent Continuum Rubrics to assess student work, guide students to self-assess and reflect, and provide effective formative feedback. You will continue to use your own formative and summative assessments of the content standards and learning objectives.

Let's walk through the process of composing rubrics to assess the cross-domain and domain-specific aptitudes of (1) *creativity*, (2) *insight*, (3) *spatial reasoning*, and (4) *communication*.

1. Assess a Cross-Domain Aptitude: Creativity

The talent goal for *creativity* presented in Chapter 4 is from the *Stop Sports Injuries* STEM study. In the performance of understanding, students use *creativity* to collect and interpret data on classmates' sports injuries in order to propose an idea to prevent youth sports injuries. Using the Talent Aptitude Learning Progressions (Figure 7.0), you can generate a rubric to assess the performance of understanding for *creativity*.

Cross-Domain Talent Aptitudes	Emerging	Progressing	Advancing
1. **Curiosity** Seeks new ideas; asks thoughtful, searching questions; is inquisitive; observes, explores, and investigates keenly and alertly in any environment.	Asks questions on topics of interest; observes, explores, and investigates when prompted.	Shows interest in new ideas; asks questions; observes, explores, and investigates.	Seeks out new ideas; asks searching questions; observes intently, widely explores, and investigates.
2. **Logical Reasoning** Draws conclusions from facts or premises; observes patterns and infers rules; hypothesizes and tests; uses a systematic process to make sound judgments and form sensible arguments.	With guidance and modeling, can draw conclusions from evidence to make sound judgments and arguments.	Applies systematic thinking to draw conclusions from evidence in order to make sound judgments and sensible arguments.	Consciously selects a systematic process to form a hypothesis, draw conclusions from evidence, make sound judgments, and develop sensible arguments.
3. **Creativity** Has unusual or clever ideas; enjoys divergent thinking, brainstorming, or imagining; is inventive; discovers unusual connections; initiates new projects.	Demonstrates typical ideas; makes literal connections; works on assigned projects.	Demonstrates divergent thinking when prompted; makes appropriate connections; is open to new projects.	Demonstrates divergent thinking through unusual or clever ideas; makes unexpected or imaginative connections; initiates new projects.
4. **Insight** Is keenly observant and aware; is intuitive; perceives new patterns and relationships; readily grasps concepts and applies them to new situations.	Sees patterns and relationships when modeled; acquires concepts through experience and applies them to new situations with practice.	Observes patterns and relationships; acquires concepts through examples and applies them to new situations with modeling	Grasps patterns and relationships quickly and easily transfers them to new situations; applies concepts independently in novel ways.
5. **Persistence** Focuses time and energy on a topic of interest; looks for more than one way to accomplish a task; continues in spite of difficulty; strives to improve and refine; tests and verifies; may resist closure.	Stays on task for a reasonable period of time, if not bringing it to completion.	Continues in a task with sufficient time and energy to bring it to completion, if not refinement.	Focuses energy and time to accomplish a task in spite of difficulty; examines alternatives; strives to test, refine, and improve.
6. **Metacognition** Understands own thought processes; self-selects appropriate problem-solving strategies; plans; self-monitors, reflects, assesses, and corrects; learns from mistakes.	Can identify own thinking when prompted; uses problem-solving strategies as provided; may correct mistakes if asked; typically acts before deliberating.	Aware of own thought processes; chooses a problem-solving strategy from those provided; applies feedback to correct mistakes when prompted; considers own thoughts and actions.	Understands own thought processes; self-selects appropriate problem-solving strategies; self-monitors; assesses and corrects; learns from mistakes; is deliberate, reflective.

Cross-Domain Talent Aptitudes	Emerging	Progressing	Advancing
7. **Leadership** Motivates others to achieve a goal; initiates ideas and listens to concerns of others; influences others to adopt and participate in a plan of action; organizes others to implement a plan.	When provided with the goals, can follow a plan of action and work with others to achieve it.	Sets goals and creates a plan of action to achieve them; influences others to participate in the plan.	Casts a vision and develops a plan of action; motivates and organizes others to participate and bring the vision into reality.

 Available for download from **resources.corwin.com/DevelopTalent**

Composing a Talent Continuum Rubric for *Creativity*

The learning progressions for *creativity* assume that all learners are "emerging" in the aptitude, meaning that they are at-promise for creative thinking and production. At the *emerging* level, learners have typical rather than unusual or "out-of-the-box" ideas. At the *progressing* level, learners are open to divergent, out-of-the-box thinking, particularly when prompted to do so. At the *advancing* level, learners' divergent thinking is habitual and leads them to make new connections and start new projects. Table 7.0 presents the teacher rubric for *creativity*.

Table 7.0 *Creativity* Talent Continuum (Teacher Rubric)

The student performance in this talent-targeted task . . .			
Talent Aptitude	**Emerging**	**Progressing**	**Advancing**
Creativity Has unusual or clever ideas; enjoys divergent thinking, brainstorming, or imagining; is inventive; discovers unusual connections; initiates new projects.	Demonstrates typical ideas; makes literal connections; works on assigned projects.	Demonstrates divergent thinking when prompted; makes appropriate connections; is open to new projects.	Demonstrates divergent thinking through unusual or clever ideas; makes unexpected or imaginative connections; initiates new projects.

Use the Talent Continuum Rubrics to Assess Performances of Understanding

Clearly, students differ in the ways that they receive and use feedback. Based on the age level and needs of your students, you can decide how to use the teacher version of the Talent Continuum Rubric in assessing performances of understanding. Early in the talent-targeted teaching and learning process, and with younger students and struggling learners, the learning progressions may be used to focus on accomplishments. As an alternative to providing students with rubric scores, you might use the language from the rubric to write simple descriptive formative feedback statements for those students (see Table 7.1).

> Early in the talent-targeted teaching and learning process, and with younger students and struggling learners, the learning progressions may be used to focus on accomplishments.

Table 7.1 Teacher Assessment Summary Statements: *Creativity*

In this talent-targeted task,
1. I see the aptitude of creativity *emerging*. Continue to develop creativity by *seeking to have many different ideas.*
2. I see the aptitude of creativity *progressing*. Continue to advance by seeking to *make new connections and think of different, unusual ideas.*
3. I see the aptitude of creativity *advancing*. Continue to make *unusual connections and think how you might put imaginative ideas into practice.*

A Word About Student–Teacher Conferences

Students and teachers can share their respective rubric assessments during informal one-on-one conferences. Together, students and teachers can agree on the final rubric ratings to be recorded in the Talent Development Portfolios. In these conferences, "the feedback students give is just as important as the feedback they get."[8] As students express what they think they need to improve, the teacher learns ways to support their growth.

Student Self-Assessment of *Creativity*

Now that you have generated your teacher rubric as the touchstone for teaching and learning, use the student versions of the Talent Aptitude Learning Progressions to compose the student's self-assessment rubric (see Figure 7.1).

Student Self-Directed Goal for *Creativity*

I express creativity through new or unusual ideas that are imaginative or inventive, making new connections, and initiating new projects.

The student versions of the Talent Aptitude Learning Progressions are written as statements of *ability*, focusing on strengths rather than deficits, while at the same time providing a direction for growth. Students who are *emerging* in creativity see that they have the abilities to think of ideas and follow a model or pattern. *Progressing* in creativity will entail thinking of new ideas and improvements and how to put them into practice. *Advancing* in creativity is characterized by intrinsic motivation and engagement that leads to creative achievement. Table 7.2 presents the student's rubric for *creativity*.

Figure 7.1 The Talent Aptitude Learning Progressions: Cross-Domain Aptitudes of Innovators (Student Version)

Cross-Domain Talent Aptitudes	Emerging	Progressing	Advancing
1. Curiosity Seeks new ideas; asks thoughtful, searching questions; is inquisitive; observes, explores, and investigates keenly and alertly in any environment.	I am mostly interested in ideas and environments that are familiar to me.	I am interested in new ideas and environments, and I ask questions that I can explore.	I am eager to learn new ideas, and I investigate new environments to find answers to my questions.
2. Logical Reasoning Draws conclusions from facts or premises; observes patterns and infers rules; hypothesizes and tests; uses a systematic process to make sound judgments and form sensible arguments.	I use evidence to draw conclusions and form arguments.	I draw conclusions and form sensible arguments based on evidence.	I use evidence to make convincing arguments and justify sensible solutions.
3. Creativity Has unusual or clever ideas; enjoys divergent thinking, brainstorming, or imagining; is inventive; discovers unusual connections; initiates new projects.	I sometimes think of ideas about how things could be improved. I like to follow a model or pattern that already exists.	I think of ideas for new projects and can imagine how things could be improved. I sometimes put these new ideas into practice.	I enjoy thinking of different and unusual ideas. I often imagine what could be improved and discover new ideas for projects.
4. Insight Is keenly observant and aware; is intuitive; perceives new patterns and relationships; readily grasps concepts and applies them to new situations.	I recognize patterns and relationships when given examples. I understand by following models.	I recognize patterns and relationships and understand ways to apply these to new situations.	I look for and quickly recognize patterns and relationships. I think of ways to apply understandings in new situations.

(Continued)

(Continued)

Cross-Domain Talent Aptitudes	Emerging	Progressing	Advancing
5. Persistence Focuses time and energy on a topic of interest; looks for more than one way to accomplish a task; continues in spite of difficulty; strives to improve and refine; tests and verifies; may resist closure.	I work on a task for what I think is enough time and then stop, even if I am not finished.	I continue working on a task with enough time and energy to complete it, unless it's too difficult.	I focus my energy and time on a task and keep working when it is difficult, trying different ways to improve and refine.
6. Metacognition Understands own thought processes; self-selects appropriate problem-solving strategies; plans; self-monitors, reflects, assesses, and corrects; learns from mistakes.	I start working on a task or solving a problem before thinking about the best way for me to complete it. I'm not sure how to use the feedback I'm given to improve my work.	I think about the best way for me to solve a problem or complete a task before I start it. I can use the feedback I'm given to improve my work and learn from my mistakes.	I understand how I think, learn, and solve problems, and I use that knowledge to complete tasks. I think about how I can improve and learn from my mistakes.
7. Leadership Motivates others to achieve a goal; initiates ideas and listens to concerns of others; influences others to adopt and participate in a plan of action; organizes others to implement a plan.	I can work with others to follow a plan of action to achieve a goal.	I can set goals and work with others to achieve a plan of action.	I have a vision for what I want to achieve and can persuade others to participate in my plan of action.

 Available for download from **resources.corwin.com/DevelopTalent**

Table 7.2 *Creativity* Talent Continuum (Student Rubric)

My work on this talent–targeted task shows that . . .			
Talent Aptitude	Emerging	Progressing	Advancing
Creativity I express creativity through new or unusual ideas that are imaginative or inventive, making new connections and initiating new projects.	I sometimes think of ideas about how things could be improved. I like to follow a model or pattern that already exists.	I think of ideas for new projects and can imagine how things could be improved. I sometimes put these new ideas into practice.	I enjoy thinking of different and unusual ideas. I often imagine what could be improved and discover new ideas for projects.

Helpful Tips for Student Self-Assessment Using Rubrics

Students can become adept at self-assessment after initial experiences. Teachers have reported that students were able to use the rubrics to self-assess their progress and were able to explain why they chose the levels of emerging, progressing, or advancing in each talent aptitude. Initially,

The student versions of the Talent Aptitude Learning Progressions are written as statements of *ability*, focusing on strengths rather than deficits, while at the same time providing a direction for growth.

provide students with guidance about how to use the rubric to reflect on the evidence of the talent aptitude in their work (see Table 7.3). All begin with *emerging* as the baseline. As they move forward to read the descriptors of the *progressing* and *advancing* levels, there is the opportunity to say "not yet" and move back to the level that is the best-fit assessment at this time. The learning progressions of the *advancing* level show students what the aptitude looks like when cultivated, thus enabling them to set individual goals for growth.

Table 7.3 Guidance for Students: How to Self-Assess Using the Talent Aptitude Continuum Rubrics

Emerging	Progressing	Advancing
1. Begin your self-assessment here by reading the *Emerging* descriptors. These behaviors are evidence of the talent aptitude that you will recognize in your work. Continue on to read the *Progressing* and *Advancing* talent aptitude descriptors. You may come back to the *Emerging* category if it is the best fit for you now.	2. Next, read the *Progressing* descriptors. This level adds new behaviors to the *Emerging* evidence. Does your work demonstrate these? If the answer is "not yet," then your best self-assessment is *Emerging*. If the answer is "yes," then you are *Progressing* in this aptitude. But before stopping, continue to read about *Advancing*.	3. Finally, read the *Advancing* descriptors. This level adds new behaviors to *Progressing*. At the *Advancing* level, there is strong evidence of the talent aptitude. Is this evident in your work now? If "not yet," then your best self-assessment may be *Progressing* or *Emerging*. The *Advancing* descriptors show what goals you can set to develop this talent aptitude.

2. Assessing a Cross-Domain Talent Goal: Insight

The talent goal for *insight* presented in Chapter 4 is from the *Perspectives in Art and Culture* humanities study. In the performance of understanding, students use *insight* to identify an object that is a symbol in the novel and create a slide show to communicate the meaning it holds for different characters as well as for themselves. Using the learning progressions for *insight* (see Figure 7.0), you can compose a rubric to assess the "Symbol Slide Show" for that aptitude.

Composing the *Insight* Talent Aptitude Continuum Rubrics

The Talent Aptitude Learning Progressions for *insight* assume that all learners are "emerging" in the aptitude, meaning that they are at-promise for *intuitive perceptions*. At the *emerging* level, the learner sees patterns and relationships through modeling. At the *progressing* level, the learner observes patterns and relationships at a more independent level and can apply these to new situations with modeling. At the *advancing* level, the learner independently makes intuitive leaps in thinking and applies insights in novel ways (see Table 7.4).

Student Self-Assessment of *Insight*

Use the student versions of the learning progressions to compose the self-assessment rubric. Introduce the rubric early in the instructional sequence to establish expectations. A template for preparing a Talent-Targeted Task Prompt

Table 7.4 *Insight* Talent Continuum (Teacher Rubric)

This talent–targeted task demonstrates that the student . . .			
Talent Aptitude	**Emerging**	**Progressing**	**Advancing**
Insight Is keenly observant and aware; is intuitive; perceives new patterns and relationships; readily grasps concepts and applies them to new situations.	Sees patterns and relationships when modeled; acquires concepts through experience and applies them to new situations with practice.	Observes patterns and relationships; acquires concepts through examples and applies them to new situations with modeling.	Grasps patterns and relationships quickly and easily transfers them to new situations; applies concepts independently in novel ways.

and Self-Assessment (see Figure 7.6) is presented in the section on cluster goals. Students will self-assess their demonstration of *insight* in the performance of understanding, Symbol Slide Show.

Self-Directed Talent Goal for *Insight*

I use *insight* to recognize patterns and see relationships, which I apply to understanding new situations.

The student versions of the Talent Aptitude Learning Progressions, like the teacher versions, are written as *statements of ability*, focusing on strengths rather than deficits, while also providing a direction for growth. For the aptitude of *insight*, students who are *emerging* are able to recognize patterns and relationships from the examples that are provided. Students who are *progressing* gain insights more independently and understand ways to apply them; those who are *advancing* actively and independently look for patterns and relationships and apply them to new situations. Table 7.5 presents the student rubric for assessing *insight*.

Table 7.5 *Insight* Talent Continuum (Student Rubric)

My work in this talent-targeted task shows that . . .			
Talent Aptitude	**Emerging**	**Progressing**	**Advancing**
Insight I use insight to recognize patterns and see relationships, which I apply to understanding new situations.	I recognize patterns and relationships when given examples. I understand by following models.	I recognize patterns and relationships and understand ways to apply to these to new situations.	I look for and quickly recognize patterns and relationships. I think of ways to apply understandings in new situations.

3. Assessing a STEM Talent Goal: Spatial Reasoning

To assess each of the five domain-specific STEM aptitudes, we'll apply the same process, this time using the Talent Aptitude Learning Progressions for STEM aptitudes (see Figure 7.2). The talent goal for *spatial reasoning* presented in Chapter 5 is from the STEM study *Healthy Community by Design*. In the performance of understanding "Building to Scale," students use *spatial reasoning* to create a scale drawing or model of a building in their Healthy Community by Design plan. Use the Talent Aptitude Learning Progressions for STEM aptitudes to compose a rubric to assess the product for *spatial reasoning*.

Figure 7.2 The Talent Aptitude Learning Progressions: STEM Aptitudes (Teacher Version)

STEM Talent Aptitudes	Emerging	Progressing	Advancing
1. Engagement in STEM Exhibits high interest in science, technology, engineering, or mathematics content; enthusiastic, observant and involved in STEM activities; self-motivated to pursue STEM knowledge and skills.	Demonstrates some interest in STEM activities; completes the required STEM activities with external prompting.	Demonstrates interest in STEM through involvement in activities; is self-motivated to complete the required activities without external prompting.	Demonstrates high interest in and enthusiasm for STEM through active and focused involvement; initiates new tasks beyond requirements.
2. Investigation Uses a systematic approach to explore natural phenomenon; collects, examines, analyzes, and summarizes data; offers logical explanations; interprets and communicates findings.	Implements methods to explore natural phenomenon; uses prescribed procedures to collect, analyze, and summarize data.	Selects appropriate procedures to explore natural phenomenon and methods to collect, analyze, and summarize data to communicate findings.	Develops procedures to explore natural phenomenon and methods to collect, analyze, and summarize data; explains and interprets findings.
3. Problem Solving Identifies and frames problems; analyzes causes and effects to generate solutions; selects appropriate strategies and technologies; develops a plan of action; tests and verifies.	Solves problems with guidance and modeling of cause and effect; uses the tools and strategies provided to follow a plan of action.	Identifies problems and applies strategies to analyze causes and effects; selects appropriate tools and processes to find solutions.	Frames new problems and determines appropriate strategies, tools, and processes to generate verifiable solutions.
4. Spatial Reasoning Visualizes and interprets images; understands and remembers relationships among three-dimensional objects; mentally manipulates objects to solve problems.	Recognizes and remembers simple images; visualizes three-dimensional objects and identifies relationships.	Recognizes and remembers complex images; visualizes and manipulates three-dimensional objects to solve problems.	Mentally manipulates, constructs, and interprets relationships among three-dimensional objects to solve problems.
5. Mathematical Reasoning Perceives patterns and relationships; quickly and accurately applies mathematical knowledge to solve problems; selects appropriate strategies; analyzes and evaluates results; proposes alternate solutions.	Recognizes patterns and relationships from multiple examples; uses strategies to solve mathematical problems with modeling and practice.	Recognizes patterns and relationships after a few examples; selects strategies to accurately solve mathematical problems.	Readily perceives patterns and relationships; proposes, implements, and evaluates multiple strategies to accurately solve problems.

 Available for download from **resources.corwin.com/DevelopTalent**

Composing the *Spatial Reasoning* Talent Continuum Rubrics

The Talent Aptitude Learning Progressions for *spatial reasoning* assume that all learners are "emerging" in the aptitude, meaning that they are at-promise for visualizing and remembering three-dimensional objects. At the *emerging* level, the learner recognizes and remembers simple images and can identify relationships among objects. At the *progressing* level, the learner recognizes and remembers more complex images and can manipulate three-dimensional objects to solve problems. At the *advancing* level, the learner mentally manipulates, constructs, and interprets relationships among three-dimensional objects in order to solve problems (see Table 7.6). You will continue to use your own formative and summative assessments of the content standards and learning objectives.

Table 7.6 *Spatial Reasoning* Talent Continuum (Teacher Rubric)

The performance in this talent-targeted task shows that the student . . .			
Talent Aptitude	**Emerging**	**Progressing**	**Advancing**
Spatial Reasoning Visualizes and interprets images; understands and remembers relationships among three-dimensional objects; mentally manipulates objects to solve problems.	Recognizes and remembers simple images; visualizes three-dimensional objects and identifies relationships.	Recognizes and remembers complex images; visualizes and manipulates three-dimensional objects to solve problems.	Mentally manipulates, constructs, and interprets relationships among three-dimensional objects to solve problems.

Student Self-Assessment of *Spatial Reasoning*

Use the student version of the Talent Aptitude Learning Progressions for STEM Aptitudes (see Figure 7.3) to compose a rubric for *spatial reasoning*. Have students assess their *spatial reasoning* as demonstrated in the performance of understanding, "Building to Scale."

Student-Directed Talent Goal for *Spatial Reasoning*

I use *spatial reasoning* to visualize, remember, and understand relationships among three-dimensional objects.

STEM Talent Aptitudes	Emerging	Progressing	Advancing
1. Engagement in STEM Exhibits high interest in science, technology, engineering, or mathematics content; is enthusiastic, observant, and involved in STEM activities; is self-motivated to pursue STEM knowledge and skills.	I have some interest in science, technology, engineering, and mathematics (STEM) topics, and I am sometimes engaged by the activities.	I am interested in science, technology, engineering, and mathematics (STEM) topics and motivated to complete the activities.	I am very interested and engaged in science, technology, engineering, and mathematics (STEM) topics. I am self-motivated to engage in STEM activities.
2. Investigation Uses a systematic approach to explore natural phenomenon; collects, examines, analyzes, and summarizes data; offers logical explanations; interprets and communicates findings.	I follow the procedures that are provided to explore and find answers to questions, collect data, and summarize findings.	I explore and search out answers to questions. I select appropriate strategies to collect and display data and summarize findings.	I propose questions and search out answers, developing a system to accurately collect, display, analyze, and interpret findings.
3. Problem Solving Identifies and frames problems; analyzes causes and effects to generate solutions; selects appropriate strategies and technologies; develops a plan of action; tests and verifies.	I solve problems using the strategies and tools that are provided for me to use.	I solve problems selecting from the strategies and tools I have learned and test my solutions for accuracy.	I identify new problems to solve and select appropriate strategies and tools to find solutions that I test and verify.
4. Spatial Reasoning Visualizes and interprets images; understands and remembers relationships among three-dimensional objects; mentally manipulates objects to solve problems.	I recognize and remember images and three-dimensional objects.	I visualize, remember, and understand relationships among three-dimensional objects.	I understand the relationships among three-dimensional objects and mentally manipulate them to solve problems.
5. Mathematical Reasoning Perceives patterns and relationships; quickly and accurately applies mathematical knowledge to solve problems; selects appropriate strategies; analyzes and evaluates results; proposes alternate solutions.	I see how the patterns in numbers or shapes follow rules when these are modeled for me. I follow the strategy provided to solve mathematical problems.	I see the rules in patterns of numbers or shapes, which I apply to select strategies to accurately solve mathematical problems.	I find new patterns in numbers or shapes, propose rules, and use multiple strategies to accurately solve mathematical problems.

online resources — Available for download from **resources.corwin.com/DevelopTalent**

TEACH TO DEVELOP TALENT

Table 7.7 *Spatial Reasoning* Talent Continuum (Student Rubric)

My work on this talent-targeted task shows that . . .			
Talent Aptitude	**Emerging**	**Progressing**	**Advancing**
Spatial Reasoning I use *spatial reasoning* to visualize, remember, and understand relationships among three-dimensional objects.	I recognize and remember images and three-dimensional objects.	I visualize, remember, and understand relationships among three-dimensional objects.	I understand the relationships among three-dimensional objects and mentally manipulate them to solve problems.

The student learning progressions for *spatial reasoning* are statements of ability, focusing on strengths rather than deficits, while at the same time providing a direction for growth. Students who are *emerging* in spatial reasoning know how to recognize and remember images and three-dimensional objects. Students who are *progressing* visualize, remember, and understand relationships; those who are *advancing* can do these things as well as mentally manipulate three-dimensional objects to solve problems (see Table 7.7). Continue to provide guidance to students, as stated earlier, about how to use the rubric to reflect on the evidence of the talent aptitude in their work (see Table 7.3).

4. Assessing a Humanities Talent Goal: Communication

To assess the five domain-specific humanities aptitudes, we'll apply the same process using the teacher version of the Talent Aptitude Learning Progressions for Humanities Aptitudes (see Figure 7.4). The talent goal for *communication* presented in Chapter 6 is from the humanities study *Creating Sustainable Communities*. In the performance of understanding, students use *communication* to compose a multi-voice poem, which they then perform with a partner in a poetry café. Use the learning progressions to compose a rubric to assess the product for *communication*.

Talent Aptitudes	Emerging	Progressing	Advancing
1. Engagement in Humanities Shows active interest in human society and culture, contemporary and historical issues, academic disciplines, languages, or the arts; is self-motivated to expand knowledge and experiences in these areas.	Demonstrates some interest in humanities activities; completes required humanities activities with external prompting.	Demonstrates interest in humanities through involvement in activities; is self-motivated to complete the required activities with external prompting.	Demonstrates high interest in and enthusiasm for the humanities through active and focused involvement; initiates new tasks beyond requirements.
2. Empathy Readily makes personal associations; understands and shares the feelings of others; identifies with human concerns beyond one's own cultural group.	Recognizes that others' feelings and circumstances differ from their own.	Recognizes and identifies with others' feelings and circumstances, including those from different groups and cultures.	Readily identifies with others' feelings and circumstances outside of own group or culture; shows concern by meeting needs.
3. Resourcefulness When presented with a problem, can locate and effectively use a variety of resources to extract relevant information and significant ideas; uses existing materials effectively and in new ways.	Uses existing resources and materials to find facts and ideas to solve a problem.	Uses and adapts existing resources and materials to extract information and ideas that are effective in solving a problem.	Searches for new and relevant resources to solve a problem; experiments with and adapts existing resources; extracts and applies significant information and ideas.
4. Verbal Reasoning Demonstrates depth and complexity of comprehension by making inferences and forming interpretations; integrates prior knowledge and monitors comprehension; synthesizes and applies reading in creative problem solving.	Attains literal comprehension of facts and ideas; with prompting, makes connections and applications.	Makes inferences and forms interpretations by integrating prior knowledge; suggests applications.	Demonstrates depth of understanding by synthesizing and applying what is read to solve problems.
5. Communication Expresses ideas fluently and effectively in written, oral, or visual forms; expands and elaborates on ideas in ways that others understand; conveys meaning through symbol and emotion; develops a personal voice or style.	Expresses ideas in written, oral, or visual forms in ways that others understand.	Expresses ideas in written, oral, or visual forms; expands and elaborates on ideas to convey meaning.	Expresses ideas in written, oral, or visual forms, using elaboration, symbol, and emotion to convey a personal voice or style.

 Available for download from **resources.corwin.com/DevelopTalent**

TEACH TO DEVELOP TALENT

Compose the *Communication* Talent Continuum Rubrics

The Talent Aptitude Learning Progressions for *communication* assume that all learners are "emerging" in the aptitude, meaning that they are at-promise for expressing ideas in written, oral, or visual form in ways that others understand. At the *progressing* level, the learners expand and elaborate on their ideas to convey meaning. At the *advancing* level, the communication becomes more complex and adept through use of emotion and symbol to create a personal voice or style (see Table 7.8).

Table 7.8 *Communication* Talent Continuum (Teacher Rubric)

The student performance in this talent-targeted task . . .			
Talent Aptitude	**Emerging**	**Progressing**	**Advancing**
Communication Expresses ideas fluently and effectively in written, oral, or visual forms; expands and elaborates on ideas in ways that others understand; conveys meaning through symbol and emotion; develops a personal voice or style.	Expresses ideas in written, oral, or visual forms in ways that others understand.	Expresses ideas in written, oral, or visual forms; expands and elaborates on ideas to convey meaning.	Expresses ideas in written, oral, or visual forms, using elaboration, symbol, and emotion to convey a personal voice or style.

Student Self-Assessment of a *Communication* Talent Goal

Use the student version of the Talent Aptitude Learning Progressions for Humanities Aptitudes (see Figure 7.5) to compose the student rubric for communication. Have students self-assess their *communication* goal as demonstrated in the performance of understanding, "Poetry Café: Multi-Voice Poem."

Student Self-Directed Goal for *Communication*

I use *communication* to express and expand upon ideas and effectively convey my meaning to others.

Figure 7.5 The Talent Aptitude Learning Progressions: Humanities Aptitudes (Student Version)

Talent Aptitudes	Emerging	Progressing	Advancing
1. Engagement in Humanities Shows active interest in human society and culture, contemporary and historical issues, academic disciplines, languages, or the arts; is self-motivated to expand knowledge and experiences in these areas.	I have some interest in humanities topics, but I am not always motivated by the activities.	I am interested in humanities and am usually motivated to complete the activities.	I am very interested in humanities and am self-motivated to complete the activities.
2. Empathy Readily makes personal associations; understands and shares the feelings of others; identifies with human concerns beyond one's own cultural group.	I recognize that other people have feelings and circumstances that are different from my own.	I recognize and make connections to other people's feelings and circumstances, including those who are very different from me.	I understand and identify with other people's feelings and circumstances; I reach out to others who are very different from me.
3. Resourcefulness When presented with a problem, can locate and effectively use a variety of resources to extract relevant information and significant ideas; uses existing materials effectively and in new ways.	I use the resources and materials that are provided and available to solve a problem.	I use, adapt, and obtain new resources and materials to find information and ideas that are effective in problem solving.	I experiment with using existing resources to solve a problem; I search for suitable resources to gain and apply important information and ideas.
4. Verbal Reasoning Demonstrates depth and complexity of comprehension by making inferences and forming interpretations; integrates prior knowledge and monitors comprehension; synthesizes and applies reading in creative problem solving.	I understand what I read and make connections between reading and real life. I select reading materials that are required.	I interpret what I read based on my prior knowledge and apply reading in real life to solve problems. I select reading based on interest.	I compare and contrast things I have read and apply my interpretations to solve problems. I select reading that is interesting and challenging.
5. Communication Expresses ideas fluently and effectively in written, oral, or visual forms; expands and elaborates on ideas in ways that others understand; conveys meaning through symbol and emotion; develops a personal voice or style.	I express my ideas to others using writing, speaking, or art.	I express my ideas and develop them with details so that others understand my meaning.	I develop my ideas with emotion and imagery to engage others with my personal style.

 Available for download from **resources.corwin.com/DevelopTalent**

TEACH TO DEVELOP TALENT

The student learning progressions for *communication* are written as statements of ability, focusing on strengths rather than deficits, while at the same time providing a direction for growth. Students who are *emerging* have the ability to express ideas to others, whether it is through writing, speaking, or art. Students who are *progressing in* communication develop their expression of ideas with details in order for others to understand their meaning; those who are *advancing* use emotion and imagery to engage others with their personal style (see Table 7.9).

Table 7.9 *Communication* Talent Continuum (Student Rubric)

My work on this talent-targeted task shows that . . .			
Talent Aptitude	Emerging	Progressing	Advancing
Communication I use communication to express and expand upon ideas and effectively convey my meaning to others.	I express my ideas to others using writing, speaking, or art.	I express my ideas and develop them with details so that others understand my meaning.	I develop my ideas with emotion and imagery to engage others with my personal style.

Assessing Talent Cluster Goals

In Chapters 4, 5, and 6, we learned how to develop talent cluster goals that target several aptitudes in the goal and performance of understanding. Students require multiple exposures to the talent aptitudes, and creating cluster goals increases this frequency. The talent-targeted performances of understanding are rich enough to accommodate cluster goals.

Assessing cluster goals uses the same process as with the single aptitude goals. Use the Talent Aptitude Learning Progressions to compose the teacher and student rubrics. The cluster goal that follows is from the *metacognition* section in Chapter 4. The goal is from the human-

> Students require multiple exposures to the talent aptitudes, and creating cluster goals increases this frequency.

ities study *Perspectives in Art and Culture* and targets the cross-domain aptitudes of *metacognition* and *persistence* along with the *humanities engagement* aptitude.

Humanities Cluster Goal

Demonstrate *metacognition*, *persistence*, and *humanities engagement* by creating a personal photo essay and composing an artist's statement to interpret it.

The talent-targeted performance of understanding is a product-based authentic application of the novel study, which develops the theme of photojournalism as both a form of self-expression and social consciousness. The task has sufficient complexity to warrant a cluster goal. Students have the opportunity to demonstrate *metacognition* as they examine their own values to choose a subject for the essay and then explain their creative process and the message they are trying to convey in the artist's statement. They must *persist* in a task that is complex with multiple steps, including shooting and selecting photos that convey the personal message. Throughout this process, their level of *engagement in the humanities* will be evident (see Table 7.10).

Table 7.10 Talent Continuum Rubric for Humanities Cluster Goal (Teacher Version)

Talent Aptitudes	Emerging	Progressing	Advancing
Metacognition	Can identify own thinking when prompted; uses problem-solving strategies as provided; may correct mistakes if asked; typically acts before deliberating.	Aware of own thought processes; chooses a problem-solving strategy from those provided; applies feedback to correct mistakes when prompted; considers own thoughts and actions.	Understands own thought processes; self-selects appropriate problem-solving strategies; self-monitors; assesses and corrects; learns from mistakes; is deliberate, reflective.
Persistence	Stays on task for a reasonable period of time, if not bringing it to completion.	Continues in a task with sufficient time and energy to bring it to completion, if not refinement.	Focuses energy and time to accomplish a task in spite of difficulty; examines alternatives; strives to test, refine, and improve.

Talent Aptitudes	Emerging	Progressing	Advancing
Humanities Engagement	Demonstrates some interest in humanities activities; completes required humanities activities with external prompting.	Demonstrates interest in humanities through involvement in activities; is self-motivated to complete the required activities with external prompting.	Demonstrates high interest in and enthusiasm for the humanities through active and focused involvement; initiates new tasks beyond requirements.

Create a Talent-Targeted Task Student Prompt and Self-Assessment

When composing the student version of the cluster goal rubric, it is effective and efficient to create a Talent-Targeted Task Prompt and Self-Assessment form that students use to self-assess and file in their Talent Development Portfolios. The prompt contains the task description, talent goal, student rubric, and self-reflection questions (see Figure 7.6).

Figure 7.6 Talent-Targeted Task Prompt and Self-Assessment

Student Name _____ Date _____

Perspectives in Art and Culture **Talent-Targeted Task Description: Photo Essay and Artist's Statement**

Demonstrate your *humanities engagement*, *persistence*, and *metacognition* by becoming an "image-maker," creating a photo essay and writing a personal artist's statement. Your photo essay should communicate an emotion, value, or idea that is important to you. Write an artist's statement to explain your personal perspective on the topic, what you hope to communicate to the audience, and the techniques you chose and why.

Talent-Targeted Task Rubric

In this project, you had opportunities to develop your talent aptitudes of *humanities engagement*, *persistence*, and *metacognition*. Use the Talent Continuum Rubric to assess your current level of development as demonstrated in your work.

1. For each talent aptitude, circle the description that best represents your performance on this task.
2. Complete the self-reflection questions.
3. Place this in your Talent Development Portfolio and bring it with you to your teacher conference.

My work on the talent-targeted task shows that . . .

(Continued)

Figure 7.6 (Continued)

Talent Aptitude	Emerging	Progressing	Advancing
Humanities Engagement	I have some interest in humanities topics, but I am not always motivated by the activities.	I am interested in humanities and usually motivated to complete the activities.	I am very interested in humanities and self-motivated to complete the activities.
Persistence	I work on a task for what I think is enough time and then stop, even if I am not finished.	I continue working on a task with enough time and energy to complete it, unless it's too difficult.	I focus my energy and time on a task and keep working when it is difficult, trying different ways to improve and refine.
Metacognition	I start working on a task or solving a problem before thinking about the best way for me to complete it. I'm not sure how to use the feedback I'm given to improve my work.	I think about the best way for me to solve a problem or complete a task before I start it. I can use the feedback I'm given to improve my work and learn from my mistakes.	I understand how I think, learn, and solve problems, and I use that knowledge to complete tasks. I think about how I can improve and learn from my mistakes.

Photo Essay and Artist's Statement Self-Reflection: *Humanities Engagement, Persistence, and Metacognition*

1. What were some things that you *did really well*?
2. What could you have *done differently*?
3. What did you *learn about your own talents* as a result of this task?
4. How can you use this self-knowledge in *future learning tasks*?
5. How *motivated* were you to complete this task? Why?
6. Did you find this lesson content *interesting*? Why or why not?
7. Which of the targeted talents do you feel are your *strongest*? Which of the targeted talents *need to be developed*?

Use the rubric *to set a growth goal* for developing a talent aptitude:

My talent goal is . . .

 Available for download from **resources.corwin.com/DevelopTalent**

The Student Self-Reflection Questions

Up to this point, we have focused on composing and implementing the Talent Continuum Rubrics without addressing the other component of the student self-assessment process, the reflection questions. As part of their self-assessment, they will respond to structured reflection questions that focus on identifying strengths and goals for growth. The students also reflect on the lesson's content, which helps them to identify areas of engagement (interest) that may be new discoveries for them. They self-assess their own motivation level and reflect on why they were or were not "motivated." This provides the teacher with information for future planning. Perhaps the challenge was too great or not enough. Perhaps the activity didn't provide them with sufficient choice or the autonomy to become intrinsically motivated. Perhaps they failed to make a personal connection. Of course, students will not find all tasks equally motivating and engaging. Figure 7.6 presents the student self-reflection questions that can be used with any talent goal and performance of understanding.

Part II. Talent-Targeted Assessment During Learning

The Talent Aptitude Learning Progressions provide the targets for formative feedback during instruction and opportunities to capture student data through "kid-watching." In this section, we'll see how to use the learning progressions to prepare Talent-Targeted Think-Aloud statements for descriptive feedback. We'll also see how the feedback we receive from students "makes learning visible."[9] Through structured observations and anecdotal records, we can capture rich information to share with students and families.

> Through structured observations and anecdotal records, we can capture rich information to share with students and families.

Talent-Targeted Think-Alouds

Formative assessment begins with teacher modeling. Chapter 3 introduced the Talent-Targeted Think-Aloud statements that explicitly focus learners' attention on how and when the talent aptitudes occur in the context of daily instruction. It's helpful to use the learning progressions to prepare some generic think-aloud statements in advance. Once you have set the talent goal for the lesson, try preparing several think-aloud statements that repeat and reinforce attributes of the talent aptitude (the aptitude definitions are helpful for this). For example, if the targeted aptitude is *insight*, these are some think-aloud statements that reinforce the concept:

- Use your insight to *recognize the pattern*.
- That *connection* shows insight.
- That's an insightful idea about *how to apply the concept*.

Recall that when using these statements, we do not include the person's name or pronoun (i.e., *Lisa's* connection shows insight or *your* idea is insightful) in order to focus attention on the quality of the work and the understanding that we are all capable of achieving it. Think-alouds take some practice and preparation. Until we become familiar with the talent aptitudes, it's best to write out a few prompts ahead of time. Table 7.11 presents sample think-alouds for cross-domain and domain-specific aptitudes.

Table 7.11 Sample Talent-Targeted Teacher Think-Aloud Statements

Curiosity	• We showed curiosity because we were *open to new experiences.*
	• That *thoughtful question* showed curiosity.
	• We'll use our curiosity as we are *observing and investigating.*
Insight	• Use your insight to *recognize the pattern.*
	• That *connection* showed insight.
	• That's an insightful idea about *how to apply this concept.*
Leadership	• That's what leaders do—*pay attention to other people's needs.*
	• Having a *plan of action* like that shows leadership.
	• Our task requires leadership *to organize others.*
Empathy	• That *concern for others* showed empathy.
	• We'll use empathy to *see what it is like to walk in someone else's shoes.*
	• This shows an empathetic *understanding of a different group's situation.*
Problem Solving	• The explanation of *cause and effect* showed problem solving.
	• Today, we will *test and verify* our problem solutions.
	• That's another *strategy/tool* we can use in solving the problem.

Think-Aloud Question Prompts

In addition to think-aloud statements that affirm talent aptitude examples as they occur, teachers can ask prompting questions designed to either elicit the behavior or move students' thinking to the next level. Using the Talent Aptitude Learning Progressions, you can compose think-aloud question prompts designed to challenge students' expression of the aptitude. Note that *all* levels of expression deserve further challenge, including the *advancing* level. For example, if the targeted aptitude is *creativity*, these questions prompt all students to expand and refine their thinking:

- *For an emerging response* (typical): Tell me more. What other **connections** might we make?

- *For a progressing response* (makes connections/divergent): Of these ideas, **which one is the most unusual**, or the one that most people would not think of?

- *For an advancing response* (imaginative): How might **we put into practice or apply** that imaginative idea?

Structured Observations: Talent-Targeted Kidwatching

Teachers are constantly observing student behavior. Structured observations, however, begin with a specific purpose in mind. What do we want to see? Observing through the lens of the talent aptitudes focuses our attention in targeted areas. This practice of "kidwatching," a term coined by early childhood educator Yetta Goodman, is an intentional process of observation and keeping "anecdotal records."[10] We teach to develop talent as we observe and record formative data, adjust instruction, set goals, and communicate findings with students and parents.

As introduced in Chapter 3, the practice of structured observation using "anecdotal records" is familiar to early childhood educators, but it is not as widely used in the upper grades. However, kidwatching is an authentic ongoing assessment and an essential practice in talent-targeted teaching and learning. Through observation, we capture student contributions and document expertise on the targeted aptitudes. Having the observation criteria established ahead of time in a checklist or recordkeeping chart assists in objectivity.

> Through observation, we capture student contributions and document expertise on the targeted aptitudes.

Behaviors and responses can be recorded without interpretation or value judgments because the notes document student performance relative to the criteria of targeted aptitudes.

Kidwatching Is Value-Added

Keeping talent-targeted anecdotal records creates the value-added in what we normally observe anyway, those moment-in-time perceptions that likely will be forgotten if we aren't able to capture them. When we do, we can reflect on that data and use it to more fully understand and communicate student performance to parents and the students themselves. You can start with simply a clipboard and paper, be resourceful with technology, or use premade forms that make this more manageable. Decide what, where, when, and who you want to observe and then put one of these on your clipboard or tablet:

1. **Talent Aptitude Anecdotal Note-Taking Chart:** Create a chart with three columns labeled *Date*, *Targeted Aptitude*, and *Task/Lesson*. Copy the definition of the talent aptitude in the second column. Use the third column to capture evidence of the aptitudes as they emerge, progress, or advance during instruction. Later, you'll go back over your notes to code them as **E** (*emerging*), **P** (*progressing*), or **A** (*advancing*). Can you identify these levels in the notes on Figure 7.7?

Figure 7.7 Talent Aptitude Anecdotal Note-Taking Chart

Date	Targeted Aptitude	Task: Perspectives in Art and Culture: Photo Essay and Artist's Statement
4/22	**Persistence** Focuses time and energy on a topic of interest; looks for more than one way to accomplish a task; continues in spite of difficulty; strives to improve and refine; tests and verifies; may resist closure.	Jamie: Asked Antoine and Sal to model in her photo essay shoot. Tried three different poses before deciding on the one to shoot. Ava: May I revise my artist's statement? Chris: I don't like how this one turned out. I'm going to shoot it again. Trevor (after one shot): I'm done now. Manuel: I need more time. Are we going to work on this tomorrow? Sammie: My battery died (sits down and stops working).

online resources — Available for download from **resources.corwin.com/DevelopTalent**

2. **Student Roster Aptitude Chart:** This chart is particularly useful for recording evidence of cluster goals with more than one targeted aptitude. Create a chart with four columns labeled *Date*, *Student Names*, *Targeted Aptitudes*, and *Comments*. If you complete the roster ahead of time, you only have to circle the aptitude being observed and record the behavior. Once again, when you can reflect on your notes later, you can code the behaviors as **E**, **P**, or **A** (see Figure 7.8).

Figure 7.8 Student Roster Anecdotal Record for Cluster Goal

Date	Student Names	Targeted Aptitudes			Comments
3/7	Sammy B.	(Problem Solving)	Mathematical Reasoning	(Persistence)	Surveyed every student regarding sports injuries; followed up with those who were absent.
3/8	Chris A.	(Problem Solving)	Mathematical Reasoning	Persistence	Asked, "How do we know the actual cause of the sports injury?"
3/8	Nina R.	(Problem Solving)	(Mathematical Reasoning)	Persistence	Composed ratio scenarios to explain greatest need for intervention.

3. **Talent Aptitude Continuum Record:** Create a chart with three columns labeled *Date, Student Names,* and *Targeted Aptitude.* In the third column, insert the learning progression descriptions (*emerging, progressing, advancing*) for the targeted aptitude. For a given day, record the students' names under the level of response you observe. When reflecting on your lesson, think about how the student responses inform the effectiveness of its design in targeting the talent aptitude (see Figure 7.9).

Figure 7.9 Talent Continuum Note-Taking Chart

		Curiosity		
		Emerging	**Progressing**	**Advancing**
Date	Student	Asks questions on topics of interest; observes, explores, and investigates when prompted.	Shows interest in new ideas; asks questions, observes, explores, and investigates.	Seeks out new ideas; asks searching questions; observes intently; widely explores and investigates.
2/22	Alex	✓		
2/22	Sal			✓
2/22	Jamie		✓	
2/22	Munroe		✓	
2/22	Sarah	✓		

How to Use the Talent-Targeted Kidwatching Data

Teachers can have confidence in their kidwatching anecdotal records because they document student performance relative to the established criteria of targeted aptitudes. The data are useful in instructional planning, and as presented in Part III, teachers can discuss kidwatching observations with students in portfolio conferences and with parents/families in student-led conferences.

Part III. The Talent Development Portfolio

As students experience sustained opportunities to target their humanities, STEM, and cross-disciplinary aptitudes of innovators, their unique strengths and patterns of growth become evident. The Talent Development Portfolio documents student progress over time and provides opportunities for students to self-assess and set goals. You will find that the benefits of the process justify the investment of time. The Talent Development Portfolio gives the teacher valuable insights for planning a balance of tasks to meet different students' strengths. Students and teachers interact in periodic portfolio reviews, which can be shared with parents at student-led conferences. "The magic of portfolios lies not in the portfolios themselves, but in the process used in creating them and the school culture in which documented learning is valued."[11] Overall, the Talent Development Portfolio documents essential student learning not reflected in traditional assessments.

> Overall, the Talent Development Portfolio documents essential student learning not reflected in traditional assessments.

Portfolio Design

The Talent Development Portfolio shares characteristics of a *working* portfolio and an *assessment* portfolio.[12] First, it is a work in progress that documents growth over time in specific learning targets—the cross-disciplinary and domain-specific talent aptitude goals. The portfolio also shows strengths and areas for improvement in a specific content area (STEM or humanities aptitudes). The audience is primarily the student, followed by the teacher and parents. The Talent Development Portfolio shares characteristics of an assessment portfolio in that it shows the level of performance (emerging, progressing, advancing) in the talent aptitudes, benchmarking student performance against the rubric criteria of the Talent Aptitude Learning Progressions. The Talent Development Portfolio, however, is not used as a summative assessment or as data for high-stakes decisions.

Benefits of Portfolios

To reap the benefits, portfolios must be directly integrated into the learning process or actively used to improve teaching and learning. Benefits of portfolios are that they encourage student ownership and communication between school and home when they are reviewed and discussed in student-led conferences. The basic components of the Talent Development Portfolio are the following:

1. Talent Development Portfolio Record

2. Talent-Targeted Task Prompt and Student Self-Assessment

3. Student Self-Reflection (on Task Prompt)

4. Teacher Rubric or Rubric Summary Statements

5. Teacher/Student Periodic Reviews

> Benefits of portfolios are that they encourage student ownership and communication between school and home when they are reviewed and discussed in student-led conferences.

1. The Talent Development Portfolio Record Sheet

The Talent Development Portfolio Record summarizes student performance in the talent-targeted tasks and provides an ongoing assessment of strengths and growth in the talent aptitudes. On the chart, the student fills in the date and the talent-targeted task title and then records the talent aptitude ratings of E (emerging), P (progressing), or A (advancing). These ratings are from either the teacher rubric or are the ratings agreed upon by both teacher and student in work conferences. The record provides a visual pattern of strengths that is easy to use in conducting periodic portfolio reviews. Figure 7.10 shows a sample STEM Talent Development Portfolio Record. Blank record sheets can be found in the online appendix at https://resources.corwin.com/DevelopTalent.

Reviewing Sammy B.'s STEM Talent Development Portfolio Record

Let's conduct a "periodic review" of Sammy B.'s STEM Talent Development Portfolio Record. Figure 7.10 shows ratings for the STEM talent-targeted performances of understanding (Chapter 5) using the targeted aptitudes from the cluster goals, which provide more opportunities for students to develop the talent aptitudes. The chart provides a visual pattern of strengths when looking horizontally across the rows (tasks) and vertically down the columns (aptitudes).

Figure 7.10 STEM Talent Development Portfolio Record: Sammy B.

Directions:

1. Complete the self-assessment for your talent-targeted task: the Talent Aptitude Continuum Rubric and Reflection.

   Keep these documents in your Talent Development Portfolio.

2. On the chart, fill in the date and talent-targeted task. Record the rubric ratings for the talent aptitude(s):

   E (emerging), P (progressing), or A (advancing).

3. Periodic review: Looking at the talent aptitudes, where do you see growth? Where do you see a pattern of strengths?

Date	Talent-Targeted Task	STEM Engagement	Investigation	Problem Solving	Spatial Reasoning	Mathematical Reasoning	
9/4	Sports Injuries Problem Statement	P		E			
9/15	Greatest Need Investigation		E				
10/12	Safest Running Shoe Experiment			P		E	
11/20	Building to Scale				A	P	
12/7	Sustainable Materials Estimate					P	

Reviewing the Rows (Tasks)

In reviewing the list of talent-targeted tasks, we see that Sammy's strongest talent aptitudes were demonstrated in "Building to Scale" (*spatial reasoning* and *persistence*) and the "Sustainable Materials Estimate" (*curiosity* and *insight*). Reflecting on these tasks, the teacher can see that both involve building design and construction. This provides further insight into what motivates and engages Sammy, who may be a budding architect or engineer.

Reviewing the Columns (Aptitudes)

Next, looking vertically down the aptitude columns, we see that Sammy's areas for growth are *investigation, problem solving*, and *logical reasoning* (emerging). Given Sammy's strengths in *curiosity* and *persistence*, he can use these to cultivate *logical*

Curiosity	Logical Reasoning	Creativity	Insight	Persistence	Metacognition	Leadership
	E					
A				P		
			P			
				A		
A			A			

reasoning, and the teacher can fill in gaps with explicit instruction in critical thinking and problem-solving methodology.

Sammy's Growth Over Time

The columns on the chart also document growth over time. *Mathematical reasoning* is an aptitude for which Sammy set a goal after completing the "Safest Running Shoe Experiment." Growth in mathematical reasoning is apparent in the "Building to Scale" task, which applied Sammy's strength in *spatial reasoning*. We also see that mathematical reasoning is progressing in the "Sustainable Materials Estimate," a task about which Sammy showed strong *curiosity*. From these data, we can infer that being able to draw upon strengths may have motivated Sammy to accurately apply mathematical knowledge to solve problems.

Reviewing Chris R.'s Humanities Portfolio

Let's conduct a periodic review of Chris R.'s Humanities Talent Development Portfolio Record (see Figure 7.11). The record shows hypothetical ratings for the humanities talent-targeted performances of understanding (Chapter 6) using the targeted aptitudes from the cluster goals, which provide more opportunities for students to develop the talent aptitudes. The chart provides a visual pattern of strengths when looking across the rows (tasks) and down the columns (aptitudes).

Reviewing the Rows (Tasks)

In reviewing the list of talent-targeted tasks, we see that Chris's strongest aptitudes (advancing) were demonstrated in the "Resources Mind Map" aptitudes of *resourcefulness*, *curiosity*, and *persistence*. Reflecting on the design of this task, the teacher can see that brainstorming a mind map of materials and resources for a neighborhood redevelopment plan is visual, practical, and real-life. This provides further insight into what motivates and engages Chris, whose neighborhood's needs may impact the quality of life.

Figure 7.11 Humanities Talent Development Portfolio: *Chris R.*

Directions:

1. Complete the self-assessment for your talent-targeted task: the Talent Development Continuum Rubric and Reflection.

2. Keep these documents in your Talent Development Portfolio.

   On the chart, fill in the date and talent-targeted task. Record the rubric ratings for the talent aptitude(s):

3. E (emerging), P (progressing), or A (advancing).

   Periodic review: Looking at the talent aptitudes, where do you see growth? Where do you see a pattern of strengths?

Date	Talent-Targeted Task	Humanities Engagement	Empathy	Resourcefulness	Verbal Reasoning	Communication	
9/15	Book Talk: Take It With You!	P					
10/6	Kiva Discussion		P			E	
11/2	Resources Mind Map			A			
11/30	Meeting of the Minds				P		
12/18	Poetry Café					E	

Reviewing the Columns (Talent Aptitudes)

Next, looking vertically down the aptitude columns, we see that Chris's greatest area for growth is *communication* (emerging). Reflecting on the design of the Kiva discussion and poetry café tasks, we see that both involved oral performance. This attribute of communication needs explicit instruction and practice. During the portfolio review conference, Chris can be encouraged to apply *persistence*, a strength displayed in the mind map, to tasks requiring oral communication.

Chris's Growth Over Time

The columns on the chart also document growth over time. *Leadership* is an aptitude for which Chris set a talent goal after the Kiva discussion of different character's perspectives in the novel. Growth in leadership is apparent from the "progressing" rating in the Meeting of the Minds Summit on community sustainability. The aptitude is demonstrated at different levels on dissimilar tasks. In the Meeting of the Minds, Chris also demonstrated advanced *insight*. Using the data on Chris's Talent Development Portfolio Record, we can infer that community advocacy is a

Curiosity	Logical Reasoning	Creativity	Insight	Persistence	Metacognition	Leadership
			P		P	
						E
A				A		
			A			P
		P	P			

promising arena to develop emerging oral *communication*, hone progressing *leadership*, and apply advancing *resourcefulness*.

Conducting Student-Led Talent Development Portfolio Conferences

As we learned in Chapter 3, the language of talent development creates a learning community of students, families, and educators. This culminates through the student-led conference, a meeting during which the student shares his or her portfolio.[13] The Talent Development Portfolio provides the structure. Students are engaged in their own learning process and are motivated to improve. During the conference, the goal is for the students to present their talent development journey.

Now Teach to Assess Talent!

Equipped with the practical tools presented in this chapter, we are confident that we can "teach to assess talent." We have shared understandings about the aptitudes of innovators, and the Talent Aptitude Learning Progressions guide us in knowing the extent to which students are achieving our talent goals. These clear targets—translated into analytic rubrics—provide descriptive feedback that shows learners how they can improve. The Talent-Targeted Teacher Think-Alouds provide ongoing formative feedback and assessment, capturing moments-in-time data through anecdotal records. The Talent Development Portfolio is a tool for collaborative scoring, self-monitoring, and reflection that completes the feedback loop. We are well on our way to achieving our WHY: engaging and motivating tomorrow's innovators. Chapter 8 presents the final step as we learn how to "Design for Innovation."

Table 7.12 presents a summary of the stages of teaching to assess talent.

Table 7.12 Teach to Assess Talent

Teachers . . .	Students . . .
1. Begin with the end: Introduce the talent goal, performance of understanding, and Talent Continuum Rubric.	1. Use the Talent Continuum Rubric and self-directed goal to understand the criteria for success.
2. Use Talent-Targeted Think-Alouds and question prompts to explicitly model and encourage talent behaviors.	2. Have clear targets to assess their progress along the way.

Teachers . . .	Students . . .
3. Capture and reflect on anecdotal records as formative data to adjust instruction.	3. Self-assess their performance against the established learning progressions.
4. Use rubrics to provide feedback that sets clear targets for growth.	4. Reflect on strengths and set goals for growth.
5. Maintain Talent Development Portfolios to document student strengths and progress.	5. Monitor their growth across time in their Talent Development Portfolios.
6. Teach to develop talent: Motivate and engage tomorrow's innovators.	6. Are motivated, engaged, and develop their talents.

Notes

1. Kim, H., & Care, E. (2018). Learning progressions: Pathways for 21st century teaching and learning. *Education Plus Development*. Brookings. https://www.brookings.edu/blog/education-plus-development/2018/03/27/learning-progressions-pathways-for-21st-century-teaching-and-learning/
2. Brookhart, S. M. (2010). *Formative assessment strategies for every classroom* (2nd ed., p. 3). ASCD.
3. Black, P., & Wiliam, D. (1998). Assessment and classroom learning. *Assessment in Education: Principles, Policy and Practice, 5*(1), 7–74. https://doi.org/10.1080/0969595980050102
4. OECD/CERI. (2008). Formative assessment. International Conference: *Learning in the 21st century: Research, innovation, and policy* (p. 5).
5. Great Schools Partnership. (2014). Learning progressions. *The Glossary of Educational Reform*. https://www.edglossary.org/learning-progression/
6. Popham, J. W. (2007, April). All about accountability: The lowdown on learning progressions. *Educational Leadership, 64*(7), 84. http://www.ascd.org/publications/educational-leadership/apr07/vol64/num07/The-Lowdown-on-Learning-Progressions.aspx
7. Kim & Care, 2018.
8. Tovis, C. (2012). Feedback is a two-way street. *Educational Leadership, 70*(1), 48–51.
9. Hattie, J. (2012). *Visible learning for teachers: Maximizing impact on learning*. Routledge.
10. Owocki, G., & Goodman, Y. (2002). *Kidwatching: Documenting children's literacy development*. Heinemann.
11. Danielson, C., & Arbutyn, L. (1997). *An introduction to using portfolios in the classroom*. ASCD.
12. Danielson & Arbutyn, 1997.
13. Berger, R., Ruger, L., & Woodfin, L. (2014). *Leaders of their own learning: Transforming schools through student-engaged assessment*. Jossey-Bass.

Chapter
EIGHT

Teach Today to Develop Tomorrow's Innovators

Don't quit. Never give up trying to build the world you can see, even if others can't see it. Listen to your drum, and your drum only. It's the one that makes the sweetest sound.

—Simon Sinek

It is today that we create the world of the future.

—Eleanor Roosevelt

Who are tomorrow's innovators? Using Howard Gardner's *Five Minds for the Future* as a framework, tomorrow's innovators are *disciplined* thinkers; having mastered the content and processes of their crafts over time, they continue to be lifelong learners. They are *synthesizers*, drawing elements from their expertise to blend into narratives, theories, images, or metaphors. They use *creativity* to ask new questions and seek new answers. They are *respectful* citizens who value human diversity and put those beliefs into action. And finally, they are *ethical* innovators, seeking in their creative endeavors to do "good work" for the benefit of others.[1]

Tomorrow's innovators are *your* students *today*.

We can teach today to develop these disciplined, creative, and ethical future innovators. We do this when we develop curriculum and instruction using seven "Design Essentials," a framework synthesized from other effective models. Implementing this "Design for Innovation" framework ensures that you are creating a context in which learners can discover and develop their aptitudes of innovators, STEM, and humanities aptitudes.

With the many competing demands on what our programming needs to be and do, it's imperative to know, "What are the essentials?" These are not the latest fads, and they don't need any abundant funding or special technology to implement. It is likely that these seven Design Essentials are not new to you (they are not new!). We need to be reminded of their efficacy in achieving our long-term aims for students, for their role in our WHY to engage and motivate tomorrow's innovators. This chapter provides practical examples of how the seven Design Essentials are used in talent goals and talent-targeted tasks so that you can apply them to your own curriculum.

> With the many competing demands on what our programming needs to be and do, it's imperative to know, "What are the essentials?"

Key Understandings: *The Seven Design Essentials*

1. **Organize content using overarching concepts** to generate interdisciplinary essential questions that engage students in higher-level thinking to develop the aptitudes of innovators.

2. **Structure learning around open-ended problems** to motivate and engage learners in authentic talent-targeted tasks that can be designed using the Five-P Problem Planner.

3. ***Align for acceleration*** to challenge all learners by matching depth and complexity with students' readiness levels and interests.

4. ***Develop expert thinking*** to foster the talent aptitudes inherent in innovation and creative problem solving.

5. ***Engage differing perspectives*** with divergent thinking and questions applied in talent-targeted tasks.

6. ***Analyze patterns, relationships, and trends*** using concept-attainment and mind-mapping strategies to achieve talent-targeted goals and performances of understanding.

7. ***Consider ethical implications*** of innovation by using discussions of moral dilemmas to generate alternative courses of action at higher levels of moral reasoning.

Why Are These Design Principles *Essential*?

You might conclude, after reading one or more of the following Design Essentials sections, that "we are already doing this." Good! This chapter will continue to bolster your commitment. You can use the Design for Innovation framework as standards for evaluating your existing instructional programming and as guidelines for developing new programming. To encourage reflection, each section is written in the form of a question: "***To what extent do we*** . . . ?" I encourage you to explicitly document where these Design Essentials already occur in your written curriculum, to observe their actual implementation during instruction, and to look for new ways to integrate them into your own talent goals and talent-targeted studies.

Use the Design Essentials as Talent Goals

Just as we have targeted and assessed the cross-domain and domain-specific aptitudes in talent goals, we need to design curriculum to support talent development. In each of the seven sections that follow, you'll see examples of how the design essential is used to create a goal and a talent-targeted task. Just as you are explicit about targeting the talent aptitudes in your goals, you can be straightforward with students about the instructional Design Essential you are using and its potential benefits to their learning. Brain research tells us that "goals drive the nervous system," so both educators and the learners need to be clear about the nature of intended learning outcomes.[2]

> Just as you are explicit about targeting the talent aptitudes in your goals, you can be straightforward with students about the instructional Design Essential you are using and its potential benefits to their learning.

Design Essential #1: *To What Extent Do We . . .* Organize Content Using Overarching Concepts?

Concepts are big ideas or universal themes that cross domains, such as *change* or *relationships*. Organizing a unit of study around an overarching concept provides students with opportunities to see interrelationships, think creatively and critically, and make personal connections. According to Wiggins and McTighe, these big ideas act as "conceptual Velcro" to generate essential questions that foster inquiry and real-world application.[3]

Using overarching concepts to structure units of study enables interdisciplinary teaching and the formation of essential questions that are touchstones for both content mastery and developing talent aptitudes. Interdisciplinary teaching draws on multiple disciplines to examine an overarching theme, issue, or question. It promotes student engagement, higher-level thinking, and the transfer of learning. Learning experiences are more authentic because they mirror real life, which is multifaceted.

Innovation Is Interdisciplinary

Innovators use concept-based thinking to see interrelationships and make new associations across disciplines. These "forced associations" lead to new discoveries. Innovators need a broad, transdisciplinary range of knowledge and experiences to create new associations.

Real-world problems are complex, and no single discipline can adequately describe and resolve these issues. Findings from neuroscience, cognitive science, social psychology, and human development support that interdisciplinary instruction helps students develop their cognitive abilities needed to acquire a deep and thorough understanding of complex issues and challenges.[4] Innovators use interdisciplinary thinking to synthesize multiple perspectives and create new ideas, alternative approaches, and problem solutions. Social innovators use interdisciplinary understandings to challenge preconceived ideas, dispel biases, and integrate conflicting perspectives to solve complex problems.[5]

Interdisciplinary Concepts in Talent-Targeted Teaching and Learning

The four talent-targeted teaching and learning studies sampled throughout this book are organized using interdisciplinary concepts of *perspective*, *community*, *relationships*, and *sustainability*. Organizing a language arts novel study for *Shooting Kabul* around the concept of *perspective* allows for interdisciplinary connections to the concept in art and social sciences. Organizing the language arts novel study for *Watership Down* around the concepts of *community* and *sustainability* makes an acclaimed classic about rabbit warrens more accessible, engaging, and relevant to today's students.

The concept of *relationships* (*Stop Sports Injuries*) is a disciplinary big idea in mathematics that engages students in using data to solve real problems that are of personal importance to them. The concept of *sustainability* (*Healthy Community by Design*) integrates the content disciplines of mathematics, health, economics, environmental science, and architecture to model the way that real-world interdisciplinary teams collaborate to solve today's complex problems. The overarching concepts lead to overarching essential questions that continue to be explored throughout the study and applied in performances of understanding.

Concepts Generate Essential Questions

Educators are adept at asking questions that guide students to respond with the one right answer, the one that we want them to know, the one that is assessed on the standardized test. *Essential questions* differ in that the teacher doesn't have one right answer in mind because there *isn't* just one. According to Wiggins and McTighe, essential questions that organize discussion around concepts, or big ideas, in a discipline are open-ended, engage students personally, are thought-provoking, and promote inquiry. "By tackling such questions, learners are engaged in *uncovering* the depth and richness of a topic that might otherwise be obscured by simply *covering* it."[6]

The talent-targeted teaching and learning studies are organized around *overarching* essential questions, which means that they are not relegated to one lesson, one unit, or one grade level. Essential questions can continue to be explored in different grade levels and life stages. These questions can be revisited over and over again because they explore key issues, the same ones that adults ask in real life. Table 8.0 presents essential questions that address the core concepts in the talent-targeted teaching and learning humanities and STEM studies.

> Essential questions can continue to be explored in different grade levels and life stages. These questions can be revisited over and over again because they explore key issues, the same ones that adults ask in real life.

Table 8.0 Overarching Concepts and Essential Questions in Talent-Targeted Studies

Talent-Targeted Study	Concept	Essential Question
Humanities (Grades 4–6)	*Perspectives in Art and Culture*	Perspective	How do our perspectives shape our perceptions?
Humanities (Grades 6–8)	*Creating Sustainable Communities*	Sustainability Community	What makes communities thrive?
STEM (Grades 4–6)	*Stop Sports Injuries*	Relationships	How does data help us make good decisions?
STEM (Grades 6–8)	*Healthy Community by Design*	Sustainability	How does form follow function?

Use Concept-Based Learning to Develop Talent Aptitudes

Your current curriculum may already use overarching concepts and essential questions. Now, you can extend and deepen their impact by using them to create *concept-based* talent goals! Just as you created *content*-based talent goals, use the same process to target the aptitudes that will drive the exploration of concepts and essential questions. For example, if the goal is to discuss the essential question "How does our perspective shape our perceptions," you can target the aptitude of *metacognition* in the goal. Or if the goal is to explore the overarching concept of *sustainability*, it can at the same time target the talent aptitude of *problem solving* (see Table 8.1). Concept-based talent goals provide a "value-added" means to integrate higher-order, interdisciplinary thinking in the process of talent development.

Table 8.1 Talent Goals for Exploring Essential Questions and Concepts

• Use your *curiosity* to discuss the essential question "What makes communities thrive?"
• Apply your *insight* to explore the concept of *perspective*.
• Use *metacognition* to discuss the essential question "How does our perspective shape our perceptions?"
• Use *problem solving* to explore the concept of *sustainability*.
• Show your *engagement in the humanities* as we explore the overarching concept of *community*.
• Apply *logical reasoning* as we discuss the essential question "How does form follow function?"

Design Essential #2: *To What Extent Do We . . .* Structure Learning Around Open-Ended Problems?

Overarching concepts and essential questions prepare the way for Design Essential #2: *Structure Learning Around Open-Ended Problems*. Units of study organized around open-ended problems are often referred to as problem-based learning (PBL) or project-based learning. Problem-based learning (PBL) is an approach that motivates and challenges students to learn through engagement in a real problem in which the students see themselves as active stakeholders. While the problem becomes the purpose for learning, the problem-solving process is carefully structured by what students need to learn and be able to do to create a solution, thus ensuring that students reach the required learning objectives.[7] Research shows that middle school students who engaged in problem-based learning showed superior mastery of science concepts when compared to students learning in traditional methods.[8] PBL investigations culminate in student-created projects, exhibitions, or other artifacts that address the overarching concepts and essential questions.

Innovators use problem-based learning techniques when they approach "messy" or ill-structured problems for which there are no known solutions and multiple directions for exploration and inquiry. Problem-based learning develops intrinsic motivation and the discovery skills of curiosity, observation, questioning, and experimenting.[9]

Use the Five-P Problem Planner to Create Talent-Targeted Tasks

Each of the four humanities and STEM talent-targeted studies is structured around an open-ended problem or issue that is "designed backward" from the required content standards and skills. The problems are not just interesting, engaging, or fun, but must provide evidence of transfer, or the independent application of deep understanding.[10] The Five-P Problem Planner (adapted from one by Wiggins and McTighe) aims at transfer but also explicitly integrates social and emotional learning to develop social and self-awareness, responsible decision-making, and relationships.[11]

> The Five-P Problem Planner explicitly integrates social and emotional learning to develop social and self-awareness, responsible decision-making, and relationships.

Use the Five-P to craft a talent-targeted task that is prompted by a local need or issue with a personalized purpose in which the students have an authentic part to play in creating a professional product that meets the established performance criteria. Figures 8.0 and 8.1 present the Five-P Problem Planners for the four talent-targeted teaching and learning STEM and humanities studies. The Five-P Problem Planner is available online at www.resources.corwin.com/DevelopTalent.

1. **Problem Prompt:** What circumstances surround or have prompted the problem or challenge? What is the immediate need? An authentic context can be established using current issues and events in the community that encourage the students to become personally involved. For example, there is an increase in youth sports injuries that has prompted a campaign to *Stop Sports Injuries* (see Figure 8.0).

2. **Personalized Purpose:** What challenge is presented? The challenge has a personalized purpose and community connection, which activates student motivation and engagement. For example, students are asked to create community redevelopment plans for an area in their neighborhood that needs revitalizing (see Figure 8.1).

3. **Part to Play:** What part do students play in solving the problem? Aim for the students having an authentic role as *themselves*. This is a key factor for engagement. Often, problem-based studies are "simulations" in which students play a role other than themselves. These roles may or may not be engaging on a personal level. In the talent-targeted studies, the students are invited to participate as community stakeholders through a "call for proposals" campaign, contest, or exhibit. For example, students are amateur photographers who create a photo essay to communicate a personal perspective to the community in a local exhibit (see Figure 8.1).

4. **Professional Product:** What is being created to solve the problem? The problem-solving process culminates in a product or performance that mirrors what professionals do in that field. For example, students create a scale model for a healthy community design that applies professional standards (see Figure 8.0). In most cases, there is an audience beyond the school—ideally, a community stakeholder. Local business and community experts are often very willing to participate as mentors/judges in developing and assessing products. However, also consider how you might also use school-based audiences who have a stake in a school-based problem, such as administrators, staff, other teachers, parents, or students from a different grade.

5. **Performance Criteria**: These define what is considered a proficient demonstration of the content standards and skills applied in the problem solution. The criteria are presented to students "up front" in the initial problem scenario and scored in the final product assessment. For example, the students create a scale model that must accurately demonstrate the mathematical principles of similarity and congruence (see Figure 8.0). The problem-solving process entails direct instruction on the knowledge and skills that are needed to effectively reach that goal.

Figure 8.0 The Five-P Problem Planner for Talent-Targeted Studies (STEM)

Five-P *Problem Elements*	STEM (Grades 4–6) Stop Sports Injuries	STEM (Grades 6–8) Healthy Community by Design
1. **Problem Prompt** *Aim for an authentic, local community need or challenge.*	• There is a growing epidemic of youth sports injuries. • The *Stop Sports Injuries* campaign is a partnership of a sportswear designer, Safe Kids USA, and the American Academy of Pediatrics.	• The Department of Planning believes that citizens are active partners in planning and implementing communities. • It is soliciting designs for *Livewell*, a new mixed-use healthy community to be built locally.
2. **Personalized Purpose** *Aim for a local need or issue.*	• Propose an idea for a product that helps to prevent or reduce youth sports injuries.	• Create a design for a mixed-use sustainable community to be built on a local tract of undeveloped land.

Five-P Problem Elements	STEM (Grades 4–6) Stop Sports Injuries	STEM (Grades 6–8) Healthy Community by Design
3. **Part to Play** *Aim to create an authentic student role over a simulated role.*	• You are submitting your idea to the sports apparel designer as part of their *Stop Sports Injuries* campaign.	• You are submitting your design to the local Department of Planning, which is seeking development ideas from the community.
4. **Professional Product** *Target the product and present it to a real audience (preferably from the community).* *Who are local experts in this field?*	• Present your proposal to an audience of experts (e.g., local school physical education teachers and athletic coaches, young athletes, sports medicine specialists, sporting goods store personnel, etc.), who will judge it based on the criteria and provide feedback. • The final proposal will be submitted to the *Stop Sports Injuries* campaign.	• Create a *Livewell* community plan with a scale drawing, three-dimensional model for one mixed-used building, and include supporting data on how design decisions were made. • Present your design to a team of experts (e.g., local community planners, environmental activists, community organizations, architects, builders, interested citizens, etc.) for judging and feedback.
5. **Performance Criteria** *Determine the criteria necessary to show mastery of the content standards. These would be assessed using a scoring tool.*	• The proposal must be based on a topic related to youth sports injuries. • The proposal shows evidence of following the seven steps of the engineering design process. • Conclusions accurately apply knowledge of how to collect and interpret data.	• The design is based on the principles of sustainable communities. • The scale drawing and key accurately apply the targeted mathematics skills. • The model demonstrates principles of congruence and similarity. • Research analyzes and displays data from a random sample survey of stakeholders.

Figure 8.1 Five-P Problem Planners for Talent-Targeted Studies (Humanities)

Five-P Problem Elements	Humanities (Grades 4–6) Perspectives in Art and Culture	Humanities (Grades 6–8) Creating Sustainable Communities
1. **Problem Prompt** *Aim for an authentic, local community need or challenge.*	• You saw how photojournalism was used to communicate different perspectives about a recent conflict in your city. • You read about how Fadi entered a photojournalism contest in order to resolve a conflict.	• You read about The STAR Community Rating system that was used to evaluate your city. • You read in *Watership Down* about the ways in which communities can either thrive or decline.

(Continued)

Figure 8.1 (Continued)

Five-P Problem Elements	Humanities (Grades 4–6) Perspectives in Art and Culture	Humanities (Grades 6–8) Creating Sustainable Communities
2. Personalized Purpose *Aim for a local need or issue.*	• Create a photo essay and artist's statement to communicate your perspective on a topic of personal importance.	• Create a plan for the sustainable redevelopment of an area in need that will fundamentally transform the neighborhood.
3. Part to Play *Aim to create an authentic student role over a simulated role.*	• Like Fadi (*Shooting Kabul*), you are a photographer entering your photo essay in a photojournalism exhibit.	• You are a community member applying what you have learned about the characteristics of sustainable communities as portrayed in literature and life.
4. Professional Product *Target the product and present it to a real audience (preferably from the community).* *Who are local experts in this field?*	• Display your photo essay and artist's statement at the school photojournalism exhibit attended by photographers from the local paper, local art teachers, students, families, and community members. • Enter your photo in a local contest.	• Display your plan at our school booth at the community fair attended by local experts in community planning and redevelopment and other community residents. • Present your plan to local stakeholders at a community meeting.
5. Performance Criteria *Determine the criteria necessary to show mastery of the content standards. These would be assessed using a scoring tool.*	• The photo essay addresses the essential question "How do our perspectives shape our perceptions?" • A series of three photos communicates a personal value, emotion, or experience. • The artist's statement explains methods used to communicate the message.	• The plan is aligned with the requirements of the STAR rating system. • The plan develops a vision statement, describes what currently exists, provides a rationale for redevelopment, and addresses leadership and community engagement. • Visuals show the projected site.

Adapted from: Wiggins, G., & McTighe, J. (2005). Understanding by Design (2nd Ed.). Alexandria: ASCD

Design Essential #3: *To What Extent Do We ... Align for Acceleration?*

As we structure learning around authentic, open-ended problems, we naturally create opportunities for acceleration. Acceleration as an educational practice is one of the most misunderstood and maligned. Yet there are decades of research that show its effectiveness in supporting student achievement.[12] "Acceleration" simply means to advance the progress of students.[13] The term is used in two main ways: to advance the progress of struggling students to achieve grade level, or to advance above-grade-level students into more challenging content that matches their achievement level. In talent-targeted teaching and learning, we use acceleration to meet both of these goals.

Accelerate Learning for All Students

The talent-targeted teaching and learning practices of creating a talent development mindset, using the language of talent development, and creating and assessing talent goals introduce higher levels of thinking that accelerate learning for *all* students. For those who are considered to be struggling or at-risk (i.e., not scoring proficient on standardized tests), these practices develop their metacognition, self-efficacy, intrinsic motivation, and engagement. While remediation focuses on filling in skill gaps, an acceleration mindset concurrently challenges higher-level thinking (along with targeted intervention) as a strategy to advance student mastery. Acceleration for these students means maintaining consistent high expectations:

> The concept of high expectations is premised on the philosophical and pedagogical belief that a failure to hold all students to high expectations effectively denies them access to a high-quality education, since the educational achievement of students tends to rise or fall in direct relation to the expectations placed upon them. In other words, students who are expected to learn more or perform better generally do.[14]

For students who are functioning above grade level or those identified as gifted and talented, acceleration is essential for them to maintain continual progress and fulfill their potential. While we typically think of acceleration as grade skipping, there are actually 20 different types of acceleration, which include in-grade content acceleration, subject acceleration, and college-level courses such as Advanced Placement and International Baccalaureate. Researchers have found that, overall, acceleration influences these students' academic achievement in positive ways that continue throughout college and career.[15]

In "aligning" for acceleration, we are "putting things in the correct position" so that learners are appropriately matched with adequate challenge. We are also "aligning" our beliefs with the concept of acceleration as essential to student success.[16] The process of creating talent goals and assessing them using the Talent Aptitude Learning Progressions provides clear targets for advancement for *all* learners.

> In "aligning" for acceleration, we are "putting things in the correct position" so that learners are appropriately matched with adequate challenge.

How to Align for Acceleration: Analyzing Content Standards

You'll recall that the sample talent-targeted teaching and learning studies referenced throughout this book are categorized in grade spans, such as Grades 4–6 or Grades 6–8 rather than single grades. This practice allows you to align for acceleration. At the lower level of the span, the study would be an appropriate match for above-grade-level learners who need content acceleration. At the upper grade in the band, the study is a match for struggling or at-risk learners. You may have noticed that the sample talent goals for each study were aligned with content standards from all three grades. How can we use our required content standards to accelerate learning? By analyzing your grade-level standards, you can identify where it is possible to extend concepts for students who show readiness. This type of "vertical planning" enables you to achieve the "optimal match" of challenge and skill with the readiness and interests of the student.

How One Teacher Aligns for Acceleration

Figure 8.2 presents a Grade 6 language arts teacher's analysis of the learning targets in one language arts reading standard across grade levels. The Grade 5 below-level standard provides a starting point for pre-assessment. The Grade 6 on-level standard defines what students should know and be able to do but also suggests more complex concepts useful for acceleration and differentiation. Looking ahead at the Grade 7 above-level standard, the teacher knows from pre-assessments and interest inventories that there are students who are ready for acceleration and would be interested in how authors of historical fiction use or alter history. Finally, when analyzing the Grade 8 standard, the teacher applies the "could, would, should" principle for acceleration.[17] *Could* my advanced students decode the modern novel and the biblical archetypes? Probably. *Would* they be interested in doing so? Probably not. *Should* they be doing this at this time in their lives, or is there something else just as challenging and more interesting to them at their age? This teacher decides that the Grade 7 standard would do both, so the Grade 8 standard can wait.

Figure 8.2 Aligning for Acceleration: Content Standards Across Grade Levels

You can analyze the learning targets of your content standards across grade levels to determine how to achieve an optimal match of challenge/skill with the readiness levels and interests of the students.

Content Standard Across Grade Levels	Match With Students' Readiness Level/Interests
Below-Grade-Level Standard (Grade 5) Compare and contrast stories in the same genre (e.g., mysteries and adventure stories) on their approaches to similar themes and topics. (CCSS.ELA-LITERACY.RL.5.9)	The Grade 5 standard focuses on key disciplinary concepts—theme and genre—and requires that students use critical thinking to compare and contrast. The standard is limited to stories in one genre. Pre-assessments show that my Grade 6 on-level students have mastered this, and there is more to understand about theme and genre that they can explore.

Grade-Level Standard (Grade 6) Compare and contrast texts in different forms or genres (e.g., stories and poems; historical novels and fantasy stories) in terms of their approaches to similar themes and topics. (CCSS.ELA-LITERACY.RL.6.9)	The Grade 6 standard allows for a more complex integration of knowledge and ideas. The students are now comparing and contrasting themes across different genres. This points to the more complex concept of universal themes, which is a big idea that would challenge and engage the more advanced students and foster depth and complexity.
Above-Grade-Level Standard (Grade 7) Compare and contrast a fictional portrayal of a time, place, or character and a historical account of the same period as a means of understanding how authors of fiction use or alter history. (CCSS.ELA-LITERACY.RL.7.9)	The Grade 7 standard expands on the concept of genre, comparing and contrasting fictional and historical accounts. The emphasis is on the author's craft and the authenticity of historical fiction. The interdisciplinary approach is intellectually rigorous but age appropriate. I could use this standard to challenge my advanced Grade 6 students.
Two Grades Above Level (Grade 8) Analyze how a modern work of fiction draws on themes, patterns of events, or character types from myths, traditional stories, or religious works such as the Bible, including describing how the material is rendered new. (CCSS.ELA-LITERACY. RL.8.9)	The Grade 8 standard greatly expands the disciplinary big ideas and concepts through an analytical study of universal themes and patterns across time and culture. Here is where I must consider my students' age and interests. Although they could decode the modern novel and biblical archetypes, is there something more relevant for their age? I think the Grade 7 standard is more appropriate for my advanced Grade 6 students.

Design Essential #4: *To What Extent Do We . . . Develop Expert Thinking?*

Providing opportunities for acceleration is essential for learners to develop expertise in a domain. We may not know how to prepare today's students for tomorrow's inscrutable careers, but we can prepare them to become expert thinkers, to develop *expertise*. "Understanding expertise is important because it provides insights into that nature of thinking and problem solving . . . the study of expertise shows us what successful learning looks like."[18] Two decades ago, the seminal research report *How People Learn* showed us how experts reason and think differently than novices. Experts differ from novices in six key ways: pattern recognition, conceptual understanding, contextualized knowledge, fluent recall, metacognition, artistry, and vision.

We must teach our students these thinking skills of experts, and we can be confident that, as we create and assess goals that target the aptitudes of innovators, we are developing expert thinking (see Table 8.2). For example, a talent goal to develop the aptitude of *insight* also develops the expert skill of *pattern recognition*, the ability to notice features that novices do not see. A talent goal for *persistence*

We can be confident that, as we create and assess goals that target the aptitudes of innovators, we are developing expert thinking aligns with the expert's fluent recall of the knowledge they have persistently gained and now can apply to solving problems. A talent goal for *creativity* develops the expert's adaptive, flexible thinking, which enables them to see a problem as just the starting place for new discoveries.[19]

Table 8.2 How Talent Aptitudes Align With the Characteristics of Expert Thinking (Adapted From *How People Learn*)

Expert Characteristic	Description	Seven Talent Aptitudes of Innovators
Pattern Recognition	Experts have a depth of knowledge that enables them to see things differently; they notice features and patterns novices do not see.	*Insight*: Is keenly observant and aware; is intuitive; perceives new patterns and relationships; readily grasps concepts and applies them to new situations.
Conceptual Understanding	Experts' knowledge is organized efficiently and meaningfully around principles and concepts.	*Logical Reasoning*: Draws conclusions from facts or premises; observes patterns and infers rules; hypothesizes and tests; uses a systematic process to make sound judgments and form sensible arguments.
Contextualized Understanding	Experts transfer knowledge to solve problems in new contexts.	*Curiosity*: Seeks new ideas; asks thoughtful, searching questions; is inquisitive; observes, explores, and investigates keenly and alertly in any environment.
Fluent Recall	Experts try to understand the problem first. Then, they retrieve knowledge from their large storehouse.	*Persistence*: Focuses time and energy on a topic of interest; looks for more than one way to accomplish a task; continues in spite of difficulty; strives to improve and refine; tests and verifies; may resist closure.

Expert Characteristic	Description	Seven Talent Aptitudes of Innovators
Metacognition	Experts understand how they learn, can teach themselves to learn, and are aware of their limits.	*Metacognition*: Understands own thought processes; self-selects appropriate problem-solving strategies; plans; self-monitors, reflects, assesses, and corrects; learns from mistakes.
Artistry and Vision	"Adaptive experts" are flexible virtuosos. Problems are new opportunities to explore, expand, discover, improve.	*Creativity*: Has unusual or clever ideas; enjoys divergent thinking, brainstorming, or imagining; is inventive; discovers unusual connections; initiates new projects. *Leadership*: Motivates others to achieve a goal; initiates ideas and listens to concerns of others; influences others to adopt and participate in a plan of action; organizes others to implement a plan.

Source: Bransford, J.D., Brown, A.L. & Cocking, R.R. (Eds). (2000). *How people learn: Brain, mind, experience, and school.* Washington, D.C.: National Academies Press. (pp. 33–36).

Develop Adaptive Expert Thinkers With Creative Problem Solving (CPS)

Problem solving is the essence of the creative process. The creative problem solving (CPS) method developed by Alex Osbourne, Sidney Parnes, Donald Treffinger, and others has 50 years of research and development in the deliberate teaching and learning of creativity and the creative process.[20] We can teach students to use CPS to develop their talent aptitudes and the problem-solving strategies of adaptive experts.

Creative thinking is an interplay of convergent and divergent thinking. *Divergent thinking* requires one to go beyond predetermined responses to explore broad possibilities; *convergent thinking* requires a focus on a single answer or a limited set of responses. Both types of thinking are essential to the creative thinking process. While the creative person must be open to new ideas and willing to take risks, the creative product requires focus and discipline.

The CPS model has five steps, with a preliminary stage called "mess finding" or the sensing of a challenge, opportunity, need, or problem.[21] One feature of CPS that distinguishes it from other problem-solving models is that each step begins with an *open, divergent* thinking phase that generates many ideas, facts, problems, criteria, solutions, or implementation strategies. This open, divergent stage is followed by a second *focused, convergent* phase in which the most promising ideas are selected for further exploration. The individual steps of the CPS process can be integrated into your current instruction, even though you may not have the latitude or time in your curriculum to complete the entire process. The key is to design lessons that use both the divergent and convergent thinking stages and to make it explicit to students when they should use "open/divergent" or "closed/convergent" thinking. Table 8.3 presents the divergent and convergent stages in CPS.

Table 8.3 Divergent and Convergent Thinking Stages in Creative Problem Solving (CPS)

CPS Step	Divergent Stage (Open)	Convergent Stage (Focused)
Mess Finding (Preliminary) *What can be improved?*	Sense what is missing, causing uneasiness or concern, or needs to be improved.	Identify a concern that should be addressed.
Fact Finding (Preparation) *What do we know about the problem?*	Observe; collect data. Ask questions: who, what, when, where, why, how.	Look for important ideas (hits) and group-related ideas (hot spots).
Problem Finding (Definition) *How can we define the problem?*	Look at different viewpoints. Restate the problem, "In what ways might we ..."	Select the problem based on what you want to accomplish.
Idea Finding (Brainstorming) *What are all the possible solutions?*	Generate ideas without criticism or evaluation.	Select the best solutions to evaluate.
Solution Finding (Evaluation) *Which are the best solutions?*	Develop criteria for the evaluation of the alternatives.	Evaluate and select a solution using the evaluation matrix.

CPS Step	Divergent Stage (Open)	Convergent Stage (Focused)
Acceptance Finding (Implementation) *How can we put our ideas into practice?*	Develop a plan of action to put the idea into practice.	Consider all stakeholders. Assess assistance and resistance to the plan.

Use Creative Problem Solving (CPS) in Talent-Targeted Teaching and Learning

The six stages of CPS also provide opportunities to develop the talent aptitudes. For example, the "mess-finding" stage is an opportunity to use *curiosity* and *insight* to sense "what can be improved? what is missing?" A mess-finding talent goal would be, "Use *curiosity* and *insight* to survey your community about which recreational activities they would like." Next, the fact-finding stage is an opportunity to use *resourcefulness* and *persistence* to find out "What do we know about the problem?" A fact-finding talent goal would be, "Use persistence and resourcefulness to collect data about the lengths of people's feet." The final CPS stage, Acceptance Finding, applies the aptitudes of *leadership*, *communication*, *metacognition*, and *empathy* to put ideas into practice. An Acceptance Finding talent goal would be, "Use *leadership* and *communication* to compose a speech that defends your community redevelopment plan and motivates others to adopt the plan." Table 8.4 shows how each stage of CPS aligns with the STEM and humanities talent goals and tasks.

Table 8.4 Creative Problem Solving in Talent-Targeted Tasks

CPS Steps	Talent Aptitudes	Talent-Targeted Task
Mess Finding *What can be improved?* *What is missing?*	Curiosity Insight	Use *curiosity* and *insight* to survey your community in order to draw conclusions about which recreational activities to include in your community plan (STEM, *Healthy Community by Design*).
Fact Finding *What do we know about the problem?*	Resourcefulness Persistence	Use *persistence* and *resourcefulness* to collect data about the lengths of people's feet in order to determine a better, safer way to designate running shoe sizes (STEM, *Stop Sports Injuries*).

(Continued)

Table 8.4 (Continued)

CPS Steps	Talent Aptitudes	Talent-Targeted Task
Problem Finding *How can we define the problem?* *In what ways might we . . .*	Logical Reasoning Problem Solving	Use *logical reasoning* and *problem solving* to design and conduct an experiment to determine which running shoe best reduces foot strike impact. (STEM, *Stop Sports Injuries*)
Idea Finding *Brainstorming: What are all the possible solutions?*	Creativity Investigation	Use *creativity* and *investigation* to collect data on youth sports injuries in order to identify the greatest area of need for a new product to reduce youth sports injuries. (STEM, *Stop Sports Injuries*)
Solution Finding *Based on our criteria, which are the best solutions?*	Verbal Reasoning Mathematical Reasoning Spatial Reasoning	Use *verbal, mathematical,* and *spatial reasoning* to research sustainable building materials, calculate the amount needed and cost to cover a community building, and make a recommendation for the best material to use based on these criteria. (STEM, *Healthy Community by Design*)
Acceptance Finding *How can we put our ideas into practice?*	Leadership Communication	Use *leadership* and *communication* to compose a speech that defends your community redevelopment plan and motivates others to adopt the plan. (Humanities, *Creating Sustainable Communities*)
	Metacognition Empathy	Use *metacognition* and *empathy* to create a photo essay that communicates a personal perspective that may help others solve problems. (Humanities, *Perspectives in Art and Culture*)

Design Essential #5: *To What Extent Do We ... Engage Differing Perspectives?*

Creative problem solvers use flexible thinking to generate new ideas and solve problems by taking different perspectives. Looking at the familiar from new angles enables us to "Think Different," as states the Apple mission established by innovative founder Steve Jobs. Perspective can be defined as a point of view, viewpoint, position, stance, or attitude. Our perspectives are limited by and will differ based on our knowledge and experiences. Perspective in the visual arts is a way of portraying three-dimensional objects on a flat, two-dimensional surface by suggesting depth or distance. Perspective provides the right impression of their height, width, depth, and position in relation to each other. Integrating both definitions, we *engage differing perspectives* when we prepare learners to "see with new eyes," to view the big picture, expand knowledge and experiences, and recognize interrelationships.

In this section, we'll see how engaging differing perspectives develops talent aptitudes through the strategies of divergent thinking, divergent questioning, and mind mapping.

Engage Differing Perspectives With Divergent Thinking

E. Paul Torrance, known as the "Father of Modern Creativity," derived four creative thinking abilities from studying the real-life creative achievements of famous scientists and inventors, as well as from examples of "everyday creativity."[22] He maintained that creative thinking abilities can be improved through "creative teaching."[23] Creative thinking as defined by E. Paul Torrance consists of four distinct processes:

- Fluency: The ability to produce a large number of ideas.
- Flexibility: The ability to see from different perspectives; a wide range of ideas.
- Originality: The ability to produce ideas that are unique (statistically infrequent).
- Elaboration: The ability to develop an idea with details.

Torrance's work proved that these abilities can be developed or enhanced through practice. Creative thinking expands perspective through a future orientation: What could exist that does not exist now? [24]

Develop Divergent Thinking Through Divergent Questioning

Expanding perspective depends upon students acquiring and implementing effective questioning strategies. Teachers have direct control over the types of questions asked and discussed, and these questions directly affect the quantity and quality of students' responses. The ability to recognize, generate, and respond to questions at various levels can be developed, and taxonomies of thinking, such as Bloom's taxonomy, provide models for composing levels of questioning.[25] The divergent questioning model (DQM) is a strategy for developing higher-level questions and responses at Bloom's *synthesis* level.[26] Synthesis uses creative thinking to solve problems and produce original ideas and products. Many new inventions have resulted from asking a divergent "What If?" question or thinking about how an object or situation is similar to another (forced association). Table 8.5 presents the five creative thinking perspectives used in the DQM: quantity, supposition, viewpoint, involvement, and forced association. The DQM questions may be used individually, as they are here, or as a system for the elaboration of a single concept.

> Many new inventions have resulted from asking a divergent "What If?" question or thinking about how an object or situation is similar to another (forced association).

Use Divergent Questioning in Talent-Targeted Goals and Tasks

The divergent questioning model can be used to compose talent goals and tasks that engage divergent perspectives (see Table 8.5). For example, the supposition question "What would happen if?" was used to create the talent-targeted task "Use *creativity* to imagine **what would happen if** General Woundwort (from *Watership Down*) was elected mayor of your town." Because Woundwort is the tyrannical leader of the Efrafa warren, this task requires a creative change of perspective. The *forced association* question "Take ideas from—to improve—" was used to compose the talent-targeted task, "Use *resourcefulness* **to take ideas from** the Watership Down warrens **to solve problems** in your neighborhood." These tasks, which are relatively easy to compose using the DQM and the talent aptitudes, accomplish a threefold purpose to encourage divergent thinking, advance talent development, and accomplish transfer of learning.

Table 8.5 Divergent Questioning in Talent-Targeted Tasks

Divergent Questioning Model		Talent-Targeted Task
Quantity	*List all the _____.* *What are all the solutions you can think of?*	Use *persistence* to **list all** the types of youth sports injuries that might occur. (STEM *Stop Sports Injuries*)

Divergent Questioning Model		Talent-Targeted Task
Supposition	*What would happen if _____? Suppose _____ happened?*	Use *creativity* to imagine **what would happen if** General Woundwort (in *Watership Down*) was elected mayor of your town. (Humanities, *Creating Sustainable Communities*)
Viewpoint	*How would this look to a _____? How would _____ view this?*	Use *insight* to understand how your community design **would look to a** dog. (STEM, *Healthy Community by Design*)
Involvement	*How would _____ feel if it were human? If you were _____, what would you do (think, feel)?*	Use *empathy* to understand **what you would think and feel if you were** Miriam, the sister left behind (in *Shooting Kabul*). (Humanities, *Perspectives in Art and Culture*)
Forced Association	*How is _____ like a _____? Take ideas from _____ to improve _____.*	Use *resourcefulness* to **take ideas from** the *Watership Down* warrens **to improve** your neighborhood. (Humanities, *Creating Sustainable Communities*)

Design Essential #6: *To What Extent Do We . . . Analyze Patterns, Relationships, and Trends?*

Divergent thinking and questioning shift our perspective so that we are open to seeing new patterns, relationships, and trends. Innovators analyze these to detect changes that predict issues and shifts that could profoundly affect our future. Trend and pattern analysis help us to see the big picture, think strategically, and challenge the status quo, leading to discoveries and ideas that break new ground.[27]

The analysis of patterns, relationships, and trends promotes critical and creative thinking. Patterns are repetitive and predictable recurring elements in ideas, objects, stories, and events. We see patterns across disciplines. Being able to move beyond simple pattern identification to defining the cause and effect of a pattern or the relationships among patterns requires the ability to think deeply and critically.

Trends represent the external social, economic, political, and cultural forces that shape actions and events. They show the prevailing tendency and the general direction of change over time. In analyzing trends, it is important to examine the "why" and the "so now what?" questions and examine the consequences of trends, both intentional and unintentional.

Use Concept Attainment to See Patterns and Relationships

A time-honored and effective strategy for recognizing patterns and relationships is concept attainment, based on the work of psychologist Jerome Bruner, who conducted extensive research into the process of *concept formation*. Bruner concluded that in order to cope with our diverse environment, humans naturally group information into categories based on common characteristics.[28]

Concept attainment uses a structured inquiry process to engage students in seeing patterns and relationships by identifying the attributes that distinguish *examples* of a given group or category from *nonexamples* of a group or category that has already been formed by the teacher. To do so, students compare and contrast examples that contain the attributes of the concept with examples that do not contain those attributes. The relevance to this section on engaging differing perspectives is that students must critically observe attributes, think inductively to determine patterns, hypothesize, test, and "find the rule." Concept attainment integrates strategies that help students extend and apply knowledge and that are known to raise student achievement.[29] This is an approach that we can take to the next level in teaching to develop talent.

A Talent-Targeted Concept Attainment Lesson

Talent goals can drive a concept attainment lesson that engages different perspectives. To design a concept attainment lesson, there are three major principles to consider: "conceptual clarity, multiple examples, and conceptual competence."[30] This means that the examples and nonexamples must be thoughtfully chosen to exemplify essential attributes of the concept. With multiple examples, students can refine and test their initial hypotheses. Finally, students must be able to apply the concept in a new context, which is, as we know, the test of transfer.

In talent-targeted teaching and learning, the content focus of the lesson is set in motion by a talent goal for the process. For example, in the talent-targeted STEM study *Stop Sports Injuries*, the overarching concept of relationships is explored through the essential question "How does data help us make good decisions?" A key mathematical concept in the study is *correlation*, defined as a mutual or reciprocal relationship between two or more things (variables). To use concept attainment to define the concept of correlation, first create a talent goal: Use *curiosity and mathematical reasoning* to observe patterns and explain relationships among examples to "find the rule" and apply it to solve a real problem.

In the talent-targeted concept attainment lesson plan on correlation (see Figure 8.3), students will apply and develop the targeted talent aptitudes as they inductively define the concept. The teacher begins by (Step 1) introducing the student-directed goals for *curiosity* and *mathematical reasoning* and by (Step 2) using Talent-Targeted Think-Alouds, such as "Today, you'll use *curiosity* to explore a new idea." The concept attainment begins with the presentation of the concept attribute examples and nonexamples (Step 3), followed by hypothesis formation and testing (Step 4) and definition formation (Step 5). At this stage, formative assessment is needed to assess understanding of the concept, with reteaching provided if needed (Step 6). Students will then apply the concept in the talent-targeted performance of understanding (Step 7) that will be assessed (Step 8) using the procedures explained in Chapter 7.

Figure 8.3 Talent-Targeted Concept Attainment Lesson: Correlation

Talent Goal: Use your *curiosity and mathematical reasoning* to observe patterns and explain relationships among examples to "find the rule" and apply it to solve a real problem.
Essential Question: *How do we use data to make good decisions?*
Mathematics Standard: Statistics and Probability: Represent and Interpret Data
Performance of Understanding: Safest Running Shoe? Use your *curiosity* and *mathematical reasoning* to design and conduct an experiment to determine which running shoe best reduces foot strike impact. Graph the data and analyze the results for correlation.
Concept Attainment: Correlation
1. **Introduce the talent goal and student-directed goals:** • I demonstrate *curiosity* by being open to explore new ideas and experiences, asking thoughtful questions, observing, and investigating. • I use *mathematical reasoning* to recognize the patterns in numbers or shapes, determine the rules, and apply mathematical knowledge to solve problems.
2. **(Ongoing) Use Talent-Targeted Think-Alouds:** • Use your *curiosity* to explore a new idea today. • We'll use *mathematical reasoning* to recognize the pattern and determine the rule. • That hypothesis shows *mathematical reasoning*.
3. **Present positive and negative examples of the attributes:** Carefully observe these examples. What do you see? • Examples: Doing your homework and getting good grades; smoking and dying of lung cancer • Nonexamples: Playing football and having blond hair; owning a dog and liking to read

(Continued)

Figure 8.3 (Continued)

4. Have students form a hypothesis and initiate more examples to test it:

- What similarities, patterns, or relationships do you see among the examples? What concept do you see?

"In the first group, there is a relationship between the two things, but in the second group, there is no connection."

"Height and weight go in the first group. Height and hair color go in the second."

5. Define the concept:

- Using what you observe in the examples and your prior knowledge, generate a working definition:

Correlation is a mutual or reciprocal relationship between two or more things (variables).

6. Conduct formative assessment of the concept of correlation:

- Reteach/reinforce the concept as needed.

7. Apply the concept to solve a problem:

- Introduce the talent-targeted performance of understanding called "Safest Running Shoe?" experiment.
- Use direct teaching for skills that will be applied in the task.

8. Assess the talent goal:

- Use the Talent Aptitude Learning Progressions to compose rubrics for *curiosity* and *mathematical reasoning*.
- Have students self-assess their student-directed goals (#1) and complete the self-reflection for their Talent Development Portfolios.

Use Mind Mapping to See Patterns and Relationships

Integrating a powerful strategy such as concept attainment with talent-targeted teaching and learning is efficient and effective for developing both content expertise and the aptitudes of innovators. Another powerful strategy is *mind mapping*, a visual thinking technique invented by Tony Buzan. Our minds naturally seek patterns. Mind mapping models the way the brain works, by making associations among ideas. Given one example, our minds seek a second and third, branching out like trees. Mind maps help us to understand ideas and concepts, make connections and recognize relationships, brainstorm ideas, recall information, plan tasks, and organize and communicate ideas.[31]

A mind map starts with a big idea or concept like *community* or *sustainability* and uses color, lines, and images to branch out organically with details and insights to show the association of ideas and levels of relationships. The diagrams always take the same basic format of a tree, with a single starting point in the middle that branches out and divides again and again. The lines that connect the words are part of the meaning. There are many software programs available that can be used to create mind maps. However, learners need only paper and colored markers to create their maps. Here are Tony Buzan's seven steps for visually mapping the way the brain works:[32]

1. Start the map in the center of a blank page turned sideways.

2. Consider using an image to communicate the central concept.

3. Use color throughout.

4. Connect the main branches to the central image and then connect the second- and third-level branches.

5. Make your branches curved, not straight.

6. Use one key word per line.

7. Use images throughout.

> Our minds naturally seek patterns. Mind mapping models the way the brain works by making associations among ideas.

Mind Mapping in a Talent-Targeted Teaching and Learning Lesson

A powerful strategy in its own right, mind mapping is ideal for developing the talent aptitudes of tomorrow's innovators. In a lesson from the humanities study *Creating Sustainable Communities*, mind mapping is used to explore the essential question "What makes communities thrive?" (see Figure 8.4). This technique enables students to engage and integrate differing perspectives on this question, which they will infer from both literature and real life. First, they'll explore the principles of the STAR Communities Rating System[33] as applied to their own city. They'll apply these principles to analyze and evaluate local case studies of redevelopment in their community. Next, they explore the essential question in the fantasy adventure novel *Watership Down*, in which a band of rabbits embark on a quest for a sustainable warren after theirs was destroyed by irresponsible community development.

Through the ongoing process of mind mapping their ideas, learners are developing their talent aptitudes of *insight*, *creativity*, and *engagement in the humanities* as they read and think about "what makes communities thrive." They will explore the problem, gain information, brainstorm ideas, see patterns, and make connections to apply in the performance of understanding a sustainable community redevelopment plan to create a "thriving" area in their own neighborhoods. For an example of a mind map, see Figure 8.5.

Talent Goal:

Demonstrate *insight*, *creativity*, and *engagement in the humanities* by developing the concepts of community and sustainability in a mind map of ideas for community redevelopment.

Content Standards:

- Determine the meaning of words and phrases as they are used in a text, including vocabulary specific to domains related to history/social studies. (ELA.LITERACY-RH.6-8.4)
- Demonstrate the understanding of figurative language, work relationships, and nuances in word meanings. (ELA.LITERACY.L.7.5)

Essential Question:

What makes communities thrive?

Performance of Understanding:

Apply your *insight*, *creativity*, and *engagement in the humanities* to develop a mind map that explores the concepts of community and sustainability in relation to the essential question and real-world challenge, *Creating Sustainable Communities*.

Sustainable Community Mind Map

You read about the STAR Community Rating system used to evaluate our city for characteristics of sustainable communities. We'll continue to explore the essential question "What makes communities thrive?" through case studies from literature and life.

We'll read the fantasy adventure *Watership Down*, which features a band of rabbits in search of a sustainable community. We'll also explore real-life case studies of community redevelopment in our city. The goal is for you to apply the principles you learn from these to create a community redevelopment plan for an area in your own neighborhood.

Reading, studying, and thinking about "what makes communities thrive" in order to create our own sustainable community plan is an exciting, but perhaps overwhelming task. We need to explore the problem, gain information and knowledge, brainstorm ideas, see patterns, and make connections. We need to find a way to effectively organize information and ideas.

We're going to use a technique that many real-world creative problem solvers use. It's called mind mapping, a visual way of note-taking that works the way that your brain works, by making associations among ideas.

Mind maps are graphic organizers that start with big ideas or concepts (like community and sustainability) and use color, lines, and images to branch out organically with details and insights to show the association of ideas and levels of relationships (hierarchy). Single key words are printed along the branches.

Use your *insight*, *creativity*, and *humanities engagement* to develop a mind map of ideas from our reading about what makes communities thrive.

Design Essential #7: *To What Extent Do We . . . Consider Ethical Implications?*

The emphasis on open, divergent thinking may at first seem contradictory to a focus on ethical considerations, which seek the one "right" course of action. However, when we aim to develop the talents of tomorrow's innovators, we have to consider the ways in which ethics are core to innovation. Ethics are moral principles about what is right or wrong, good or bad, for society. While it is generally accepted that

Figure 8.5 Sample Mind Map

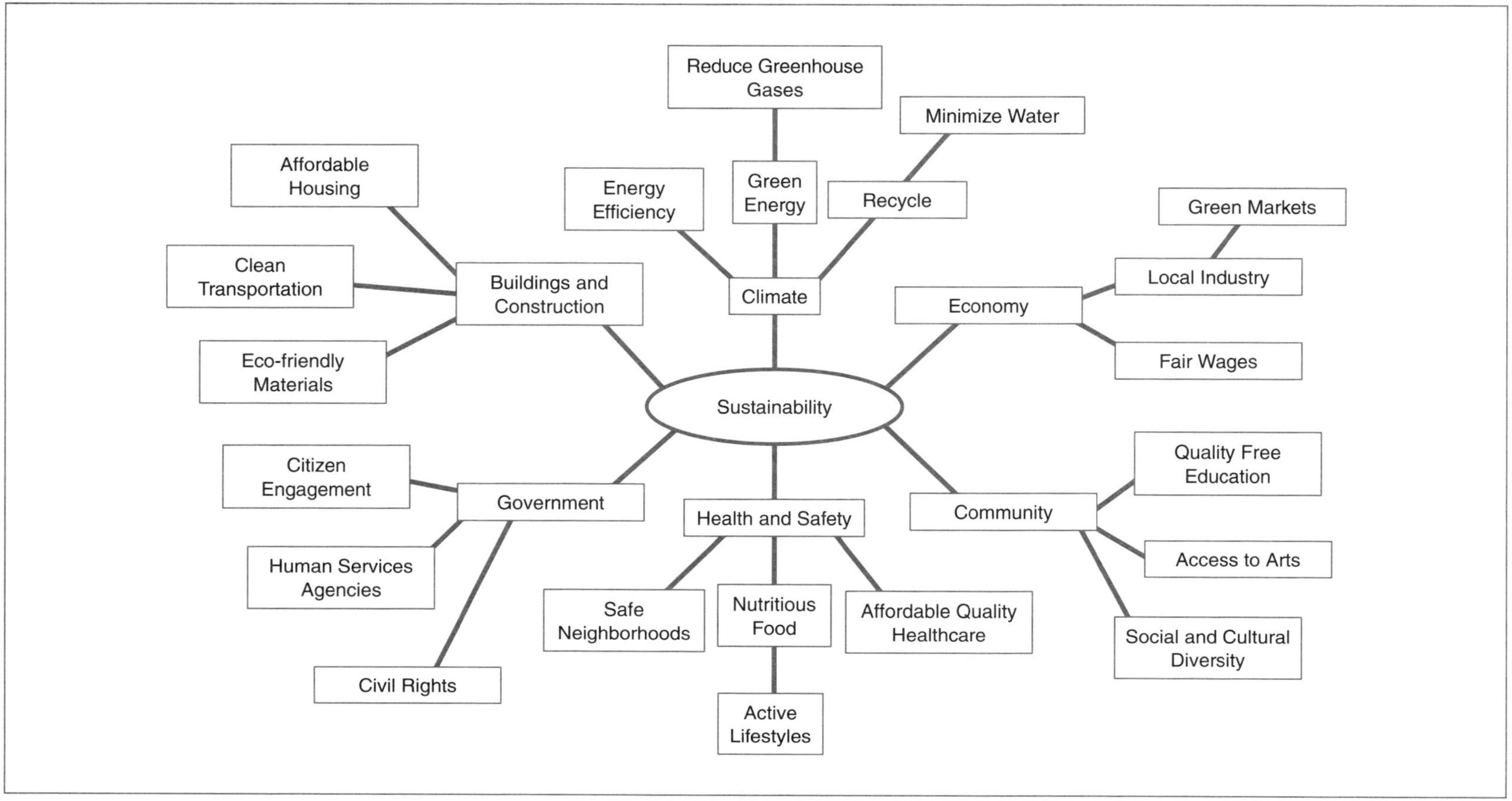

innovation improves our lives with "better things for better living,"[34] the goals of innovation, as in all human behavior, do matter. Gardner reminds us:

> As disciplined minds, it is our job to understand the world. But if we are ethical human beings, it is equally our job to use that understanding to improve the quality of life and living and to bear witness when understanding (or misunderstanding) is being used in destructive ways.[35]

The root word of ethics, "etho," means *character*. Character building in children begins early with discussions about what is right or wrong, using case studies that are close to home and connect with students' lives. While some may say that ethics vary from community to community and therefore can't really be taught, the values of peace, freedom, rule of law, equality, and dignity are universally agreed upon.[36]

The development of ethics begins with the concept of "respect" in young children, but by adolescence, they begin thinking more abstractly, seeing themselves taking the responsibilities of citizens and reflecting on the advantages/disadvantages of various courses of action. Respect is how one behaves toward *others*. However, ethics is how I behave in fulfilling a particular *role*.[37] Good work, writes Howard Gardner, "regularly takes into account its implications for the community within it is situated. . . . Education should prepare young persons for a life marked by good work."[38]

Design Strategy: Discussions of Moral Dilemmas

One strategy for teaching ethics is the discussion of moral dilemmas based on a theory of moral reasoning developed by Lawrence Kohlberg. He developed a hierarchy of six stages of moral, or ethical, thinking about what is right and wrong. The stages are associated with age, and while individuals proceed through them sequentially, rates of development vary. Learners benefit from discussions of moral dilemmas through hearing others' responses that are at a higher level. This exposure to a higher moral reasoning encourages their own development.[39]

STEM and humanities studies present many moral dilemmas, problems for which there are at least two equally defensible courses of action, based on competing moral or ethical principles. Teachers can introduce the concept of *moral dilemma* with the essential question "How do you decide what to do when there are two courses of action that seem right?" The discussion of moral dilemmas as they occur in life or literature challenges students to higher levels of critical thinking as they analyze and evaluate a course of action based on the Levels of Moral Reasoning framework. Students can use the framework to evaluate the moral level of problem solutions and to pose new solutions at a higher level. Table 8.6 presents Kohlberg's hierarchy of moral reasoning in kid-friendly language.

Table 8.6 Kohlberg's Levels of Moral Reasoning

Level I: Pre-Conventional (Most Children)			
	Focus	**Motivation**	**Reasoning**
Stage 1	Self (physical needs)	Avoid punishment	I won't do that because I don't want to get a "time out."
Stage 2	Self (others)	Satisfy needs "fair share"	If I do that, I will get a candy. "If you scratch my back, I'll scratch yours."

Level II: Conventional (Most Adults)			
	Focus	**Motivation**	**Reasoning**
Stage 3	Others (individuals)	Earn approval	I will do what makes me look good. I want to be seen as nice.
Stage 4	Others (society and authority)	Do your duty Obey authority	I will follow the rules because it maintains order.

Level III. Post-Conventional, Principled (Minority of Adults)			
	Focus	**Motivation**	**Reasoning**
Stage 5	Law (concrete)	Maintain individual rights agreed upon by society	We must develop laws that maintain social welfare (the American Constitution).
Stage 6	Principles of conscience (abstract)	Maintain personal integrity consistent with principles of justice, equality, etc.	I must disregard the law if it is inconsistent with my principles (Martin Luther King Jr.).

A Talent-Targeted Moral Dilemma Lesson

The Design Essential *Consider Ethical Implications* promotes student motivation and engagement and advances talent goals. Figure 8.6 presents a sample lesson from the *Perspectives in Art and Culture* humanities study in which learners develop *logical reasoning, empathy*, and *communication* by using Kohlberg's framework to analyze and evaluate the thoughts, feelings, and actions of characters in resolving conflict.

In the novel *Shooting Kabul,* the young protagonist Fadi is faced with the moral dilemma in this essential question: "Am I ever justified in taking revenge?" His friends and fellow victims of bullying have planned a sneak attack to get even with the bullies. While Fadi was not in on the planning, he joins them in their scheme, albeit with conflicting and contradictory thoughts, feelings, and actions. For the young readers, this story conflict involves them in a relevant moral dilemma. Applying the framework for moral reasoning to analyze and evaluate the characters' choices shows students how we can use our autonomy to make ethical decisions. The talent goal challenges them to use their *empathy* and *logical reasoning* to determine alternative courses of action and *communicate* the ethical impacts of these alternatives.

Figure 8.6 Talent-Targeted Moral Dilemma Lesson in *Perspectives in Art and Culture*

Talent Goal: Use *logical reasoning, empathy, and communication* to analyze and evaluate how a character's thoughts, feelings, and actions reflect their level of moral reasoning.

Content Standard: Compare and contrast two or more characters, settings, or events in a story or drama, drawing on specific details in the text (e.g., how characters interact).
(CCSS.ELA-LITERACY.RL.5.3)

Essential Question: *Am I ever justified in taking revenge?*

Performance of Understanding: *Different Choices: A Moral Reasoning Storyboard*

Use *logical reasoning, empathy*, and *communication* to create a storyboard presentation that shows how the plot of Chapter 23 would differ if the characters' thoughts, feelings, and actions were based on higher levels of moral reasoning.

Fadi's Moral Dilemma

In Chapter 23 of *Shooting Kabul by* N. H. Senzai, Fadi has the opportunity to "get even" with the two boys who have continuously bullied him and his friends, stealing their lunch money and calling them names. One boy had even broken Fadi's camera, a precious gift from his father. His friends have planned an ambush meeting in a remote spot, luring the bullies there with a promise of a lunch money payoff that was actually in a paper bag filled with marbles. Throughout this scene, we experience Fadi's conflicting thoughts and feelings about the rightness of the ambush.

For Fadi and your choice of two other characters from this scene, use Kohlberg's framework for moral reasoning to analyze the characters' speech, thoughts, and behavior in order to evaluate their levels of moral reasoning. Determine what other choices the characters could have made if operating on a higher level of moral reasoning and determine how these changes would affect the plot.

Use *logical reasoning, empathy*, and *communication* to create a storyboard presentation that shows how the plot of Chapter 23 would differ if the characters' thoughts, feelings, and actions were based on higher levels of moral reasoning.

Notes

1. Gardner, H. (2006). *Five minds for the future.* Harvard Business School Press.
2. CAST (2018). UDL and the learning brain. Wakefield, MA: Author. Retrieved from http://www.cast.org/products-services/resources/2018/udl-learning-brain-neuro science
3. Wiggins, G., & McTighe, J. (2005). *Understanding by Design* (2nd ed.). ASCD.
4. Bransford, J. D., Brown, A. L., & Cocking, R. R. (Eds.). (2000). *How people learn: Brain, mind, experience, and school.* National Academies Press.
5. Wagner, T. (2012). *Creating innovators: The making of young people that will change the world.* Scribner.
6. McTighe, J., & Wiggins, G. (2013). *Essential questions: Opening doors to student under-standing.* ASCD.
7. Torp, S., & Sage, S. (2002). *Problems as possibilities: Problem-based learning for K–16 educators* (2nd ed.). ASCD.
8. Wirkula, C., & Kuhn, D. (2011). Problem-based learning in K–12 education: Is it effective and how does it achieve its effects? *American Educational Research Journal, 48*(5), 1157–1186.
9. Dyer, J., Gregersen, H., & Christensen, C. M. (2011). *The innovator's DNA: Mastering the five skills of disruptive innovators.* Harvard Business Review Press.
10. Wiggins & McTighe, 2005, p. 156–159.
11. Collaborative for Academic, Social, Emotional Learning. (2020). *Core SEL competencies.* CASEL. https://casel.org/core-competencies/
12. Colangelo, N., Assouline, S., & Gross, M. U. M. (2004). *A nation deceived: How schools hold back America's brightest students* (Vol. 1). Connie Belin & Jacqueline N. Blank International Center for Gifted Education and Talent Development.
13. Acceleration. (2013). *Glossary of Educational Reform.* https://www.edglossary.org/acceleration/
14. High expectations. (2013). *Glossary of Educational Reform.* https://www.ed glossary.org/high-expectations/
15. Colangelo, N., Assouline, S., & VanTassel-Baska, J. (2015). *A nation empowered* (Vol. 1). Connie Belin & Jacqueline N. Blank International Center for Gifted Education and Talent Development.
16. Colangelo, Assouline, & Gross, 2004, p. 66.
17. Passow, H. (1988). Differentiated curricula for the gifted/talented: Some further reflections. In M. Awad (Ed.), *Priorities in curriculum planning for the gifted and talented* (pp. 11–18). National/State Leadership Training Institute.
18. Bransford, Brown, & Cocking, 2000, p. 19.
19. Bransford, Brown, & Cocking, 2000, pp. 33–36.
20. Isaksen, S. G. (2008). *A compendium of evidence for creative problem solving.* The creative problem solving group. Available from https://www.cpsb.com/research-articles-1.
21. Treffinger, D. J., & Firestien, R. L. (1989). *Handbook of creative learning* (Vol. 1). Center for Creative Learning.
22. Hebert, T., Cramond, B., Neumeister, K., Millar, G., & Silvian A. (2002). *E. Paul Torrance: His life, legacy, and accomplishments.* National Research Center on the Gifted and Talented.
23. Torrance, E. P., & Myers, R. E. (1970). *Creative learning and teaching.* Dodd, Mead.

24. Dyer, Gregersen, & Christensen, 2011.

25. Bloom, B. S., & Krathwohl, D. R. (1984). *Taxonomy of educational objectives: Handbook 1. Cognitive domain.* Longman.

26. Maryland State Department of Education. (2009). *Primary talent development early learning program, preK–2.* https://gtdiscover.org/educators/primary-talent-development/

27. Marx, G. (2014). *Twenty-one trends for the 21st century: Out of the trenches and into the future.* Education Week Press.

28. Bruner, J., Goodnow, J. J., & Austin, G. A. (1986). *A study of thinking.* Transaction Books.

29. Dean, C. B., Hubbell, E. R., Pitler, H., & Stone, B. J. (2012). *Classroom instruction that works: Research-based strategies for increasing student achievement* (2nd ed.). ASCD.

30. Silver, H. F., Strong, R. W., & Perini, M. (2007.) *The strategic teacher: Selecting the right research-based strategy for every lesson.* ASCD.

31. Buzan, T. (2009). *The mind map book: Unleash your creativity, boost your memory, change your life.* BBC Active.

32. Buzan, T., 2009.

33. Star Communities. (2020). *About us.* http://www.starcommunities.org/about/

34. Callahan, S. (1999). *DuPont replaces 1935 tagline to reflect corporate change.* https://adage.com/article/btob/dupont-replaces-1935-tagline-reflect-corporate-change/247761

35. Gardner, 2006, p. 142.

36. Annan, K. (2003). *Do we still have universal values?* Press Release of the United Nations. https://www.un.org/press/en/2003/sgsm9076.doc.htm

37. Gardner, 2006, pp. 142–143.

38. Gardner, 2006, p. 128.

39. Kohlberg, L. (1976). Moral states and moralization: The cognitive developmental approach. In T. Lockona (Ed.), *Moral development and behavior.* Holt, Rinehart, & Winston.

Teach to Touch the Future

And let us not be weary in well-doing, for in due season, we shall reap, if we faint not.

—Galatians 6:9

Here we are at the end of our journey, a hero's journey, one that I promised would make all the difference and bring you home, never the same, with a treasure. This is a time to reflect: What is that treasure? I can't tell you this exactly because you are on your own unique pathway to teaching tomorrow's innovators today. But now let's explore together some of what we've gleaned, and if you don't mind, I'll use the stages of the hero's journey to guide us.[1] Each stage presents an opportunity to review where we have been, but also to prepare for the new challenges we face as we teach to touch the future.

> Let's explore together some of what we've gleaned, and if you don't mind, I'll use the stages of the hero's journey to guide us.

1. Leaving the Place of Safety

One benefit we experienced is the opportunity to look at our current "place of safety" and recognize how the short-term focus on incentives to manipulate the outcomes we seek is robbing our school culture of inspiration for both students and teachers. Incentives, both the carrots and the sticks, do produce results, but the effects are fleeting, producing stress about how to maintain the gains that reduce students to data-points. These insights about incentive-driven education initiate the call to a new WHY, or long-term purpose: to motivate and engage learners, believing that they all have the potential to become tomorrow's creative problem solvers and change our world for the better.

2. The Call to Adventure

An asset of our new or renewed WHY, the long-term aim to educate innovators, lies in the opportunities it presents. These come in the form of challenges, to be sure, and the hero (that means you!) initially experiences "the refusal," or fear of the unknown. Equipped with the knowledge of how to foster intrinsic motivation (autonomy, competency, involvement) and student engagement (challenge, novelty, purpose), we can move forward with creating and assessing goals for talent development, the deliberate process of identifying and nurturing our students' unique aptitudes.

3. Meeting With a Mentor

There is great value in having a mentor, someone with experience who can provide helpful advice that builds confidence. While I hope that I have been such a mentor to you throughout this book, you will need the help of counselors and confidantes that emerge as you create a talent development mindset in your school. This three-phase process involves uncovering misconceptions, pre-assessing talent aptitudes, and strategically using the language of talent development in daily instruction and communication with families. In these ways, you build a community of learners, your new mentors, focused on the same goal: to identify and nurture individual talents.

4. Friends, Foes, and Trials

The riches discovered in this "teach to develop talent" adventure come through the many "friends," or in this case, practical tools and models, you can trust as allies in achieving your goals and overcoming challenges. In fact, the overarching purpose of *Teach to Develop Talent* is to be for you a wealth of resources that turns potential foes into friends and possible trials into triumphs. These "gems" include the shared definitions of talent aptitudes that are rooted in research on what motivates innovation and the student-directed goals that engage self-efficacy. You've gained the Talent Goal Frame process for creating goals based on challenging content standards and demonstrated in talent-targeted performances of understanding in STEM and the humanities. The process for assessing goals using the Talent Aptitude Learning Progressions is a new friend to cherish because we all have experienced the trial of "what gets assessed counts," and what doesn't, *doesn't*. Now, we have exemplars of what the cognitive and psychosocial talent aptitudes look like as they are emerging, progressing, and advancing.

5. The Ordeal

Amidst all this positive talk about adventure, mentors, and friends, I am sure you were waiting for a different reality to break through. In this stage of the journey, that reality is an *ordeal*: a serious, severe, and painful experience or test of virtue. *Ordeal* is not a term I want to use to describe the talent development journey, but here it is, so how do we find the value?

Right now, as I am writing this, the world is in the early stages of emerging from a global pandemic, which surely qualifies as a serious, severe, and painful experience for all of us. This ordeal has had an impact on every aspect of our lives, including, of course, education. Teaching and learning have been forcibly thrust into the virtual schoolhouse, which may be a temporary move but likely will result in some permanent changes that could, I think, become the treasures in the trial.

As we see the proliferation of online educational resources, we need a framework by which to evaluate them. An ordeal is a test of virtue. Will we remain true to our transformed purpose? Do these new resources align with our WHY: our long-term aim to motivate and engage tomorrow's innovators? To what extent do these resources align with our talent development goals? Are we assessing for understanding? Do we chart the growth of students' talent aptitudes over time using Talent Development Portfolios?

I believe that we can teach to develop talent in a virtual school just as in a bricks-and-mortar schoolhouse. In fact, there are advantages in the online environment for implementing the five stages of talent-targeted teaching and learning and the tools that support them. Let's review those and think about the virtual applications for each stage: (1) Prepare mindsets and pre-assess with the talent aptitude surveys; (2) set goals using the Talent Goal Frame process; (3) develop targets using the Talent Aptitude Learning Progressions; (4) design talent-targeted tasks using the seven principles of the Design for Innovation framework; and (5) assess and reflect using the processes integrated into the Talent Development Portfolio.

> I believe that we can teach to develop talent in a virtual school just as in a bricks-and-mortar schoolhouse.

Perhaps by the time you are reading this, we will have already partnered with talented technology experts to make talent-targeted teaching and learning a virtual reality.

6. The Resurrection

Following the ordeal is resurrection: a return from death, a rebirth, a transformation. I and many others have called for "transforming education," but what does that look like at this stage in our "teach to develop talent" journey? We will experience rebirth as we experience the following:

REvolutionize the Vision: Overturn the current focus on WHAT we produce—students who are college and career ready according to standardized tests. Return to WHY most teachers enter the profession—to make a difference in their students' lives by motivating and engaging them to develop their unique potentials.

> Overturn the current focus on WHAT we produce—students who are college and career ready according to standardized tests. Return to WHY most teachers enter the profession—to make a difference in their students' lives.

REcast Our Goals: Sir Ken Robinson reminds us that curriculum standardization, like fast food, aims at producing a uniform product, which is typically not of the quality that can compete in our "Michelin-star" global economy.[2] Nor does it "nourish" the discovery of creative solutions to social problems. The pivotal shift in the talent-targeted teaching and learning approach is the recast of short-term goals for content and skill acquisition into long-term aims to develop the aptitudes of innovators in STEM and humanities.

REshape Assessment: We have had few classroom-friendly assessments of the aptitudes of innovators, those cognitive and psychosocial traits that we know motivate high achievement, such as *curiosity, creativity, persistence*, or *metacognition*. Now, we have the Talent Aptitude Learning Progressions, which describe a continuum of how these qualities can emerge, progress, and advance. The learning progressions are used to create rubrics to assess our recast goals, and as formative assessments to communicate learning.

REinvent Teaching and Learning: Teaching tomorrow's innovators requires creating a context in which they can discover and develop their innovation, STEM, and humanities talent aptitudes. With the many competing demands on what our programming needs to be and do, it's imperative to know "What are the essentials?" Talent-targeted tasks use seven design principles that rekindle motivation and reenergize engagement. These are not the latest fads but have an evidence base that supports their efficacy to reinvent teaching and learning. We teach to develop talent when we organize content using overarching concepts to generate interdisciplinary questions, structure learning around personalized open-ended problems with professional products, accelerate expectations for all students, develop the creative thinking of "adaptive" experts, engage diverse perspectives, analyze patterns, and consider ethical implications.

7. **Return With the Elixir**

The hero returns home from the journey with an elixir to share with the world. An elixir is a magical potion that can change base metal into gold; it is a medicine with life-giving potential; it heals and restores. Given the many wounds we have in today's world, how can teaching to develop talent be a healing elixir? I have seen how my graduate students (who are teachers) are increasingly overwhelmed by children's needs attributable to circumstances outside of the teachers' control. Shouldn't attention to these immediate, pressing needs surpass a long-term focus on talent development?

The elixir of teaching to develop talent is far from a magic potion, but it is aimed at giving life to that which we can control: the time that students spend with us in our classrooms (virtual or otherwise). We have control over our WHY—our vision, goals, and expectations for all learners. We can control the design of the learning opportunities to motivate and engage children, enabling them to discover their unique callings and contributions. We *can* teach to touch the future.

> The elixir of teaching to develop talent is far from a magic potion, but it is aimed at giving life to that which we can control: the time that students spend with us in our classrooms (virtual or otherwise).

8. Back to the Place of Safety

The hero returns home, but it is a place where nothing is the same. The hero is changed; we are changed, for the better. Take the treasures you've gained along this journey and sow them as seeds in the soil of your schools and classrooms. Start small. Start now. Faint not! We must not grow weary in well-doing. One day, we will reap a harvest of transformed lives who will change the world for the better.

> Take the treasures you've gained along this journey and sow them as seeds in the soil of your schools and classrooms. Start small. Start now. Faint not!

Heed these words of Dr. Martin Luther King Jr.: "If you can't fly then run, if you can't run then walk, if you can't walk then crawl, but by all means, keep moving."[3]

Notes

1. Campbell, J. (2014/1990). *The hero's journey: Joseph Campbell on his life and work.* New World Library.
2. Robinson, K., & Aronica, L. (2009). *The element: How finding your passion changes everything* (p. 250). Penguin Books.
3. King, M. L. (1967). *What is your life's blueprint?* https://www.youtube.com/watch?v=ZmtOGXreTOU

INDEX

Note: Page numbers followed by "t" and "f" refer to pages containing tables and figures respectively.

Helping educators make the greatest impact

CORWIN HAS ONE MISSION: to enhance education through intentional professional learning.

We build long-term relationships with our authors, educators, clients, and associations who partner with us to develop and continuously improve the best evidence-based practices that establish and support lifelong learning.

Solutions YOU WANT | Experts YOU TRUST | Results YOU NEED

EVENTS

>>> **INSTITUTES**

Corwin Institutes provide large regional events where educators collaborate with peers and learn from industry experts. Prepare to be recharged and motivated!

corwin.com/institutes

ON-SITE PD

>>> **ON-SITE PROFESSIONAL LEARNING**

Corwin on-site PD is delivered through high-energy keynotes, practical workshops, and custom coaching services designed to support knowledge development and implementation.

corwin.com/pd

>>> **PROFESSIONAL DEVELOPMENT RESOURCE CENTER**

The PD Resource Center provides school and district PD facilitators with the tools and resources needed to deliver effective PD.

corwin.com/pdrc

ONLINE

>>> **ADVANCE**

Designed for K–12 teachers, Advance offers a range of online learning options that can qualify for graduate-level credit and apply toward license renewal.

corwin.com/advance

Contact a PD Advisor at (800) 831-6640 or visit www.corwin.com for more information

CORWIN